GREAT SMOKY MOUNTAINS NATIONAL PARK

JASON FRYE

Contents

DISCOVER

Great Smoky Mountains National Park

The national parks are called "America's Great Idea," and I think Great Smoky Mountains National Park is the best of the bunch. But I may be biased.

My earliest vacation memories are of these green mountains in summer and their blazing color in fall, of rushing streams and black bears lazing in the afternoon sun and the fields of Cades Cove filled with deer. On one morning ride across Newfound Gap Road, I learned why these mountains are called the Smokies. The mist rising from the coves and hollows and hidden places in the hills looked like smoke: tendrils of it rose like the sure sign of a chimney or a campfire; drifts of it formed miniature cloudbanks.

The Smokies are a colorful place. In the summer, the mountains are emerald green. In the fall the leaves are a riot of color. Spring is a time when wildflowers blanket high mountain meadows and secret glades. Thickets of rhododendron, galax, mountain laurel, and flame azalea bring flowery breath to the trails and paths throughout the park. In the winter, there's the beauty of a red fox running across a field white with snow, the crystalline shine of ice at the waterfalls, the

Clockwise from top left: lane in Cades Cove; floating vacation homes on Fontana Lake; mountain laurel; Mountain Farm Museum at the Oconaluftee Visitor Center; Hi-Wire Brewing in Asheville; sunset from Clingmas Dome jewel-like glint of snow in the morning sun, and the surprising yellow blooms of witch hazel.

There's a smell to this place too—rich, wet, and fertile, the smell of dirt and decades of leaves. Moss tinges the air near the springs, seeps, and waterfalls. In the autumn, the faint cinnamon smell of leaves perfumes the breeze, and the sound as they crunch underfoot announces your passage.

Birds, cicadas, the rush of water, and the sigh of wind create a layered sonic landscape. When the elk bugle and call to one another, when a turkey gobbles, or when a hawk keens, it punctuates the soundtrack of the Smokies.

There's other music—banjos and dulcimers and guitars and voices raised in song. That music sounds so at home it feels like it's been here as long as the stream or bird or wind, but it's just evidence of us. We drive the roads and hike the trails, fish in the streams, take photos of the sunsets and vistas, adding our voices to the music of the place.

When we leave, this song stays with us. We hum it to ourselves, recalling the place, the breeze, the sun on our faces, and the smell of fall on the air. We sing because this place is song-worthy, a place like no other.

This is why we go back: to learn a new verse, to find a place or experience missed on a previous trip. I go not to lose myself in the wilds of the Smokies, but to find myself there.

Clockwise from top left: tubing in Deep Creek; the SkyBridge in Gatlinburg; Cades Cove; hiking along Abrams Creek at Cades Cove

8 TOP EXPERIENCES

1 **Watch the Sky Change from Clingmans Dome:** From the highest point in the park, sunrises and sunsets tint the mountains, the mist, and the sky in quiet, breathtaking moments you shouldn't miss (page 44).

2 **See Why They're Called The Smoky Mountains:** Mist fills the valleys and tendrils of fog rise from secret coves and hollows in the mountains. Drive **Newfound Gap Road** just after dawn or as the sun sets to see exactly what makes these mountains "smoky" (page 43).

3 **See the Firefly Light Show:** Elkmont's colony of synchronous fireflies is world-renowned. With a little luck you can catch them blinking in unison every night for a couple of weeks in early summer (page 76).

4 **Find Fall Color on a Scenic Drive:** To see the mountains awash in color, drive **Cades Cove Loop** (page 80), hear the leaves crunch underfoot on **Deep Creek Loop** (page 88), or hike to **Andrews Bald** (page 47).

13

5 **Go Wildlife Watching:** Want to see elk, deer, turkeys and even bear? You'll find them in **Cades Cove** (page 80), **Cataloochee** (page 72), and at the **Oconaluftee Visitor Center** (page 43). Just remember to bring your binoculars or zoom lens and keep a safe distance from the park's full-time residents.

6 Hike to a Waterfall: There are tons of hikes in the Smoky Mountains, so why not hit the trail and head to Hen Wallow Falls, Abrams Falls, Deep Creek, or Grotto Falls (page 27)?

<<<

7 Go for a (Thrill) Ride in Dollywood: Dolly Parton's mountain theme park is full of roller coasters and waterslides, ready to deliver the thrills you want (page 118).

>>>

8 Say "Cheers!" in Asheville: Asheville's vibrant brewery and restaurant scene makes for the perfect reward after a few days on the trail. Head to civilization for a celebratory pint (page 185).

<<<

Planning Your Trip

Where to Go

Great Smoky Mountains National Park

Great Smoky Mountains National Park, the **most-visited national park** in the country, straddles the North Carolina-Tennessee border and encompasses an incredible and varied landscape. Here you'll see rounded peaks and jagged mountaintops that are among the tallest in the Eastern United States; white-water rivers and crystal-clear streams loaded with trout; **wildlife** like elk and bears, turkeys and deer in meadows and balds throughout the park; morning mist and **evening firefly shows** that delight millions of visitors every year. It's a hiker's paradise crisscrossed by more than 800 miles of **trails** and studded with **waterfalls** that make for the perfect place to rest and refresh.

NEWFOUND GAP

Newfound Gap bisects the park and connects Cherokee, North Carolina, with Gatlinburg, Tennessee. This beautiful drive draws just about every visitor to the park, and for good reason. With the **overlooks** that give big views of the eastern and western Smokies, sunrise at **Clingmans Dome,** quiet wooded strolls and **short day hikes,** spring wildflowers, and stellar fall color, it's where you can say, "I went to Great Smoky Mountains National Park and it was great" and mean every word.

WESTERN SMOKIES

In the western Smokies you find some busy spots like **Cades Cove, Fontana Lake,** and **Deep Creek** (a little less visited, but still busy), and a

Clingmans Dome

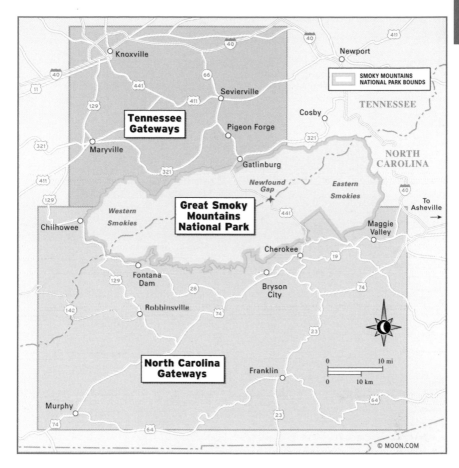

few places, like **Abrams Creek,** where visitors are infrequent. **Fly-fishing** is outstanding here, as the creeks flow into various rivers and into Fontana Lake. Long-distance hikers come here for the **Appalachian Trail, Lakeshore Trail,** and other big backpacking adventures.

EASTERN SMOKIES

The eastern Smokies are less visited, but spots like **Cosby, Cataloochee, Balsam Mountain,** and **Greenbrier** offer the remoteness and rugged beauty that characterize this park. **Camping, day hikes,** and **backpacking** adventures are the norm here. While many casual visitors don't

frequent this region, serious outdoorspeople do. The **wildlife-viewing** alone makes this part of the park worth every minute you spend here.

Tennessee Gateways

Gatlinburg, the western gateway to the Smokies, has delighted families for generations, while nearby **Pigeon Forge** is home to **Dollywood,** the mountain-themed amusement park from the country music legend. **Knoxville,** a big-time college town and one of Tennessee's music cities, offers a taste of city living at the edge of the Smokies. All three towns are tourist draws in their own right, and their blend of Southern

If You're Looking For...

- **Backpacking:** Make overnight reservations in advance to backpack to Mount LeConte, or hike a section of the Appalachian Trail and stay in one of the backcountry campsites.

- **Bicycling:** Get up early to rent a bike from the Cades Cove Store and ride the loop car-free in summer.

- **Camping:** The Cataloochee Valley offers solitude; or time it right to see fireflies at Elkmont Campground.

- **Hiking:** Follow the easy Hen Wallow Falls Trail to a lovely waterfall, take in the views from the top of Andrews Bald, or make the trek to Rocky Top, a mountain immortalized in song. Adventurous souls can step foot on the Appalachian Trail.

- **Historic Sites:** Watch living history demonstrations at the Mountain Farm Museum or explore the chapel and cemetery of Cataloochee's former communities.

- **Scenic Drives:** Cruise along Newfound Gap Road for epic views and scenic overlooks. Drive through Roaring Fork Motor Nature Trail for close-up views of the hills and hollows.

- **Solitude:** Camp at Abrams Creek or Cosby Campgrounds, drive along Balsam Mountain Road, or take a midday hike in the Cataloochee valley.

- **Waterfalls:** Hike to Grotto Falls, gear up and head to Abrams Falls, or get ready to take a dip in Midnight Hole while you hike along Big Creek Trail.

hospitality, humor, and mountain culture makes quite the impression.

North Carolina Gateways

Newfound Gap Road begins in **Cherokee, North Carolina.** This place is the ancestral home of the Eastern Band of the Cherokee Nation, and they celebrate their history and culture, past and present, on the **Qualla Boundary.** Between Cherokee and Asheville, small appealing towns like **Dillsboro, Waynesville,** and **Sylva** are rich with history and culture, while a town like **Bryson City** has embraced its place as an outdoor center and doorway to the park.

Located between the Blue Ridge and Smokies, with easy access to the mountains, **Asheville** is home to the lauded **Biltmore Estate,** some of the best **restaurants and breweries** in the South, and a number of cool **inns** and **B&Bs.** Only 90 minutes away, staying here makes getting to Great Smoky Mountains National Park easy.

When to Go

High Season

SUMMER (JUNE-AUG.)

Summer draws a **big number of visitors** escaping the summer heat at cooler high elevations and spending their vacation days in a beautiful part of the world. Beat the heat by tubing in **Deep Creek** or going **white-water rafting** on the Nantahala or Pigeon Rivers, or head to spots like Cades Cove for **early morning bike rides** or even **mountaintop hikes** throughout summer. Plan for **warm weather** and pack shorts and light tops and plenty of water as well as sunscreen and bug spray.

AUTUMN (SEPT.-MID-NOV.)

Autumn is the obvious season to visit the mountains. With leaves showing their last—and brightest—bit of **fall color** from the end of **September** through **October,** you can have as long a season of leaf-peeping as you want. This is prime time to hit some of the park's **backroads**—Balsam, Heintooga Ridge, Little Greenbrier, Rich Mountain, and Heintooga Round Bottom Roads—for great views before the **routes close (early to mid-Nov.).** Every hike becomes a color study, and around every bend you'll find towering trees and sky-scraping mountainsides alive with gold, red, even purple leaves.

Most days are warm and sunny in the daytime, chilly in the evening, and even cold at the highest elevations. You'll be fine in long sleeves and a vest or light jacket most of the time, but you'll want something a little heavier if you're visiting late in the season.

Low Season

WINTER (MID-NOV.-FEB.)

Winter in this region varies by elevation. At the highest points, the temperatures drop—plummet, even—and the chance of snow or ice is real. It's a little warmer at the lowest elevations, but make no mistake, it's still winter. **Clingmans Dome Road** and **Roaring Fork Motor Nature Trail close** in late November when inclement winter weather has the potential to arrive, but the other roads stay open as weather allows.

Expect snow several times throughout the season, with a few significant snowfalls; come with some warm layers, a hat, and gloves.

SPRING (MAR.-MAY)

Spring rains bring **wildflowers** and **waterfalls** back to life. Though trails can be muddy, it's a fabulous time to visit, especially for **wildlife-viewing.** In **Cades Cove** and **Cataloochee,** you'll see bear cubs, deer fawn, and elk calves trailing their mothers at the woods' edge. The park's back roads—Balsam, Heintooga Ridge, Little Greenbrier, Parson Branch, Rich Mountain, and Heintooga Round Bottom Roads—as well as **Roaring Fork Motor Nature Trail** and **Clingmans Dome Road reopen.**

Spring temperatures are similar to fall, with warm days and cooler or even cold evenings, so pack accordingly—just remember to throw in a rain jacket.

Before You Go

Park Fees and Passes

Great Smoky Mountains National Park (www.nps.gov/grsm) is **free** to visit. Backcountry campgrounds require permits and reservations through the **Backcountry Information Office** (Sugarlands Visitor Center, 865/436-1297, https://smokiespermits.nps.gov, 8am-5pm daily, $4 pp per night) up to 30 days in advance.

Entrance Stations

There are three main entrances to Great Smoky Mountains National Park. Each entrance is easily accessed from a nearby gateway town:

- From **Gatlinburg, Tennessee,** follow U.S. 441 south two miles to the north entrance to the park.

- From **Cherokee, North Carolina,** drive two miles north along U.S. 441 to the south entrance to the park.

- From **Townsend, Tennessee,** take Highway 73 east for three miles into the park near Cades Cove.

Reservations

Reservations are recommended at most **campgrounds** and required at others in the national park and along the Blue Ridge Parkway, especially during the peak seasons of summer and fall. Reservations for **hotels and B&Bs** in the gateway towns of Cherokee, Bryson City, and Asheville, North Carolina, or Gatlinburg, Pigeon Forge, or Knoxville, Tennessee, are recommended during summer and fall.

In the Park

Visitors Centers

The busiest information center in the park is **Sugarlands Visitor Center and Park Headquarters** (1420 Old Hwy. 73 Scenic, 865/436-1200, www.nps.gov/grsm, 8am-4:30pm daily Dec.-Feb., except Dec. 25, 8am-5pm daily Mar. and Nov., 8am-6pm daily Apr.-May and Sept.-Oct., 8am-7pm daily June-Aug.), located in Gatlinburg, Tennessee, at the north entrance to Newfound Gap Road.

If entering from the North Carolina side, **Oconaluftee Visitor Center** (1194 Newfound Gap Rd., 828/497-1904, www.nps.gov/grsm, 8am-4:30pm daily Dec.-Feb., except Dec. 25, 8am-5pm daily Mar. and Nov., 9am-6pm daily Apr.-May and Sept.-Oct., 8am-7pm daily June-Aug.) is just two miles north of Cherokee at the south entrance to Newfound Gap Road.

Where to Stay

LeConte Lodge (865/429-5704, www.lecontelodge.com, Mar. 21-Nov. 22) is the only true lodging in the park, accessible via a 5-6.8-mile hike. Even though there is no running water or electricity, the lodge books quickly. Reservations are via lottery up to **one year in advance.** For more amenities, plan to stay in the gateway towns of **Cherokee, North Carolina,** or **Gatlinburg, Tennessee.**

There are 10 developed campgrounds in the park. **Campground reservations** (877/444-6777, www.recreation.gov, $17.50-25) are accepted up to **six months in advance** for the following sites:

- **Elkmont Campground** (220 sites, Gatlinburg, TN, Mar.-Nov.), located west of Sugarlands Visitor Center, is the largest of the campgrounds and one of the most visited.

LeConte Lodge

- **Smokemont Campground** (142 sites, Cherokee, NC, year-round) is just off Newfound Gap Road, 3.2 miles north of the Oconaluftee Visitor Center.

- **Cades Cove Campground** (159 sites, Townsend, TN, year-round) is a popular spot located on the east side off Cades Cove Loop.

- **Cosby Campground** (157 sites, Cosby, TN, Apr.-Oct.) is the park's third-largest campground, located in the quiet northwest corner of the park.

- **Cataloochee Campground** (Cataloochee, NC, Mar.-Oct.) has only 27 tent and RV sites

in a valley on the west side. Reservations are required.

All other developed park campgrounds are a mix of **first-come, first-served** and **reservation only,** and are typically open April-October.

Getting Around

There are no park shuttles or public transportation available within the park—you will need **your own vehicle** (though there are a few for-hire hiking shuttles). There are also **no gas stations** in the park; fill up first in Cherokee, North Carolina; Gatlinburg, Tennessee; or Townsend, Tennessee.

Best of the Smokies

What do you do in Great Smoky Mountains National Park? Seeing how the park is mountainous and wild and that trails rather than roads lead into every corner, cove, and holler, it can be puzzling. But don't worry; we have plenty of ideas on how to spend a week you'll never forget in Great Smoky Mountains National Park.

Day 1
NEWFOUND GAP ROAD

Base yourself in **Gatlinburg,** Tennessee, where you'll have all manner of accommodations options and tempting entertainments easily at hand. Begin your exploration of the Smokies at the **Sugarlands Visitor Center,** a mere two miles from Gatlinburg at the northern end of Newfound Gap Road where you can pick up maps, trail advice, and tips on where to spot the best wildflowers and wildlife.

As you drive **Newfound Gap Road** through the park, think about what kind of hike you want to stop and take. Is it something easy like a stroll along the **Kephart Prong Trail**? Or something challenging like the 5-mile hike to **Alum Cave Bluffs** or the 10-mile (round-trip) trek to the top of **Mount LeConte**? Along the way you'll pass trailheads and marked paths aplenty, and there's something to suit your hiking style.

Stop at any overlooks that catch your interest as you climb to the crest of the mountains on Newfound Gap Road. When you reach the gap, take the time to visit **Clingmans Dome,** the highest peak in the park. From the viewing platform at the top (an easy walk), you'll have a jaw-dropping view of the surrounding country. If you haven't taken that hike yet, **Andrews Bald** is nearby, and a moderate 3.5-mile trek will lead you to a high mountain meadow often ablaze with wildflowers.

Take Newfound Gap Road to the **Oconaluftee Visitor Center** in Cherokee, North Carolina. Stop here to check out the historic cabins and

the summit of Mount LeConte

Best of the Park in One Day

If all you have is one day to spend in Great Smoky Mountains National Park, don't sweat it. You can still see a lot (and plan a return trip as soon as you can).

Start the day in Gatlinburg with a stop at Sugarlands Visitor Center to pick up maps and find out about special events. Follow Little River Road west toward Cades Cove. You never move too fast on this curvy road, so slow down and take your time to soak up the views.

At Cades Cove, grab a map and a driving guide for the scenic 11-mile Cades Cove Loop, one of the most popular drives in the park. Though there may be company—crowds, even—this wide verdant valley ringed by tall peaks is the very picture of calm rural beauty. Stop for a walk to John Oliver Cabin, the Methodist Church, or one of the many cabins that showcase the history of settlement here. Once you've seen Cades Cove, return to grab lunch in Gatlinburg.

Newfound Gap Road connects Gatlinburg, Tennessee, to Cherokee, North Carolina. Follow Newfound Gap Road up and over the Smokies. Along the way, stop at the Kephart Prong Trail or one of the other quiet walkways, and head into the woods for a short, easy walk that'll have you immersed in nature in no time. In 23 miles, you'll reach the turnoff to Clingmans Dome, the highest peak in the park. If the weather is good, you'll be able to see the observation tower at the summit as you drive up Newfound Gap. After the 8-mile drive to the parking area, make the short, steep hike to the top. If the summit is shrouded in clouds (and it may well be), continue south along the crest of the Smokies.

Stop at Newfound Gap to check out the

driving Newfound Gap Road

Rockefeller Memorial, the place where president Franklin Delano Roosevelt dedicated the park in 1940. As you continue east toward Cherokee, stop at any of the scenic overlooks along the way—you can't go wrong.

You'll draw close to the Oconaluftee Visitor Center in North Carolina by the end of the day. Perfect timing, as elk make an appearance every evening in a field adjacent to the visitors center and the Mountain Farm Museum. While checking out the collection of historic structures at Mountain Farm, keep an eye out for elk; they will often cross right through the middle of this recreated farmstead on their way to dinner.

structures at the Mountain Farm Museum and scan the field for the herd of elk that call these hills home before returning to Gatlinburg. Once you're back in Tennessee, it's time for dinner at Local Goat or Mama's Chicken Kitchen before you hit Sugarlands Distilling or Ole Smoky for a little moonshine to calm your nerves.

Day 2
ROARING FORK

In the morning, have breakfast at the Pancake Pantry, and then head for the Roaring Fork Motor Nature Trail for today's hike. Depending on how adventurous you feel, this can be a half-day exploration of a waterfall or two, or a strenuous 14-mile trek to **Mount LeConte** and back. Either way, start off by hiking to **Rainbow Falls,** an 80-foot waterfall on LeConte Creek. For a short hike, turn around and hoof it back to the trailhead once you've seen the falls; to reach the summit of Mount LeConte, continue on the trail but be ready for a long, hard day of it. **Baskins Creek Falls** is a smaller waterfall—only 30 feet—but few people make the tough hike in to see it, so it's a bit of a hidden gem.

Since you've earned your supper, go for some traditional stick-to-your-ribs country cooking at **The Pottery House Café and Grill** in Pigeon Forge before taking in a show like **Paula Deen's Lumberjack Feud** and calling it a night.

Day 3
COSBY

Head northeast to **Cosby** for a night of camping at **Cosby Campground,** where you'll have your choice of beautiful day hikes. **Hen Wallow Falls** and **Albright Grove** offer easy, wildflower-filled hikes. The trip to the stone fire tower at the top of **Mount Cammerer** is a long, tough day on the trail, but well worth it. If you've brought your fishing gear (and license), catch dinner in **Cosby Creek.**

Day 4
CATALOOCHEE

In the morning, break camp and head north on Highway 32 for breakfast in Cosby at **Janice's Diner.** From Cosby, follow Foothills Parkway east to I-40 and take the scenic route south to **Mount Sterling Road,** a drive of about an hour. Along Mount Sterling Road, roll down the windows, relax, and breathe deeply—you're almost at one of the most secluded areas of the park.

In **Cataloochee,** register at the campground (reserve a site in advance), set up your tent, and enjoy a picnic lunch before lacing up your boots and heading into the valley. Look for **elk** in the field across from **Caldwell House,** or hike to **Palmer Chapel, Little Cataloochee,** or the **Steve Woody House.** Anglers can wet a line in one of the nearby creeks and try to catch dinner. Sunset signals time for chow and

the Caldwell House in Cataloochee

Family Fun

Great Smoky Mountains National Park is an ideal place to show kids the wonders of the great outdoors and the importance of our national parks. In addition to the Junior Ranger Program and ranger-led activities, there are several places that are perfect for kids.

- **Mountain Farm Museum:** This life-size model of a working mountain farm gives kids a feel for life here years ago.

- **Synchronous Fireflies:** These rare fireflies blink in unison as they fly above a field near the Elkmont Campground four a couple of weeks each summer. And if you miss the synchronous fireflies, keep your eyes peeled for their more typical cousins in any field around dusk.

- **Elk Watching:** Visit Cataloochee to see the elk herd there or stick around the Oconaluftee Visitor Center where they make their appearance at dusk if not before.

- **Morning Bike Ride:** Head to Cades Cove bright and early (Wed. and Sat. May-Sept.) when the road is closed to cars but open to bicycles and foot traffic. Rent a bike and spend the morning pedaling around in relative solitude.

- **Big Creek Trail:** This gentle hike includes wildflowers galore, a stream for wading, a swimming hole, and a 35-foot waterfall cascade.

cycling Cades Cove Loop

- **Go Fish:** Try your hand at fly-fishing. Cherokee, North Carolina, has weekly fishing contests for kids and adults. Fontana Lake is full of fish in the deep water and feeder streams. All along Little River you'll find plenty of places to wet a line, and in Bryson City, North Carolina, you can fly-fish downtown in the Tuckasegee River.

stargazing—there's so little light pollution that the celestial show is breathtaking. Sit back and enjoy.

Day 5
CADES COVE

Today, we head west to **Cades Cove,** a mountain community that was one of the first places settled on the western side of the Smokies. The 11-mile **Cades Cove Loop** leads through the former settlement and a collection of homes and structures. Take a moderate hike to **Abrams Falls,** a 20-foot waterfall, or follow the **Rich Mountain Loop,** a big day hike; either way, you'll find plenty of scenery. Take your time exploring because you're pitching a tent in **Cades Cove Campground** (reserve in advance) tonight. Once it's dark, be sure to take a walk and admire the stars.

Day 6
FONTANA LAKE AND DEEP CREEK

The next day, follow **Rich Mountain Road** out of Cades Cove to its junction with U.S. 321 near Townsend. Soon you'll get on the **Foothills Parkway** and skirt the southern edge of the park before crossing the border into **North Carolina** at **Deals Gap.**

After Deals Gap, follow Highway 28 east along Cheoah Lake and past **Twentymile** to Fontana Village. To stretch your legs, turn north toward **Fontana Dam,** at the western end of Fontana Lake, and the trailhead for **Shuckstack Mountain,** a strenuous hike along the **Appalachian Trail.**

Or stay eastbound on Highway 28 and U.S. 74 all the way to **Bryson City.** Stop for lunch at the **Nantahala Brewing Brewpub** before turning north for your overnight at the **Deep Creek Tube Center and Campground.** For a short hike, follow the trail to **Juney Whank Falls,** or head to the **Road to Nowhere,** an abandoned highway project that terminates with a tunnel through the mountain and hike alongside Fontana Lake.

After a long day, relax at the campground in Deep Creek, which offers a relaxing treat: **tubing.** Wash away the sweat and trail dust with a float trip and some splashing in the creek. If you need more refreshment, head back to Bryson City to call on **Nantahala Brewing Brewpub, Mountain Layers Brewing Company,** or the **Taproom** at **Bryson City Outdoors** for a pint or two.

Day 7
CHEROKEE, NORTH CAROLINA

For your final day, head to Cherokee, the ancestral heart of the Cherokee Nation and home of the Eastern Band of Cherokee Indians. The drive from Deep Creek is a short one, so you'll have a full day to explore. Start by visiting the **Museum of the Cherokee Indian,** where you'll learn the Cherokee creation story, hear songs and legends, and discover the heartache of the Trail of Tears. Across the street at the **Qualla Arts and Crafts Mutual,** browse the traditional arts and crafts made by Cherokee artisans and craftspeople, then head up the hill to the **Oconaluftee Indian Village** to see how the tribe lived in the 18th and 19th centuries.

Grab a belly-busting country buffet lunch at **Granny's Kitchen.** In the evening, head to **Harrah's Cherokee Casino,** where you can entertain yourself by dropping $20 on table games or slots before dining at one of the on-site restaurants. The casino has overnight accommodations, or you can spend a quiet night at **Panther Creek Cabins.**

In the morning, it's a 1.5-hour drive to the airport in Asheville and the flight home.

Best Hikes

There are so many wonderful hikes it can be hard to choose. Here are some bonus details to keep in mind when searching for your perfect trail.

If You're Looking For...

Waterfalls:

- The popular **Grotto Falls Trail** (2.6 miles round trip) leads to a picture-perfect waterfall off the **Roaring Fork Motor Nature Trail**.

- In **Cosby** (a few miles northeast of Gatlinburg), you'll find **Hen Wallow Falls Trail** (4.4 miles round-trip) which leads to a delicate waterfall some 90 feet high.

- **Deep Creek Loop Trail and Juney Whank Falls** (5.5 miles round trip) is a double loop hike that will take you past a trio of waterfalls and alongside a stream perfect for wading. It's easy enough to give everyone in your party a good time on the trail.

- A hike suited to just about anyone? That leads to a great waterfall? The hike to the 20-foot **Abrams Falls** (5 miles round trip) is the one—and it's in **Cades Cove**, so you know you'll drive right by the trailhead.

Wildflowers:

- **Andrews Bald** (3.5 miles round trip) is a trail that starts at **Clingmans Dome,** a few miles off Newfound Gap Road, and leads to a high mountain meadow filled with wildflowers and shrubs that bloom throughout summer, making it one of the most rewarding hikes you'll find.

- Over in **Cades Cove** head to **Rich Mountain Loop** (8.5 miles round trip) and take on all or some of the hike that's loaded with wildflowers from mid-April through summer. Spring's a hot time here, with wildflowers peaking in early May, but you'll see plenty anytime you hike here.

Hen Wallow Falls Trail

The park can attract crowds, especially at certain times of the year or along popular trails. Avoid the throngs by planning a wintertime hike, or explore the seldom-seen regions of the park.

- **Balsam Mountain Road:** The road's location off the Blue Ridge Parkway means people tend to forget this beautiful corner of the park. Head here in the fall to immerse yourself in foliage and escape from the typical leaf-peeping traffic.

- **Mount Cammerer:** This strenuous hike is avoided by many, but it rewards with an unparalleled view. The few folks on this trail are here to be surrounded by the Smokies—and to dodge the crowds.

- **Lakeshore Trail:** Start this trail from Fontana Dam to avoid foot traffic. You'll see the dam and have a tough uphill right off the start, but the western end of the trail is a beautiful one.

- **Big Creek:** An almost-forgotten campground and some awesome hikes in a corner of the park most visitors overlook? That's Big Creek. Camp here, backpack to Mount Sterling, or check out the suited-for-everyone Big Creek Trail.

- **Abrams Creek:** This seasonal campground is

Abrams Creek

rarely full; even if it is, several great hikes originate here. Hit the Rabbit and Abrams Creeks Loop or hike the easy, wildflower-rich Little Bottoms Trail.

- Along the first section of the **Chestnut Top Trail** (5.4 miles one way), the number and variety of wildflowers is surprising, making it a favorite of Spring Wildflower Pilgrimage visitors.

- When you hike from **Brushy Mountain to Mount LeConte** (11.8 miles round trip), your time on the **Porters Creek Trail** is a riot of wildflowers. Along the first mile of this trail you'll find yellow trillium, wild geranium, and more.

Wildlife:

- **Rich Mountain Loop** (8.5 miles round trip) in **Cades Cove** is a long one, but it gives you views of Cades Cove and plenty of wildlife-watching opportunities, making it one of the top hikes in the park.

- Keep **Little River Trail** (12.3 miles round trip) short and sweet as you follow an old logging road alongside Little River and through the home of the **synchronous fireflies,** or follow the whole trail for an out-and-back day hike.

- The family-friendly **Oconaluftee River Trail** (3 miles round trip) follows the Oconaluftee River near the Mountain Farm Museum and a field frequented by elk, which you can spot on the trail, crossing the trail, and even basking in the river. Remember to be careful and not get too close when you see an elk nearby.

Alum Cave Trail

Swimming Holes:

- **Big Creek Trail** (10.6 miles round trip) follows a onetime logging road through the woods on a steady, easy incline that soon reaches **Midnight Hole,** a popular, and deep, swimming hole fed by a small waterfall; continue on the trail to see the 35-foot Mouse Creek Falls.

- **Chimney Tops Trail** (4-miles round-trip) leads to a fantastic view, but when you're hot from spending time on the trail, nothing is more refreshing than jumping into one of the deep holes in the creek for a shock of cold mountain water.

- Don't think **Little River Trail** (12.3 miles round trip) is just for the synchronous fireflies; there's an excellent swimming hole with rocks for sunbathing near the trailhead, and several swimming holes up the trail.

- **Alum Cave Trail** (5 miles one way) follows LeConte Creek for a little way, and along the first 1.5 miles of this trail, you'll find a few swimming holes that are 4 or 5 feet deep, which is plenty to cool off.

Views:

- **Mount Cammerer Trail** (11.2 miles round trip) is a tough hike to the summit, but you're rewarded with some of the best views in the park, courtesy of a **stone fire tower** built in the 1930s.

- More of a really steep path than a proper trail, the trek to the observation platform on the summit of **Clingmans Dome** (0.5 mile one way) is a must-do for anyone who wants big mountain views. Be sure to check the weather before you get started because your view could vary between 7 yards and 70 miles (when you can see seven states), depending on cloud cover.

- The trail to **Baskins Creek Falls** (3 miles round trip) leads you to a beautiful short view—the 30-foot namesake waterfall—but along the way you'll be rewarded with wildflowers filling meadows, the remnants of old homesites standing in the forest, and the chance to spot a white-tailed deer or two.

Great Smoky Mountains National Park

Great Smoky Mountains National Park wears a well-earned title: Great.

In its lifetime the park has seen more than 510 million visitors, with 11.4 million visiting in 2018 alone. Why do they come? The mountains, the sky, the wildlife, the waters, the peaks, the stories—all of it. The Smokies are laced with trails; rivers, streams, and waterfalls trace their courses through the wrinkled mountains; and wildlife, from rare salamanders to huge elk to black bears, call this place home.

Straddling the North Carolina-Tennessee state line, Great Smoky Mountains National Park's 522,427 acres are nearly equally split between the two states. On the slightly larger North Carolina side of the park, the mountains pile up against one another, making for tall

Look for ★ to find recommended sights, activities, dining, and lodging.

★ **Drive Newfound Gap Road:** Bisecting the park, this 33-mile route offers plenty of long views, short hikes, and streamside driving (page 41).

★ **Catch the View from Clingmans Dome:** From this third-highest peak in the eastern United States, you can see up to 100 miles on a clear day (page 44).

★ **Hike Andrews Bald:** Hike to one of the prettiest high-altitude meadows in the Smokies (page 47).

★ **Hike Hen Wallow Falls Trail:** An easy out-and-back day hike leads to one of the loveliest waterfalls in the park (page 61).

★ **Hike Big Creek Trail:** This creek-side trek is perfect for young and beginner hikers. Make it a 2- or 10-mile hike that includes waterfalls and wildflowers (page 65).

★ **Camp in Cataloochee:** Spending the night in this secluded valley—with its Milky Way views, solitude, and frequent elk sightings—is bliss (page 68).

★ **Drive Cades Cove Loop:** The most-visited spot in the park offers plenty of wildlife viewing and its largest collection of intact historic structures (page 80).

★ **Hike Abrams Falls Trail:** This Cades Cove hike brings you through the forest to the 20-foot Abrams Falls, where a picnic lunch with your feet in the plunge pool is in order (page 82).

peaks, steep slopes, and deep coves. It's wild here and more sparsely populated than on the Tennessee side, but throughout the park you'll find places so remote and so isolated they've remained undisturbed by humans for impossible stretches of time, or at least they feel that way. As wild and secret as these mountains are, you'll also find places like Cades Cove where the first pioneers to crest the mountain range and push into Tennessee found a wide, fertile valley—the perfect place to settle. Today the remote places are still remote, requiring sometimes considerable effort to reach, but Cades Cove is a sightseer's delight with its preserved historic churches, schools, and homesteads, and in the fall, droves of visitors come for one of the most impressive color shows in the eastern United States.

The park comprises more than 800 square miles of cloud-ringed peaks and rainforest. The park was designated an International Biosphere Reserve in 1976 and a World Heritage Site in 1983, and researchers, like the nonprofit organization Discover Life in America (www.dlia.org), come here to study the flora and fauna. Tens of thousands of species of plants and animals reside here, with 80 species of reptiles and amphibians alone, which is why the park is sometimes called the Salamander Capital of the World. More than 200 species of birds nest here, and 60-plus mammals—from mice to mountain lions (though the mountain lions are unofficial denizens, you can hear tales of a sighting now and again)—roam these hills. Discover Life in America's All-Taxa Biodiversity Inventory (a census of all nonmicrobial life forms) of Great Smoky Mountains National Park has turned up 970 species of plants and animals previously unknown to science.

The deep wilderness here makes an awesome refuge for outdoor enthusiasts, and the accessibility of the park's absolutely ravishing scenery makes it ideal for visitors of all ability levels and nearly all interests.

PLANNING YOUR TIME

Many visitors devote a single day to the park, driving Newfound Gap Road, taking a short hike along the way, and circling Cades Cove before moving on. To give the park a fair shake, devote at least **three days** to exploring. Spend a day in the north end of the park in Cataloochee Valley, then devote another day to savoring the sights of Newfound Gap Road, including a stop by Clingmans Dome and time to drive Cades Cove. On the third day, pick a waterfall to visit or trail to hike; on the Roaring Fork Motor Nature Trail, you'll find both.

Within the park, **lodging** is limited to camping—unless you want to pack your sleeping bag and hike to the rustic LeConte Lodge just below the summit of Mount LeConte—so your best bet for hotels, motels, inns, cabins, and B&Bs are the Tennessee towns of **Gatlinburg, Pigeon Forge, Townsend,** and **Knoxville;** or the North Carolina towns of **Cherokee, Bryson City, Maggie Valley, Sylva, Dillsboro,** or **Asheville.**

When to Go

Seasonal considerations have a big influence on park visitation. Crowds arrive for the blooming of **spring** wildflowers, and each **autumn** the park is crawling with visitors for a good long look at the mountains blazing with red, yellow, and burgundy leaves. **Summer** brings visitors for hiking and that cool mountain air, while **winter** finds the park more empty than full, but no less beautiful.

Weather can vary wildly across the park in any season, due in part to the elevation, which ranges from 900 feet at the lowest point to more than 6,600 feet at the highest. Clingmans Dome, the highest point in the park, has an average high temperature of only 65°F in July; the only time you're guaranteed *not* to see snow flurries are June-August. In contrast, you will find temperatures in the

---

Previous: Abrams Creek; stream along Chimney Tops trail; the ramp to the viewing platform on Clingmans Dome upper 60s on Clingmans Dome the same day, and it can be in the low 90s with some contentious humidity in Cades Cove.

If ever there was a place for wearing layers, this is it. Be sure to pack long sleeves or a light jacket and your rain gear, regardless of the season. Keep these extremes in mind in terms of safety as well: a snowstorm can bring two feet of snow to the highest elevations and leave ice on the curvy mountain roads while temperatures at the foot of the mountains are considerably warmer and snow-free. Thick fog and isolated storms are also a possibility year-round.

SPRING

Spring wildflowers begin to appear in late **March** and peak in mid- to late-**April.** This time of year, rain is common and there's a chance of a spring snowstorm (especially at higher elevations, but even at the base of the mountains) or a strong spring thunderstorm. It's a muddy time to hit the trail, and you'll want to pack layers and foul-weather gear if you plan on heading into the woods. Temperatures begin to climb in spring, working toward summer's warmth, but it happens in fits and starts, another reason to keep a sweater or jacket handy when visiting in the spring.

The wildflower show bleeds over into early summer as azaleas, mountain laurels, and rhododendrons put on their best show just after the season transitions to summer, but due to the park's extensive microclimates, it's possible to see flame azaleas blooming early, peaking **April-July.** Mountain laurels come next, blooming **May-June,** and rhododendrons come last with a burst of color in **June-July.** You'll find the wildflowers bloom from the bottom of the mountain to the top, with patches of color and reports of blooms occurring first at lower elevations and ending at the high balds and ridgelines.

SUMMER AND FALL

Summer and fall constitute the park's high season; the busiest times to visit are **mid-June**

to **mid-August** and throughout **October.** In summer, the most popular hiking trails don't quite resemble a queue, but you're guaranteed to encounter many groups of hikers of all ages and ability levels coming and going. In fall, these same trails are busy with picture-takers; if fall color is on your agenda, consider spending more time on the gravel roads and long hikes and in seldom-seen corners of the park's extreme north and south ends.

Fall color is on everyone's mind when they visit in October. The mountaintops are the first to show signs of the season's best and brightest show as they begin to turn in early October. Colors bleed down the mountain, descending until early November, when the trees from the foot to the crest of the mountains are aflame with color. Note that the color's arrival and departure isn't set, summer heat can alter the schedule for wildflower blooms and fall color, and rainfall can do the same. It's best to call the park or check regional websites to see how fall color is progressing. It's a safe bet to visit in **mid-October** for a solid color show.

Temperatures throughout summer and fall can get as high as the low 90s (F) at the lowest elevations, though high temperatures and humidity are relatively rare. There is an extreme of temperature to consider, though. Spots like Clingmans Dome can be chilly even in the summer, with as much as a 30°F difference from peak to valley floor. Those temperature extremes also give rise to the park's namesake "smoky" effect as layers of fog can fill valleys or wrap the peaks. If you visit Clingmans Dome and find it enshrouded in fog, try again in an hour or two, or even the next day, and the weather will likely reward you.

WINTER

Winter can be a fantastic time to visit the park, especially if you're there for a bit of snow. The crowds are nearly nonexistent, and maintained roads like Cades Cove Loop and Newfound Gap are starkly beautiful. Along the mountain ridges, trails, and streams, as well as among the historic structures, you'll find lovely, lonely sights.

Great Smoky Mountains

KNOXVILLE

French

Broad

River

Sevierville

TENNESSEE MUSEUM
OF AVIATION

FIVE OAKS MALL

West Prong
Little Pigeon
River

0   4 mi

0   4 km

Pigeon
Forge

DOLLYWOOD

Alcoa

Maryville

Wears
Valley

OBER GATLINBURG
SKI AREA

Chilhowee Mtn

PKWY

FOOTHILLS

LITTLE RIVER
RAILROAD AND
LUMBER MUSEUM

Townsend

METCALPH
BOTTOMS

LITTLE
GREENBRIER
SCHOOL

SUGARLANDS
VISITOR
CENTER

Laurel
Falls

TUCKALEECHEE
CAVERNS

(Closed in
winter)

MTN

RICH

Abrams Ck

LOOK ROCK
CAMPGROUND

ABRAMS CREEK
CAMPGROUND

ABRAMS FALLS
TRAIL

Rich Mountain

ELKMONT
CAMPGROUND

GREAT SMOKY MOUNTAINS
INSTITUTE AT TREMONT

Sugarland

Little River

CADES COVE

Creek

Great   Smoky   Mountains

Thunderhead
Mountain
5,530ft

Silers Bald
5,607ft

Spence Field
4,900ft

PARSONS BRANCH RD
(Closed in winter)

Gregory Bald
4,948ft

TN
NC

Great Smoky Mountains

National Park

129

Cherokee

National

Forest

Shuckstack
4,020ft

TWENTYMILE

Lake
Cheoah

FONTANA
DAM

Fontana
Lake

Fontana
Village

28

Nantahala   National   Forest

© MOON.COM

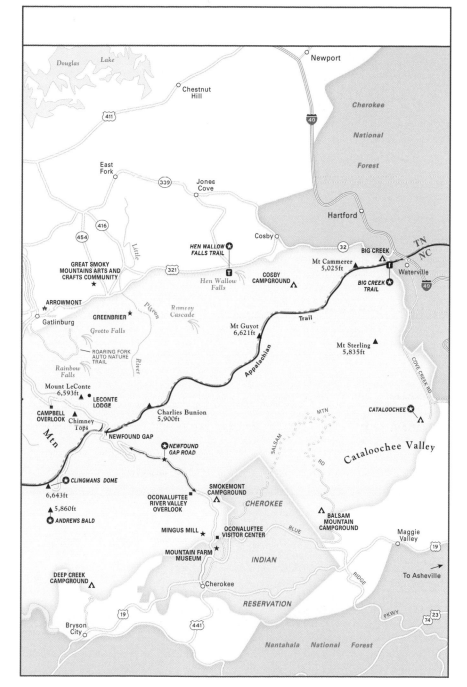

Douglas Lake

Newport

Chestnut Hill

411

Cherokee

National

Forest

East Fork

339

Jones Cove

416

Hartford

454

Little

Cosby

321

HEN WALLOW FALLS TRAIL

Hen Wallow Falls

COSBY CAMPGROUND

Mt Cammerer 5,025ft

32

BIG CREEK

Waterville

GREAT SMOKY MOUNTAINS ARTS AND CRAFTS COMMUNITY

BIG CREEK TRAIL

40

TN NC

ARROWMONT

Gatlinburg

GREENBRIER

Grotto Falls

Pigeon

Ramsey Cascade

Mt Guyot 6,621ft

Trail

Mt Sterling 5,835ft

COVE CREEK RD

ROARING FORK AUTO NATURE TRAIL

River

Appalachian

Rainbow Falls

Mount LeConte 6,593ft

LECONTE LODGE

CAMPBELL OVERLOOK

Chimney Tops

Charlies Bunion 5,900ft

MTN

CATALOOCHEE

Mtn

NEWFOUND GAP

NEWFOUND GAP ROAD

BALSAM

RD

Cataloochee Valley

CLINGMANS DOME

6,643ft

5,860ft

ANDREWS BALD

OCONALUFTEE RIVER VALLEY OVERLOOK

SMOKEMONT CAMPGROUND

CHEROKEE

BALSAM MOUNTAIN CAMPGROUND

Maggie Valley

19

MINGUS MILL

OCONALUFTEE VISITOR CENTER

BLUE

MOUNTAIN FARM MUSEUM

INDIAN

To Asheville

DEEP CREEK CAMPGROUND

Cherokee

RIDGE

RESERVATION

PKWY

23

19

441

74

Bryson City

Nantahala National Forest

Temperatures can hit highs of 50°F, but more often than not it's cold, with nighttime temperatures at or below freezing (32°F, and colder at high elevations) and daytime temperatures in the 40s. Snow is possible, with most significant snow occurring in **January-February.**

Several roads in the park are closed in the winter, though closing dates vary. Among these are Balsam Mountain, Clingmans Dome, Little Greenbrier, Rich Mountain,

and Heintooga Round Bottom Roads, and the Roaring Fork Motor Nature Trail. The **Blue Ridge Parkway,** which starts (or ends) in Cherokee, North Carolina, also closes in the winter. **Newfound Gap Road** remains open in all but the most serious of weather; however, road crews work to maintain it in the winter. Before you set out, check current road conditions (865/436-1200, ext. 631, or on Twitter by following @SmokiesRoadNPS) and the weather (865/436-1200, ext. 630).

Exploring the Park

Great Smoky Mountains National Park (GSMNP, 865/436-1200, www.nps.gov/grsm) was the first—and the largest—of three National Park Service units established in the southern Appalachians. The park was founded in 1934, followed in 1935 by the Blue Ridge Parkway and in 1936 by Shenandoah National Park. These sister facilities include some 600 miles of contiguous roads and close to 800,000 acres of land, all of it acquired from private landholders, and all of it standing testament to the wild, rugged beauty of the Appalachian Mountains and the people who helped to tame these places.

Great Smoky Mountains National Park is the most-visited national park, with visitor numbers approaching 11 million each year. In the 522,427-acre park, there are 850 miles of hiking trails, including 71 miles of the Appalachian Trail; 16 mountains over 6,000 feet; 2,100 miles of mountain streams and rivers; and an astoundingly diverse set of flora and fauna.

More than 17,000 species have been documented here, including more than 100 species of native trees, 1,500 flowering plant species, 200 species of birds, 66 types of mammals, 67 native species of fish, 39 varieties of reptiles, and 43 species of amphibians. And that's not even counting the mushrooms, mollusks, and millipedes. Researchers believe an additional 30,000-80,000 species may exist. No

other area of a similar size in a similar climate can boast a higher number of species. A multitude of factors are believed to have contributed to this astounding diversity, including the wide elevation range (875-6,643 feet), which provides a large variance in temperature, as well as the fantastic growing conditions created by summer's high humidity and abundant rainfall (apart from the Pacific Northwest, these are the rainiest mountains in the country). Plus, as some of the oldest mountains in the world—it is believed they were formed some 200-300 million years ago—the Smokies have seen a number of dramatic climatic changes. During the last ice age (10,000 years ago), the glacial intrusion into the United States didn't reach the Smokies, making them a refuge for species of plants and animals displaced from homes farther north.

VISITORS CENTERS
Begin your exploration of Great Smoky Mountains National Park with a stop at one of the park's four visitors centers. You'll find rangers who know the trail and road conditions as well as what's blooming where. You can also grab detailed maps and trail guides.

Sugarlands Visitor Center
The busiest information center in the park is also the first stop for visitors entering the

Blooms and Foliage

rhododendron

You'll find the most abundant display of spring wildflower blooms in mid- to late April. Keep in mind that the dates for wildflower blooms and fall color displays are only guidelines. A number of factors contribute to peak timing of blooms and changing leaves. Check with park officials for the best times and places to experience the finest each season has to offer. At the highest elevations, **leaves begin to change** during the first two weeks of October, creeping down the mountains and ending in late October or early November.

· **Catawba rhododendron:** Grows at elevations above 3,500 feet; blooms in June.

· **Flame azalea:** This wild shrub blooms at lower elevations in April-May, at higher elevations through June-early July.

· **Mountain laurel:** Blooms early May-June.

· **Rosebay rhododendron:** Blooms in lower elevations in June-July.

· **Witch hazel:** Blooms in late fall and into winter at low and mid-elevations.

· **Yellow fringed orchids:** Blooms throughout summer at lower elevations.

· **Trillium:** This wildflower comes in several colors and blooms in late spring and summer at low and mid-elevations.

park from Tennessee. **Sugarlands Visitor Center and Park Headquarters** (1420 Old Hwy. 73 Scenic, Gatlinburg, TN, 865/436-1200, www.nps.gov/grsm, 8am-4:30pm daily Dec.-Feb., except Dec. 25, 8am-5pm daily Mar. and Nov., 8am-6pm daily Apr.-May and Sept.-Oct., 8am-7pm daily June-Aug.) is located just inside the park, only two miles from Gatlinburg. Here you'll find the usual visitors center information as well as a 20-minute film introducing you to the park.

The **Backcountry Information Office** (865/436-1297, https://smokiespermits.nps. gov, 8am-5pm daily, permits $4 per night, $20 maximum) is located at the Sugarlands Visitor Center. This is the place to get backcountry permits, as well as thru-hiker permits for the Appalachian Trail. Facilities

By the Numbers

Great Smoky Mountains National Park puts up some impressive numbers, from the staggering number of visitors—11,421,200 in 2018—to the incredible biodiversity—970 plant and animal species new to science have been discovered within the park. Its other numbers are just as impressive.

- Size: 522,427 acres

- Elevation: From 875 feet at the mouth of Abrams Creek to the towering summit of Clingmans Dome at 6,643 feet

- 16 peaks standing at more than 6,000 feet elevation

- 850 miles of hiking trails, including 70 miles of the Appalachian Trail

- More than 400,000 hikers annually

- Only 384 miles of roadway in the park; 146 miles are unpaved

- 1,000 front-country campsites

- 730 miles of fish-bearing streams

- And all this with only 240 permanent employees

include restrooms, snack machines, and a **Great Smoky Mountains Association** (www.smokiesinformation.org) bookstore and shop.

Oconaluftee Visitor Center

If you're entering Great Smoky Mountains National Park from the North Carolina side, **Oconaluftee Visitor Center and Mountain Farm Museum** (1194 Newfound Gap Rd., Cherokee, 828/436-1200, www.nps.gov/grsm, 8am-4:30pm daily Dec.-Feb., except Dec. 25, 8am-5pm daily Mar. and Nov., 9am-6pm daily Apr.-May and Sept.-Oct., 8am-7pm daily June-Aug.), just two miles north of Cherokee on U.S. 441 (Newfound Gap Rd.), is the best place to begin your tour.

You'll find public restrooms, snack machines, and a bookstore and shop operated by the Great Smoky Mountains Association (www.smokiesinformation.org). Adjacent is the **Mountain Farm Museum,** a collection of log structures that include a farmhouse, a barn, a smokehouse, and other homestead structures; demonstrations of early farm life are held here regularly.

Clingmans Dome Visitor Contact Station

Along Newfound Gap Road is the turnoff to Clingmans Dome and the **Clingmans Dome Visitor Contact Station** (Clingmans Dome Rd., off Newfound Gap Rd., 25 miles from Cherokee, NC, and 23 miles from Gatlinburg, TN, 865/436-1200, www.nps.gov/grsm, 10am-6pm daily Apr.-May and Sept.-Oct., 10am-6:30pm daily June-Aug., 9:30am-5pm daily Nov.). Clingmans Dome is the highest peak in Great Smoky Mountains National Park and features a fantastic viewing platform. At the visitor contact station, you'll find information on the park, a bookstore operated by the Great Smoky Mountains Association (www.smokiesinformation.org), and restrooms.

Cades Cove Visitor Center

In Cades Cove, about halfway around the ever-popular Loop Road, is the **Cades Cove Visitor Center** (Cades Cove Loop Rd., Townsend, TN, 865/448-2472, 9am-4:30pm daily Dec.-Jan., except Dec. 25, 9am-5pm daily Feb., 9am-6:30pm daily Mar. and Sept.-Oct., 9am-7pm daily Apr.-Aug., 9am-5:30pm daily Nov.). Indoor and outdoor exhibits illustrate Southern mountain life and culture, and there are a number of historic structures to photograph and explore. You'll also find a gift shop and restrooms at the Cades Cove Visitor Center.

Backcountry Information Office

The knowledgeable folks at the **Backcountry Information Office** (1420 Old Hwy. 73 Scenic, Gatlinburg, TN, 865/436-1297, https://smokiespermits.nps.gov, 8am-5pm daily) are a good first resource when planning a hiking or backcountry camping trip. There are more than a dozen shelters and approximately 100 backcountry campsites sprinkled throughout the park at convenient intervals. Those on multiday hikes or interested in backcountry camping can **reserve tent sites** and shelter space (www.smokiespermits.nps.gov, permits $4 pp per night, $20 maximum) up to 30 days in advance of their trip. Hikers, campers, anglers, and equestrians are asked to follow Leave No Trace practices.

Field Schools

Two Tennessee-based organizations affiliated with Great Smoky Mountains National Park offer ways to get to know the park even better. The **Smoky Mountain Field School** (865/974-0150, www.outreach.utk.edu/smoky) teaches workshops and leads excursions to educate participants in a wide array of fields related to the Smokies. One-day classes focus on the history and cultural heritage of the park, the lives of some of the park's most interesting animals, folk medicine and cooking of the southern Appalachians, and much more. Instructors also lead one-day and overnight hikes into the heart of the park. This is a great way to discover the park far beyond what you would be able to do on your own, so check their schedule and sign up for a class that interests you. Unfortunately, new regulations from the University of Tennessee mean Field School programs are closed to minors, a situation we hope will change soon.

The **Great Smoky Mountains Institute at Tremont** (9275 Tremont Rd., Townsend, TN, 865/448-6709, www.gsmit.org) teaches students of all ages about the ecology of the region, wilderness rescue and survival skills, and even nature photography. Many of the classes and guided trips are part of Road Scholars, kids' camps, or teacher-training institutes; however, there are also rich opportunities for unaffiliated learners.

PARK ENTRANCES

Great Smoky Mountains National Park is unusual among the National Park System in that it has **no entrance fee**, so if you see a Friends of the Smokies donation box and you're so inclined (or so moved by what you see around you), toss a few bucks their way.

Main Entrances

There are three main entrances to Great Smoky Mountains National Park that access the busiest parts of the park. Each entrance is easily approached from a nearby gateway town:

- From **Cherokee, North Carolina,** drive two miles north along U.S. 441 into the park.
- From **Gatlinburg, Tennessee,** follow U.S. 441 south two miles into the park.
- From **Townsend, Tennessee,** take Hwy. 73 three miles east into the park.

Remote Entrances

There are 17 additional points at which you can enter the park via automobile. The majority of these are gravel roads in varying states of maintenance that require different degrees of driving confidence and skill. If you're up for an adventure, these roads can lead you into some beautiful corners of the park that few others experience.

Note that though these secondary entrances enter the national park, they don't provide access to the extensive trail systems and historic and recreational opportunities provided by the main entrances.

ROARING FORK MOTOR NATURE TRAIL

From **Gatlinburg, Tennessee,** turn off the main parkway in Gatlinburg at traffic light number 8 and follow Historic Nature Trail Road to Cherokee Orchard and the entrance to the national park, about one mile from Gatlinburg. Soon after you pass the Rainbow Falls Trailhead, you can enter **Roaring Fork Motor Nature Trail** (open Mar.-Nov.) or turn back to Gatlinburg. All told, it's a drive of 3.7 miles.

Roaring Fork Motor Nature Trail is located in the western-central part of the park, to the east of Newfound Gap Road. From here, you can access several trails to waterfalls as well as trails leading to **Mount LeConte;** you'll also find several historic structures and homesteads along this one-way road that give visitors a taste of the wild, rugged nature of these mountains.

RICH MOUNTAIN ROAD

Rich Mountain Road roughly follows the course of an old trading and horse trail over the mountains from Cades Cove to Townsend, Tennessee. It's a one-way gravel road, and the forest is thick here. As you climb out of Cades Cove, there are one or two spots where the views open up and you look out across the valley, but the rest is heavily wooded. Toward the end you'll reach a point where the road widens to two lanes, which provides access to a pair of trails at the parking area here.

From **Townsend, Tennessee,** follow Hwy. 73 (West Lamar Alexander Pkwy.) to Old Tuckaleechee Road, then turn left on Dry Valley Road (Old Cades Cove Rd.) and follow it to where the pavement gives way to a gravel road. Soon after, it changes to a gravel road; you'll find a small parking area and signs indicating a one-way road. This is Rich Mountain Road coming in from **Cades Cove.**

This entrance is only 7 miles from Townsend, 0.5 miles from the nearest house, and just inside the national park boundary, but it will feel much more isolated because the forest is thick and wild here. From the parking area, you can access both **Ace Gap Trail** and **Rich Mountain Trail.**

HAPPY VALLEY ROAD

From **Walland, Tennessee,** follow Hwy. 73 (East Lamar Alexander Pkwy.) to Foothills Parkway; take the Foothills Parkway south, then turn left onto Butterfly Gap Road, right on Flats Road, then follow Happy Valley Road to the unpaved **Abrams Creek Road,** a trip of 17.1 miles.

This entrance takes you into the southwestern portion of the park, just over the mountain from Cades Cove into the headwaters of Abrams Creek. The **Abrams Creek Campground** (late May-mid-Oct., $17.50) has 16 first-come, first-served campsites and can accommodate RVs up to 12 feet.

DEEP CREEK ROAD

From **Cherokee, North Carolina,** follow U.S. 19 south to Bryson City, then turn right on West Deep Creek Road until you enter the park and reach the Deep Creek Campground. At **Deep Creek Campground** (877/444-6777, www.recreation.gov, Apr.-Oct., $17.50) there are 92 campsites that fill up fast, so make reservations early if you want to explore the trails and waterfalls of the southeastern edge of the park. It's only 2.2 miles from downtown Bryson City.

LAKEVIEW DRIVE

From **Cherokee, North Carolina,** follow U.S. 19 south to Bryson City; the road name changes to Old River Road then Deep Creek Road. Turn left on Ramseur Street and then right on Depot Street. Finally, turn onto Everett Street (which changes to Fontana Road). Follow **Fontana Road** to the end, where there is a parking area a short walk from a tunnel through the mountain.

This 18.5-mile drive is known to locals at the **Road to Nowhere** (or, more properly, Fontana Road) for its strange intrusion into the national park. The road earned this name when the national park scrapped plans to build Lakeview Drive, a 26-mile parkway along the shores of Fontana Lake. The project built this first part of the road and completed a tunnel through the mountain before stopping. Today hikers, mountain bikers, and anglers use this point to access the streams and trails along the shores of **Fontana Lake.**

HEINTOOGA RIDGE ROAD

From the **Blue Ridge Parkway,** turn onto paved Heintooga Ridge Road (open May-Nov.) at milepost 458.2. You'll be in the Blue Ridge Parkway for the first four miles, but will abruptly enter Great Smoky Mountains National Park at **Black Camp Gap.** The road continues five miles, passing **Balsam Mountain Campground.** It terminates at the **Heintooga Overlook.**

Look for the one-lane gravel road at Heintooga Overlook and you've found **Heintooga Round Bottom Road** (May-Nov.). This gravel track takes you on an hour-long, 14-mile trip along **Balsam Mountain** and down into Straight Fork Valley on the lands of the Eastern Band of Cherokee Indians (the Qualla Boundary). Keep an eye out for wildlife along this seldom-traveled road, or stop for a short hike along the trails that branch off the road. This road is closed to vehicles longer than 25 feet or passenger vehicles towing trailers.

COVE CREEK ROAD

From **Asheville, North Carolina,** follow I-40 west to exit 20, then follow Highway 276 to Cove Creek Road into the Cataloochee Valley, a trip of 42 miles.

From **Knoxville, Tennessee,** follow I-40 east to exit 20, then take Highway 284 to Cove Creek Road into the Cataloochee Valley, a trip of 80 miles.

Cove Creek Road skirts the edge of the **Cherokee National Forest** before plunging into the park. The road is narrow, but paved for half the drive; it changes to a well-maintained gravel track that, while still narrow, is open to two-way traffic. The road enters **Cataloochee Valley** in the extreme northern end of the national park, where

there is camping, plenty of hiking, wildlife viewing (including herds of elk), and historic buildings.

MOUNT STERLING ROAD

From **Cataloochee Valley, North Carolina,** take the gravel Mount Sterling Road north and west out of the valley to I-40, a drive of 16.4 miles. The road is narrow but well maintained, and it winds its way out of the **Cataloochee Valley** up toward **Mount Sterling,** then back down to cross the Tennessee state line where you access I-40.

COSBY PARK ROAD

From **Gatlinburg, Tennessee,** take U.S. 321/Hwy. 73/East Parkway northeast to Cosby, then turn right on Hwy. 32 and right again onto Cosby Park Road to the **Cosby Campground** (471 Cosby Campground Rd. A, Cosby, TN, 423/487-2683, www.recreation.gov, Apr.-Oct., $17.50), a trip of 21 miles. Cosby Park Road provides access to the campground in the northwestern quadrant of the park, and also to the hiking trails and waterfalls nearby, namely Hen Wallow Falls, the hike to the top of Mount Cammerer, and as a way to connect to the Appalachian Trail.

GREENBRIER ROAD

From **Gatlinburg, Tennessee,** take U.S. 321/Hwy. 73/East Parkway northeast 5.4 miles, then turn right into the park. This narrow but paved two-lane road leads to the **Ramsey Cascades** trailhead, some excellent wildflower viewing, and trout fishing. The paved road eventually gives way to a maintained gravel road, which leads to additional trailheads.

DRIVING TOURS
★ Newfound Gap Road
33 MILES

While many visitors use this 33-mile road that bisects Great Smoky Mountains National Park as a mere thruway, it's actually one of the prettiest drives you'll find anywhere. This curvy road alternates between exposed and tree-enclosed, and a number of **scenic overlooks** provide spectacular views of the Smokies. Stop at one that has a **trail** (more than half of them do) and take a short walk into the woods, or eat a picnic lunch at one of the mountainside overlooks. Whatever you do on this road between **Cherokee** and **Gatlinburg,** take your time and enjoy the ride.

Cades Cove Loop
11 MILES

This 11-mile loop around a broad and pictur-esque valley ringed by high peaks is about as pretty as it gets. The fields, forests, those high peaks, wildlife, and historic structures are just some of the highlights the **Cades Cove Loop** (closed to vehicles until 10am Wed.-Sat. May-Sept.). One of the most popular spots in the park in any season, expect crowds, espe-cially in the fall. To avoid the crowds, show up early. Hikes include gentle strolls to home-steads, cabins, and churches, or longer hikes to **Abrams Falls.** The road is paved, and very well maintained, and although it's **one-way,** there are two points where you can cut across the valley to shorten the drive or circle back for one more look, whichever strikes your fancy.

Rich Mountain Road
8 MILES

Rich Mountain Road (open Apr.-Nov.) is a photographer's dream. Running north from Cades Cove over Rich Mountain to **Tuckaleechee Cove** and **Townsend,** this **one-way gravel road** provides a few stun-ning views of Cades Cove and Tuckaleechee Cove. You're likely to see bears, deer, turkeys, and other wildlife along the way. The road is typically in good condition and isn't too chal-lenging as far as backroads go, but I'd avoid tackling this drive in a low-clearance vehicle or your economy rental car; instead, go with a truck or SUV (no 4WD necessary). Know that the road gets a little steep once it passes outside park boundaries, but it's nothing too hair-raising.

If you're stuck with a rental or you aren't confident in your off-road driving abilities, you can always enjoy similar views on the 8.5-mile Rich Mountain Loop hike, a great way to see Cades Cove without the high-season gridlock.

Heintooga Round Bottom Road/Balsam Mountain Road
14 MILES

This 14-mile one-way gravel road goes by two names—**Heintooga Round Bottom Road** and **Balsam Mountain Road** (open May-Nov.)—but they're one in the same. Accessed from Blue Ridge Parkway milepost 458.2 (just a few miles from the Cherokee, NC, en-trance), this is an often-overlooked road through a high and wild part of Great Smoky Mountains National Park. In the spring and summer you'll find wildflowers blooming, and in the fall you'll find the road awash in color. The drive takes a little more than an hour from the **Blue Ridge Parkway** back down into **Cherokee;** as off-roading expe-riences go, it's an easy one. The road is well-maintained and generally in good condition, but don't try it in your low-clearance rental or the family minivan. You'll be fine in a truck, or even a small SUV.

Roaring Fork Motor Nature Trail
5.5 MILES

The 5.5-mile **Roaring Fork Motor Nature Trail** (open Mar.-Nov.), just a few miles from the heart of Gatlinburg, has everything Smoky Mountain visitors are looking for: rushing creeks, waterfalls, hikes, historic structures, and plenty of photo opportunities. This **one-way road** stays busy, but is seldom bumper-to-bumper, though some of the parking areas may make you feel differently. If you're look-ing for an **easy drive** with some **short walks** to homesteads and waterfalls (which make them perfect for those with mobility diffi-culty), this is the one you need. Head there just after a rainfall to see a roadside waterfall called **Place of a Thousand Drips.**

Foothills Parkway

17 MILES

It's not technically in the park, but the **Foothills Parkway** is a great scenic drive that gives you high-elevation views without the same traffic on more popular routes in the park proper. The Foothills Parkway is 5.5 miles from **Townsend**, reached via U.S. 321. The 17-mile road has plenty of places to pull off to picnic or take in the view. There's one short hike here at **Look Rock**, a 0.5-mile stroll to an observation tower. There is a second, northern, section to the Foothills Parkway, running 5.6 miles from Cosby to I-40 near Denton, Tennessee. A long stretch in the middle—some 30-odd miles—has been lingering in the planning stages for years; this section would connect the Foothills Parkway and provide visitors with another way to enjoy Great Smoky Mountains National Park.

Newfound Gap Road

Easily the most heavily traveled route in the Smokies, Newfound Gap Road (U.S. 441) connects Cherokee with Gatlinburg and sees thousands of visitors a day. Newfound Gap Road is the perfect introduction to Great Smoky Mountains National Park: Contour-hugging curves, overlooks with million-dollar views, easy hikes right off the roadway, and a 3,000-foot elevation change give you a great overview of these mountains and this spectacular park. During peak times in the summer and fall, it's not uncommon to encounter a traffic jam or two along this 33-mile scenic route, especially when bears are taking their time to cross the road.

Newfound Gap Road earned its name in 1872 when Swiss geographer Arnold Henry Guyot determined that a newly found gap was the lowest pass through the Great Smoky Mountains. Lower in elevation and easier to access than the former passage at Indian Gap, 1.5 miles away, the name Newfound Gap was soon used to refer to the entire route.

SIGHTS

Oconaluftee Visitor Center

As you begin your trip along Newfound Gap Road through the park from the North Carolina side, your first stop will probably be the "Welcome to Great Smoky Mountains National Park" sign, but the **Oconaluftee Visitor Center and Mountain Farm Museum** (1194 Newfound Gap Rd., Cherokee, 828/436-1200, www.nps.gov/grsm, 8am-4:30pm daily Dec.-Feb., except Dec. 25, 8am-5pm daily Mar. and Nov., 9am-6pm daily Apr.-May and Sept.-Oct., 8am-7pm daily June-Aug.), just two miles north of Cherokee on U.S. 441 (Newfound Gap Rd.), will likely be the second stop you make. You can pick up a park map, grab the schedule of ranger-led programs, and see exhibits on the people who called these hills home long before the park was in existence. The visitors center and adjacent comfort station are LEED Gold certified.

Oconaluftee Visitor Center is also a hot spot for elk sightings. In the field next to the visitors center, the elk come to graze, rest, and put on a show for park visitors. You might see a pair of young bull elk bugling back and forth before crashing their antlers together. Or elk calves running and playing. There may even be a few deer or turkey in the elks' entourage. Regardless of who shows up, the field is a great spot for photography and as close to a guarantee for elk sightings as you'll get. Just show up early in the morning or from late afternoon into evening and you'll find the herd there.

Mountain Farm Museum

Next to the visitor center is **Mountain Farm Museum** (sunrise-sunset daily year-round, free), which showcases some of the finest farm buildings in the park. Most date to the early 1900s, and among them are a barn, an apple house, and the Davis House, a log home built from chestnut wood and constructed before the American chestnut blight decimated the species. This collection of structures is original to the area and dates back to the turn of the 20th century. Though the barn is the only structure original to this site, the other buildings were moved here from inside and adjacent to the park and arranged much like the typical farm of the era would have been arranged. If you visit during peak times, you'll see living-history interpreters in costume, demonstrating the day-to-day chores that would've occurred on this farm: preparing meals, sewing, maintaining and harvesting the garden, taking care of the hogs, and the like.

Mingus Mill

A half-mile north of the Oconaluftee Visitor Center and Mountain Farm Museum you'll find **Mingus Mill** (9am-5pm daily mid-Mar.-mid-Nov. and Thanksgiving weekend). This historic grist mill was built in 1886; rather than use a water wheel to power the machinery and mill in the building, it uses a water-powered turbine to generate power. This cast-iron turbine still works! A miller is on hand to demonstrate how the machinery turns corn into cornmeal (for sale on-site). Walk along the millrace (the wooden trough that carries water to power the turbine), check out the abundant seasonal wildflowers, and take a good look at how well the parks service restored the structure—it looks like it was built just a few years ago.

Deep Creek Valley Overlook

The **Deep Creek Valley Overlook,** 14 miles from the Oconaluftee Visitor Center (and 16 miles from Sugarlands Visitor Center if coming from the other direction), is one of the most popular overlooks in the park for good reason. From here you'll have a long view of the mountains, which roll away from you for as far as you can see.

Oconaluftee River Valley Overlook

Halfway through Newfound Gap Road is the **Oconaluftee River Valley Overlook,** a spot where you can spy the deep cut of the valley formed by the Oconaluftee River. This place is ideal for a picnic, so if you're hungry and you've brought your blanket and something to eat, spread out and relax for a few minutes.

Newfound Gap

One of the most-visited overlooks is at **Newfound Gap.** This is the highest elevation on Newfound Gap Road, at 5,048 feet, and though the views here are fantastic, the first thing you'll probably notice is the **Rockefeller Memorial,** a simple stone terrace that straddles the Tennessee-North Carolina state line and commemorates a $5 million gift made by the Rockefeller Foundation to acquire land for the park. In 1940, President Franklin D. Roosevelt dedicated the park from this site. Plan to spend a little time here, especially early in the morning or near sunset. At sunset, you can see the Smokies' namesake haze settling into the folds and wrinkles of the mountains, and in the early morning, the mountains emerge from a blue haze in a subtle display of color that's been the subject of many a postcard and computer desktop background.

TOP EXPERIENCE

★ Clingmans Dome

At 6,643 feet, Clingmans Dome is the third-highest mountain in the eastern United States and the highest in the Great Smoky Mountains. A flying saucer-like observation tower at the end of a long, steep walkway gives 360-degree views of the surrounding mountains, and on a clear day, that view can be as far as a hundred miles. More often,

1: view from Newfound Gap Road 2: Mingus Mill 3: well-preserved cabin on Roaring Fork Motor Nature Trail 4: Clingmans Dome

though, it's misty up here in the clouds, and Clingmans Dome receives so much precipitation that its woods are actually a coniferous rainforest. The road to the summit is closed December 1-March 31, but the observation tower remains open for those willing to make the hike. To get to Clingmans Dome, turn off Newfound Gap Road 0.1 miles south of Newfound Gap, and then take **Clingmans Dome Road** (closed in winter), which leads seven miles to the parking lot. The peak is near the center of the park, due north from Bryson City.

Campbell Overlook

The **Campbell Overlook** is only 3 miles from the Sugarlands Visitor Center, and it is home to one of the best views of Mount LeConte you'll find along the road. LeConte is an interesting mountain. At 6,593 feet, it's the third-highest peak in the Smokies, but it's the tallest mountain east of the Mississippi in that it rises more than a mile from the foot of the mountain to the summit.

Sugarlands Visitor Center

The **Sugarlands Visitor Center** (1420 Old Hwy. 73 Scenic, Gatlinburg, TN, 865/436-1200, www.nps.gov/grsm, 8am-4:30pm daily Dec.-Feb., except Christmas Day, 8am-5pm daily Mar. and Nov., 8am-6pm daily Apr.-May and Sept.-Oct., 8am-7pm daily June-Aug.) is the most popular visitors center in the park due to its proximity to Gatlinburg. There's the usual visitors center stuff—restrooms, maps, guidebooks, a few gift items, some snacks— and it's also the origin point for the 1.9-mile Gatlinburg Trail.

RECREATION
Hiking

Great Smoky Mountains National Park contains hundreds of miles of hiking trails, ranging from family-friendly loop trails to strenuous wilderness treks. Before embarking on any of these trails, obtain a park map and talk to a park ranger to ascertain trail conditions and gauge whether it's suited to your hiking skills.

No dogs or other pets (other than service animals) are permitted on park trails, except the Gatlinburg Trail and Oconaluftee River Trail, though they are allowed in frontcountry campsites and picnic areas, so long as they remain on-leash.

OCONALUFTEE RIVER TRAIL

Distance: 3 miles round-trip
Duration: 45 minutes
Elevation gain: 70 feet
Difficulty: easy
Trailhead: Oconaluftee Visitor Center

This trail by the Oconaluftee River runs 1.5 miles from the **visitors center** to the outskirts of Cherokee. Flat except for a bridge or two and a few gentle rises, the Oconaluftee River Trail is a lovely walk. In the spring the banks of the Oconaluftee are blanketed with wildflowers, and throughout the year you may see a herd of elk crossing the river at any number of places. Bring bug spray because it can get a bit buggy right by the river on a still day. This is a great option for walking or jogging, and is one of only two paths in Great Smoky Mountains National Park where you can walk your **dog** or ride your **bike.**

KEPHART PRONG TRAIL

Distance: 4 miles round-trip
Duration: 2 hours
Elevation gain: 840 feet
Difficulty: easy
Trailhead: 6.9 miles north of Oconaluftee Visitor Center along Newfound Gap Road or 8.7 miles south from Newfound Gap. Trail begins on the east side of the road.

Kephart Prong offers an easy trail experience for those looking to stretch their legs a little or get more familiar with hiking in the Smokies. The trail crosses the Oconaluftee River, then follows the Kephart Prong (stream) for most of the hike, crossing it four times on log bridges. This hike ends at the Kephart Shelter, where the trail meets the Sweat Heifer Creek Trail and Grassy Branch Trail.

Begin by crossing Oconaluftee River via a **footbridge** and follow the wide, nearly flat trail. (Once this was a Jeep road, so you may spot bits of old asphalt along the way.) At 0.25 miles into the hike, you'll pass through a **Civilian Conservation Corps Camp** where you'll encounter ruins such as foundations, chimneys, and other evidence of the camp's use in the 1930s. Continue along the path and cross **Kephart Prong,** then begin to climb, passing the remains of a fish hatchery in 0.6 miles. Three more crossings of the Kephart Prong await, and you can ford the stream (use caution) or use the **log bridges** (they're narrow; use caution) at each crossing. As you continue the hike to **Kephart Shelter,** you'll pass evidence of a long-gone logging operation in the form of narrow-gauge railroad tracks. When you reach the shelter, catch your breath and get ready for the easy hike back.

APPALACHIAN TRAIL TO MOUNT LECONTE
Distance: 15.6 miles one-way
Duration: 7-8.5 hours
Elevation gain: 3,000 feet
Difficulty: strenuous
Trailhead: Appalachian Trail trailhead at the Newfound Gap Road Overlook

This is a tough hike. The trail largely follows the crest of the mountains, and thus rises and falls several times with some significant elevation gains and losses.

From the start, the trail climbs for 2 miles. You'll be on a steady incline, but there are views aplenty to give you a little boost. At 1.7 miles, just before the junction with **Sweat Heifer Creek Trail,** you'll have a good look at Mount LeConte to the north. At 2.8 miles, **The Boulevard** forks off to the left.

Continue along The Boulevard, ignoring the sign for the Jump-Off Trail (you can hike that one-mile trail on the return trip if you want). Soon you'll drop down to an elevation around 5,500 feet, after which the trail bounces back and forth between 5,500 and 6,000 feet until you begin to properly climb

Mount LeConte and make your way to the lodge there and the 6,593-foot summit.

CHARLIES BUNION
Distance: 8.1 miles round-trip
Duration: 7-8.5 hours
Elevation gain: 1,700 feet
Difficulty: strenuous
Trailhead: Appalachian Trail trailhead at the Newfound Gap Road Overlook

Originally named Fodderstack, the rock formation of Charlies Bunion earned its new name when two men, Charlie Conner and Horace Kephart, were hiking here. According to legend, they stopped to rest at Fodderstack and Conner removed his boots and socks, revealing a bunion that Kephart felt resembled the rocks around them. Impressed, Kephart promised Charlie that he'd get the name of this place changed on official maps in honor of the bunion.

The first leg of this trail follows the **Appalachian Trail** and **The Boulevard** to **Mount LeConte.** The trail climbs for 2 miles. At 1.7 miles, you'll come to the junction with Sweat Heifer Creek Trail. At 2.8 miles, The Boulevard forks off to the left; continue straight to reach Charlies Bunion.

The **Icewater Spring Shelter,** aptly named for the cold spring that flows out of the mountain here (treat the water before you drink it), is just 0.25 miles from the junction and is a good spot to rest. From the spring, continue a little less than a mile to a short **spur trail** on your left that leads out to the rock outcrop known as **Charlies Bunion.**

TOP EXPERIENCE

★ ANDREWS BALD
Distance: 3.5 miles round-trip
Duration: 3 hours
Elevation gain: 1,200 feet
Difficulty: moderate
Trailhead: Clingmans Dome parking area at the end of Clingmans Dome Road

The highest grassy bald in Great Smoky Mountains National Park, Andrews Bald is a

Clingmans Dome and Andrews Bald Trails

CLINGMANS DOME
6,643 ft
CLINGMANS DOME RD
Appalachian Trail
To Newfound Gap Road
Forney Ridge Trail
Forney Creek Trail
Forney Creek
Forney Ridge
ANDREWS BALD
© MOON.COM
0   0.5 mi
0   0.5 km

unfortunately now is dead or dying. That's because the forest has been ravaged by a tiny bug—the balsam woolly adelgid—which devours Fraser firs. However, there is a certain beauty in the white bones of the tree trunks jutting up from the land. Don't worry, though, the views get considerably better in a short time. Around 1.6 miles into the hike you'll reach the edge of **Andrews Bald,** where the forest opens up into a fantastic panorama. In spring and summer, there is a proliferation of wildflowers, flame azalea, and rhododendron.

SILERS BALD

Distance: 9.8 miles round-trip
Duration: 6-7 hours
Elevation gain: 2,100 feet
Difficulty: moderate to strenuous
Trailhead: Clingmans Dome parking area at the end of Clingmans Dome Road

This hike is a highlight for many (even though Andrews Bald is the showier of the high-altitude meadows) because it offers a nice day hike along the **Appalachian Trail.** The hike begins at the parking area for Clingmans Dome, the highest peak in Great Smoky Mountains National Park; on the way back, you can divert your path just a little and pay a visit to the summit here. While the Clingmans Dome parking area is a big lot, it can get crowded. Get here early, especially in peak seasons. Note that Clingmans Dome Road closes in winter.

Begin at the far end of the Clingmans Dome parking area and descend along **Forney Ridge Trail.** Follow this rocky path 0.1 miles to a junction: Forney Ridge leads to the left, Clingmans Dome leads to the right. Take Forney Ridge left for 0.6 miles to **Mount Buckley** and the **Appalachian Trail.** Here you can turn right to reach the summit of Clingmans Dome (which you can do on the return trip), or continue left (west) to Silers Bald.

As you continue west along the Appalachian Trail, you'll pass through wildflowers and flowering shrubs mixed with a fir and spruce forest until you reach a **clearing**

beautiful sight at the end of a nearly two-mile hike from Clingmans Dome. Balds are meadows found higher up on the mountain, and this one is absolutely lousy with flame azalea and rhododendron blooms in the summer. Note that Clingmans Dome Road is closed in the winter.

Before recent trail renovations, the Andrews Bald hike had some of the most rugged sections of rocky trails in the park. Thanks to the Trails Forever program, work crews fixed drainage issues, rebuilt parts of the trail, and even built a few stairways from native rocks and trees. Now the hike is easier and safer and leads to a spectacular view of the Smoky Mountains. A bonus: The hike is just long enough to discourage some potential hikers, but it's still short enough to be doable by everyone in your party.

The **Forney Ridge Trail** starts in a spruce-fir forest that was once beautiful but

0.9 miles into the hike. The clearing has good views, so catch your breath and keep following the ridgeline. Descending, the trail passes through clearings and back into the woods. At 2.6 miles, you'll reach the junction with **Goshen Prong Trail** (which descends toward Elkmont); continue straight along the Appalachian Trail.

At **Double Spring Gap,** in 3.4 miles, there is an **Appalachian Trail shelter** and two springs (hence the name). The gap is the low point on the trail, so begin climbing into a forest where the fir gives way to beech trees. Top out at **Jenkins Knob,** then descend through another gap. At 3.9 miles, the trail crosses an open ridge and grassy area that again provides some great views of the Smokies.

Continue along the trail to a section known as **The Narrows** (4.2 miles), and push on your final ascent toward Silers Bald. Pass the **Welch Ridge Trail** at 4.5 miles, then climb steeply to **Silers Bald,** 4.9 miles into the hike. Enjoy the view and catch your breath—or continue along the trail another 0.3 miles to the **Silers Bald Shelter** and a spring alongside the Appalachian Trail.

Despite the blooming wildflowers and shrubs along the path, Silers Bald receives some deserved criticism. The once wide-open bald is shrinking as the forest seeks to reclaim it. There's a small debate on what to do—let the forest take it back or maintain it as a bald—but it's a beautiful spot and a worthwhile hike no matter what.

When ready, reverse course and head back to Clingmans Dome. To divert to the summit and add 0.7 miles or so to your trip, continue along the **Appalachian Trail** when you reach **Mount Buckley.** The trail gets steep here, but it leads to a spot 50 yards or so from the ramp to the lookout tower at the summit of **Clingmans Dome.**

ALUM CAVE BLUFF TO MOUNT LECONTE

Distance: 5 miles one-way
Duration: 3–3.5 hours
Elevation gain: 2,560 feet

Difficulty: moderate with strenuous sections
Trailhead: Alum Cave Trailhead

As one of the most popular hikes in the park, this trail receives a lot of wear-and-tear, which can leave the trail in bad shape. Fortunately, repair work completed in 2015 and 2016 have left the trail in fantastic condition. Repairs focused on the lower portion, then the upper sections of the trail. Hikers will find sturdy handholds along the stone stairs and narrow exposed sections at the upper end of the trail.

The trail starts off fairly gently as it climbs up to Arch Rock. **Alum Cave Creek** runs alongside the trail for a while, and here you'll have the chance to snap pictures of several cascades and beautiful rhododendron thickets (which bloom in late June–July). You'll reach **Arch Rock,** which is less arch and more natural tunnel, around 1.5 miles in.

Here the trail begins to climb more steeply. A set of stone steps leads out of Arch Rock and the forest changes from hemlock and hardwood to spruce and fir trees. In another 0.5 miles you'll reach **Inspiration Point,** where the view opens onto one of the mid-elevation balds.

When you reach **Alum Cave Bluffs,** you're halfway to Mount LeConte. The rock formations aren't caves, but rather deep overhangs that create an impressive shelter from the rain. The Smokies receive more than 85 inches of rain a year, yet the majority of the soil under the bluffs remains dry and dusty, an arid spot in one of the wettest forests in the nation.

Most hikers turn around at Alum Cave Bluffs, but if you're pushing on to Mount LeConte, the path steepens and grows more challenging as you gain elevation. The trail narrows to a set of rock ledges where **steel cables** have been bolted into the mountain for use as a handhold. The drop may be precipitous, but the views are fantastic. Soon, the trail intersects with **Rainbow Falls Trail,** leading you to the summit of **Mount LeConte** in short order.

If you plan on hiking to Mount LeConte and back in a day, or spending the night at the lodge, it's in your best interest to arrive early so you can get a parking space.

CHIMNEY TOPS

Distance: 4 miles round-trip
Duration: 3.5 hours
Elevation gain: 1,400 feet
Difficulty: strenuous
Trailhead: Chimney Tops trailhead on Newfound Gap Road

This popular hike leads to an outstanding view from its namesake pinnacles. The trail has suffered some severe storm damage in the past few years, and was closed intermittently until a Trails Forever team completed repairs, fixing drainage issues, installing or refreshing rock steps and staircases, and building elevated turnpikes, as well as other laborious methods to mitigate the impact from hikers and Mother Nature. The 2016 wildfires that ravaged the Smokies and surrounding towns were started on Chimney Tops. This trail, along with others, was closed but Trails Forever crews and workers from the National Parks completed work in 2017 to make it safe and enjoyable for visitors. Today, there are signs of the wildfire but the forest has reclaimed most evidence.

Chimney Tops takes its name from the twin knobs that rise from ridge-like chimneys. These rocky summits are rare in the Smokies, but that's not the draw—what brings people up this steep, challenging trail is the 360-degree view. And it's incredibly steep, gaining nearly 1,000 feet in the last mile. To reach the pinnacles, the actual Chimney Tops, requires a very steep scramble over bare rock, which can be dangerous, and it's easier to climb up than to come back down.

Many people explore the first few hundred yards of this trail because it's right off Newfound Gap Road. The cascades, pools, and boulders found along **Walker Camp Prong** are picturesque and good for wading and sunbathing. As you climb, you'll cross **Road Prong,** another stream, twice. Just after the second crossing, the trail splits, with one part following Road Prong and the other

heading to Chimney Tops. Stay right to head to the chimneys.

After a brief ascent, the trail steepens significantly. Take a breather here before tackling this long, straight climb. The trail continues and narrows as you walk the ridgeline. Soon, you'll be at the foot of the **Chimney Tops** and you'll see a sign from the National Park Service warning you to proceed at your own risk. Heed this sign, as the last bit of "trail" to the summit is a **scramble** that doesn't require any specialized equipment but is quite risky if you're inexperienced in such terrain.

GATLINBURG TRAIL

Distance: 3.8 miles round-trip
Duration: 2 hours
Elevation gain: 20 feet
Difficulty: easy
Trailhead: Sugarlands Visitor Center

This is one of only two trails in the park to allow **pets** and **bicycles** (the other is the Oconaluftee River Trail in Cherokee). More of a walk than a hike, the Gatlinburg Trail follows the **West Prong Little Pigeon River** and Newfound Gap Road for most of the trip. It's pretty and not especially challenging, but the optional walk to **Cataract Falls**—a few hundred yards up **Cove Mountain Trail,** which splits off the Gatlinburg Trail near the trailhead—can provide some photo opportunities and a pretty, easy-to-reach waterfall.

SMOKEMONT LOOP

Distance: 6.1 miles loop
Duration: 3-3.5 hours
Elevation gain: 1,400 feet
Difficulty: moderate
Trailhead: Smokemont Campground D section

This horse-friendly trail is an enjoyable hike along forest roads and trails, but the elevation gain pushes it to moderate difficulty.

Starting at the far end of the D Section of **Smokemont Campground,** you'll see a sign marking the **Bradley Fork Trailhead;** follow

---

1: Alum Cave Trail sign **2:** trail to Andrews Bald

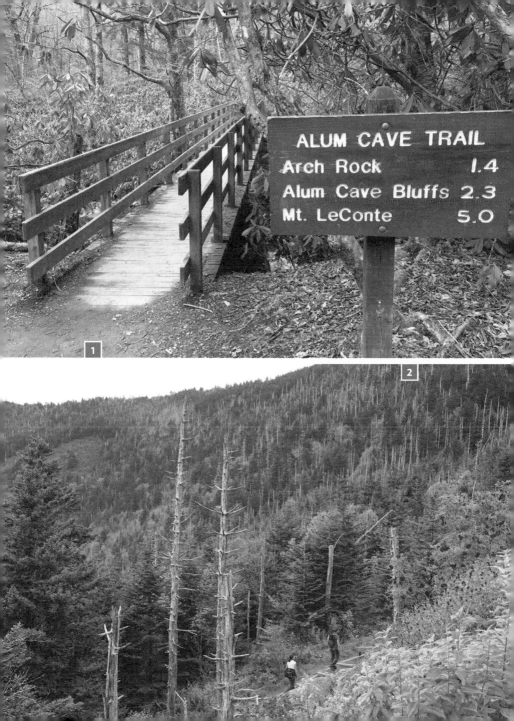

1 ALUM CAVE TRAIL
Arch Rock　　　　　1.4
Alum Cave Bluffs　2.3
Mt. LeConte　　　　5.0

this trail along Bradley Fork. In the spring, this creek-side section is packed with wildflowers, and many folks will just hike the first 0.5 miles of the trail. At 1.2 miles, the trail forks, with Chasteen Creek Trail going right and the **Bradley Fork-Smokemont Loop Trail** continuing left.

At 1.6 miles you meet up with **Smokemont Loop Trail** proper. Follow this trail left and cross **Bradley Fork** via a foot log. (Be careful; this one can be a little bouncy.) As soon as you cross, the trail forks again; the left fork follows the creek. Turn right and begin an uphill climb to **Richland Mountain.** This climb will keep going for another 2 miles at a steady incline, so pace yourself.

Once you pass through a small saddle, you'll hear the **Oconaluftee River** and, likely, cars traveling Newfound Gap Road. At the 3.4-mile mark, the trail takes a sharp left turn, marking the place you've been waiting for—the end of the climb and start of the descent. From here you have a 2-mile-long downhill trail. As you get closer to the end, you'll see the **Bradley Cemetery,** with a spur trail leading to it at 5.3 miles. At the Cemetery Trail, **Smokemont Loop** meets a gravel road leading back to the campground in another 0.2 miles.

Fishing

Smallmouth bass and rock bass are fairly abundant in Smoky's waters. Look for smallmouth bass along the **West Prong of the Little Pigeon River,** near Gatlinburg and the park's western entrance, and in the **Little Pigeon River** near Greenbrier. Smallmouth and rock bass are found in the **Little River** on the way to Cades Cove, **Abrams Creek,** and **Fontana Lake,** specifically the feeder creeks like Noland, Hazel, and Eagle Creek.

Horseback Riding

Three commercial stables in the park offer "rental" horses (around $30 per hour). **Smokemont** (828/497-2373, www.smokemontridingstable.com) is in North Carolina near Cherokee. Two are in Tennessee: **Smoky Mountain** (865/436-5634, Gatlinburg, TN, www.smokymountainridingstables.com) and **Cades Cove** (10018 Campground Dr., Townsend, TN, 865/448-9009, http://cadescovestables.com).

ACCOMMODATIONS AND CAMPING

As big as Great Smoky Mountains National Park may be, there are few places to stay

horses at a stable in Cades Cove

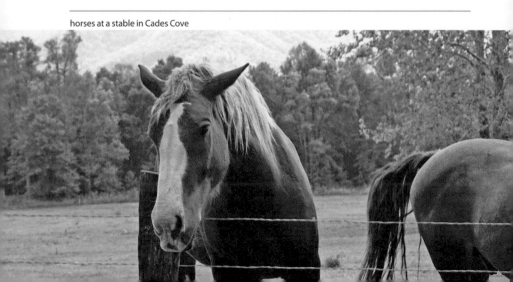

within the boundaries—and nearly all them are either campsites or backcountry shelters. The lone exception is LeConte Lodge, a collection of cabins and small lodges with a central dining room and lodge. It's only accessible by hiking in, so you have to be dedicated to stay there.

LeConte Lodge

Just below the 6,593-foot peak of Mount LeConte is the only true lodging in Great Smoky Mountains National Park, the ★ LeConte Lodge (865/429-5704, www. lecontelodge.com, Mar. 21-Nov. 22, adults $152, ages 4-12 $88, includes lodging, breakfast, and dinner). Like the mountain's summit, the lodge is accessible only via the network of hiking trails that crisscross the park. And if the accessibility limitation isn't rustic enough for you, this collection of cabins has no running water or electricity. What it does have is views for days and the seclusion of the Smoky Mountains backcountry.

For the most part the environs hark back to the lodge's 1934 opening. LeConte Lodge has no hot showers. In every cabin there is a bucket for a sponge bath—which can be surprisingly refreshing after a hot day on the trail—that you can fill with warm water from the kitchen, though you need to supply your own washcloth and towel. There are a few flush toilets in a separate building, and the only lights, aside from headlamps and flashlights, are kerosene lanterns. Your room does come with two meals: dinner and breakfast. Both are served at the same time every day (6pm for dinner and 8am for breakfast), and feature food hearty enough to fuel another day on the trail.

The lodge doesn't lack for charm, but it does for comfort, so if you're the five-star-hotel, breakfast-in-bed type, this may not be the place for you. Catering to hikers who are happy to have a dry place to sleep and a bed that's comfier than their sleeping bag, it's short on luxury amenities, and rooms are, in truth, bunk beds in small drafty cabins. But if you're a hiker or if you just love to have a

completely different experience when you travel, this is a one-of-a-kind accommodation.

RESERVATIONS

Accommodations for LeConte Lodge are made via **lottery** (www.lecontelodge.com). The lottery is competitive, but it's easy to enter; simply go to their website and fill out the online form, including your desired dates and the number in your party. If your application is chosen in the lottery, you will receive an invoice with your accommodation information. Booking information for the following season becomes available online in midsummer, so keep an eye out and get your application in early.

If you want to stay at LeConte Lodge, but you're late to the lottery party, try to get on the wait list. The process is the same, but the dates are limited—typically weeknights and the larger cabins are all that's available.

You can try one other method: calling (865/429-5704). Cancellations made with less than 30 days' notice skip the wait list and are instead offered to the first inquiry that matches availability. Frequent calls are a good way to snag these last-minute reservations.

GETTING THERE

The **Roaring Fork Motor Nature Trail** (open Mar.-Nov.) at the foot of Mount LeConte is the starting point for a trio of hiking trails that lead to LeConte Lodge. **Bull Head Trail** is a 6.8-mile trip from the trailhead to the lodge, as is **Rainbow Falls Trail.** (Bull Head and Rainbow Falls Trails share a trailhead at the designated parking area on the Motor Nature Trail.) **Trillium Gap Trail,** the trail used by the lodge's pack llamas, passes by the beautiful Grotto Falls on its 6.7-mile route (the trailhead is at the Grotto Falls parking area on the Roaring Fork Motor Nature Trail). Each of these three trails requires a four-hour hike to reach the lodge from the trailhead.

Three other trails lead to Mount LeConte from various points in the park. **Alum Cave Trail** (5 miles one-way) enters from Newfound

Gap Road; it's the shortest and easiest to access, but it's also the steepest.

Alternatively, **The Boulevard** connects the Appalachian Trail to LeConte Lodge (13.2 miles from Newfound Gap Overlook). The Boulevard is relatively easy with little elevation change, but there's the issue of exposure on this trail—the rock path has more than a few dizzying drops right beside the trail. These drops, combined with The Boulevard coming in from the Appalachian Trail, deter most day- or overnight hikers from its use. **Brushy Mountain Trail** (11.8 miles round-trip) leads to the summit from the Porters Creek Trailhead off Greenbrier Road (closed in winter). Despite the significant elevation change, this is a relatively easy trail.

Camping

Smokemont Campground (877/444-6777, www.recreation.gov, year-round, $25) is just off Newfound Gap Road, 3.2 miles from the Oconaluftee Visitor Center. There are 142 total sites available between tent campsites and RV sites. It's located on the banks of the Oconaluftee River and thus can get quite buggy, so be prepared.

Eastern Smokies

The eastern side of Great Smoky Mountains National Park was settled before the western side, so there are plenty of coves and hollows with historic structures or the ruins of cabins, barns, and other buildings in the fields and woods and along creek banks and floodplains. There are also many herds of elk here, introduced several years ago in an attempt to revive the species that once roamed these hills.

ROARING FORK
Roaring Fork Motor Nature Trail

One of the most beautiful drives in Great Smoky Mountains National Park is the **Roaring Fork Motor Nature Trail** (open Mar.-Nov.). This one-way loop passes through rhododendron thickets and dense hardwood forests as it follows the old roadbed of the Roaring Fork Community. To get here, turn onto Historic Nature Trail (Old Airport Rd.) at traffic light number 8 in Gatlinburg and follow the signs. Before you reach the trail, you'll drive a short distance on Cherokee Orchard Road, which runs through what was an 800-acre commercial orchard in the 1920s and 1930s; shortly after the orchard, you'll be at the head of the trail and have the chance to purchase an inexpensive tour booklet from a roadside exhibit.

Unfortunately Roaring Fork was one of the areas affected by the 2016 wildfires and, and just after, the road and many of the trails were closed. Today we can see evidence of the fire—the understory of the forest has been thinned out and is regrowing—but trails, cabins and the road are open for visitors. Fortunately none of the historic structures in this or any part of the park were damaged in the fires.

The roadbed here was built by hand in the 1850s, which explains both its narrowness and serpentine route. Around 25 families lived here, and though it may look quaint and primitive to our eyes, a few of the homes had running water thanks to the system of troughs—some of which are still standing—that carried water right to the houses.

As the road climbs through the forest, roll down your windows and take in a few deep breaths of that fresh, cool mountain air. There is a pair of **overlooks,** though they're overgrown and in poor repair. When you stop, take in the silence. You'll soon find yourself surrounded by the sounds of nature: wind, birds calling, and streams rumbling and echoing through the forest.

Be sure to stop at the cabins still standing

Roaring Fork and Greenbrier Cove

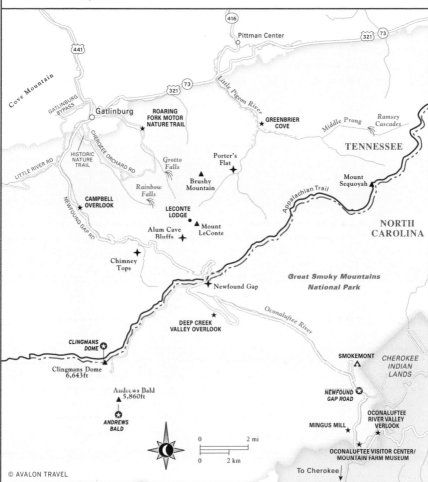

© AVALON TRAVEL

here. **Ogle Place,** a two-room cabin surrounded by rhododendrons; **Ephraim Bales Cabin,** which is smack in the middle of a boulder field; and **Alfred Regan Cabin,** which has an amazing trough system still in place, are all worth spending a few minutes exploring and photographing.

Hiking

There are three waterfalls within hiking distance of the Motor Nature Trail: **Rainbow Falls** (the most popular of the hikes), **Grotto Falls,** and **Baskins Creek Falls.** If you're not up for a hike, **Thousand Drips Falls** (sometimes called the Place of a Thousand Drips) is just off the road. In wet times, it's a great cascade plummeting down the mountain; during drier times, it's much more tame.

RAINBOW FALLS TRAIL

Distance: 5.4 miles round-trip
Duration: 3.5-4 hours

Elevation gain: 1,700 feet

Difficulty: strenuous

Trailhead: Roaring Fork Motor Nature Trail, 3.3 miles from Gatlinburg traffic light number 8, at the Rainbow Falls and Bull Head Trail parking area

This trail is strenuous due to how steep and rocky it is and how slick it can become in places where the trail nears the water and as you get closer to the falls. Note that Roaring Fork Motor Trail is closed in winter.

As you leave the parking area, you'll cross **Trillium Gap Trail** and begin to climb alongside LeConte Creek. Follow the trail as it goes through a couple of switchbacks and then crosses the creek on a **log bridge.** Here you'll enter a stretch where some impressive trees stand. Soon you'll cross LeConte Creek again. At this crossing you can see **Rainbow Falls** above you. Continue up the trail to a spot just below the falls.

Here LeConte Creek plunges 80 feet to the rocks below. During that plunge, the water becomes more of a heavy mist, giving us the name Rainbow Falls. Though you can get some good photography from the trail, there are other interesting shots to be had from different angles around the falls. Be aware that if you scramble around the falls, the rocks are slick and you could slip and hurt yourself, and with a 2.7-mile hike back to the car, who wants to do that? If you decide to explore the area around the falls, use caution and stay safe.

You may notice that the **Rainbow Falls Trail** continues on past the waterfall itself. It is possible to take this trail to the summit of Mount LeConte, but that is a strenuous, steep, full-day hike of close to 14 miles.

GROTTO FALLS TRAIL

Distance: 2.6 miles round-trip

Duration: 2–2.5 hours

Elevation gain: 585 feet

Difficulty: moderate

Trailhead: Roaring Fork Motor Nature Trail, about 2 miles into the trail, Grotto Falls parking area on the left

From the parking area, you'll follow a short unnamed spur before joining **Trillium Gap Trail,** which leads to **Grotto Falls** before continuing to the top of **Mount LeConte.** As you hike, you'll notice the path is hard-packed—that's because this trail is the re-supply route for **LeConte Lodge,** so it sees traffic from the llama trains carrying supplies up to the lodge. If you're lucky, you'll see one of these trains.

The forest was once composed mostly of hemlock trees, but thanks to a nasty little bug—the hemlock woolly adelgid—many of these trees are dead or dying. Even though some of the trees are being ravaged, the forest is still thick, and opens dramatically where the stream plunges 25 feet to form Grotto Falls.

The most intriguing part of Grotto Falls is the grotto. Trillium Gap Trail passes behind the falls thanks to a hefty rock overhang. It provides some interesting photographic opportunities that make it one of the most popular waterfall hikes on this side of the park.

BASKINS FALLS TRAIL

Distance: 3.2 miles round-trip

Duration: 3 hours

Elevation gain: 950 feet

Difficulty: strenuous

Trailhead: Roaring Fork Motor Nature Trail, on the left near the Jim Bales Place

This 30-foot waterfall is like a little secret hidden along the popular **Roaring Fork Motor Nature Trail** (closed in winter). Seldom visited, it's almost a forgotten hike, meaning you can have the falls to yourself.

As soon as you start the hike, you'll pass a cemetery before making a climb up to a ridgeline. A steep descent from the ridge will take you to **Baskins Creek.** Cross the creek (be careful, especially in high water) and make the steep climb over another ridge. From here you can see what's left of an old chimney standing in the woods. Just beyond a tiny, wildflower-filled meadow is the side path leading to the base of the falls. On the right side of this trail is an old **homesite,** followed by a steep descent down to the **falls.**

Many hikers turn around here and return to their car, but it is possible to continue along this trail another 1.5 miles and arrive near the

Mount LeConte Trails

NEWFOUND GAP RD

ROARING FORK MOTOR NATURE TRAIL

ROARING FORK MOTOR NATURE TRAIL

Rainbow Falls Trail

Bullhead Trail

LeConte Creek

Rainbow Falls

Grotto Falls

Trillium Gap Trail

ALUM CAVE

NEWFOUND GAP RD

Alum Cave Creek

Alum Cave Bluffs

Alum Rock

LECONTE LODGE

LECONTE SHELTER

Mount LeConte 6593

Trillium Gap Trail

Trillium Gap

Brushy Mountain

Boulevard Trail

Brushy Mountain Trail

Porters Creek Trail

0   0.5 km
0   0.5 mi

© MOON.COM

entrance to the Roaring Fork Motor Nature Trail. If you do this, know that you will have a 3-mile walk along the road back to your car.

Backpacking

This backpacking trip will take you from Roaring Fork to the summit of Mount LeConte, the third highest peak in the park (and sixth highest in the Appalachians). Spend the night at either the LeConte Lodge or LeConte Shelter; reservations are required for each.

RESERVATIONS

A backpacking trip to Mount LeConte from Roaring Fork requires some preparation. First, you'll need to register with the **Backcountry Information Office** (Sugarlands Visitor Center, 865/436-1297, https://smokiespermits.nps.gov, 8am-5pm daily, $4 per night) for a permit, then make a site reservation.

On Mount LeConte, you'll have only two options: LeConte Lodge, which is a hot ticket and books up early, and the LeConte Shelter, which is much easier to secure. ★ **LeConte Lodge** (865/429-5704, www.lecontelodge.com, Mar. 21-Nov. 22, adults $152, ages 4-12 $88, includes lodging and meals), requires reservations one year in advance. The LeConte Shelter is reserved through the Backcountry Information Office; reservations may be made up to 30 days before your stay. Contact the office as soon as possible to make a reservation; it's one of the most popular shelters in the park.

MOUNT LECONTE VIA GROTTO FALLS

Distance: 13.5 miles round-trip
Duration: Overnight
Elevation gain: 4,000 feet
Difficulty: strenuous
Trailhead: Roaring Fork Motor Nature Trail at the Grotto Falls Trail parking area

From the parking area, the path begins across **Roaring Fork Motor Nature Trail** for 0.1 miles before it meets with **Trillium Gap Trail.** Climb Trillium Gap Trail for 6.6 miles

(and some 4,000 vertical feet) to the summit of **Mount LeConte.** Now you're an easy 1.3 miles to **Grotto Falls,** one of the prettiest waterfalls in the park. (Grotto Falls is so named for the grotto behind the veil of water making up the falls.) The hike leads through the remains of a hemlock forest (the trees have been killed by the hemlock woolly adelgid) before it reaches the falls. At the falls you may encounter a strange sight: llamas. LeConte Lodge uses a pack train of llamas for resupply; if you're on the trail early enough, you'll see them at the waterfall.

Passing Grotto Falls, the trail will grow steeper. You'll cross a couple of small streams, but the trail is a typical woodland path with the usual rocks and roots underfoot and a decent incline. As you approach Trillium Gap you'll begin to see patches of grass along the trail. At 3.1 miles, you'll reach **Trillium Gap** proper and the intersection with **Brushy Mountain Trail.** Peak baggers can add another 0.8 miles for the round-trip hike to the summit of Brushy Mountain. Otherwise, continue along Trillium Gap Trail.

From Trillium Gap, the trail grows steeper and rockier, but the forest is quite lush. When the moss, ferns, and smaller vegetation give way to fir trees, you know you're close to LeConte Lodge. After passing a spring, you'll hit **LeConte Lodge.** Just ahead, the trail will intersect with **Bullhead Trail** and **Boulevard Trail;** turn right to approach LeConte Lodge and the spur trail leading to the summit. It's another 0.4 miles to the summit and back.

If you're staying at LeConte Lodge, check in and rest. If you've made a reservation at the **LeConte Shelter,** backtrack to the junction of Bullhead, Trillium Gap, and Boulevard Trails and continue down Boulevard Trail for another 0.2 miles.

GREENBRIER COVE

Greenbrier Cove, like many other coves in the park, was once home to a mountain community. This area was settled in the early 1800s, and families farmed, trapped, and hunted the

Ramsey Cascades Trail

land until the establishment of the national park. This cove has an interesting footnote: Dolly Parton's ancestors, Benjamin C. and Margaret Parton, moved here in the 1850s, and their descendants left when the park was formed.

Greenbrier is stunning, especially in the spring. The cove is known as a wildflower hot spot, but don't underestimate the beauty of this place in any season.

Hiking
RAMSEY CASCADES TRAIL

Distance: 8 miles round-trip
Duration: 5.5 hours
Elevation gain: 2,375 feet
Difficulty: strenuous
Trailhead: Ramsey Cascades Trailhead at the Greenbrier park entrance, 6 miles east of Gatlinburg off U.S. 321

Ramsey Cascades is the tallest waterfall in Great Smoky Mountains National Park, spilling 100 feet in a series of steps before collecting in a pool at the base. As if that wasn't reason enough to undertake this hike, this section of the park is known as a wildflower paradise, so a springtime visit is highly recommended.

The first portion of this trail is a continuation of the gravel road you took to the parking area. You'll soon cross **Little Laurel Branch** and almost immediately after, the Middle Prong of Little Pigeon River via a long **footbridge.** If you've timed your hike with the wildflower bloom, the next half mile will be a riot of color.

The hiking here is easy until you reach the 1.5-mile mark, where the Jeep trail you're on ends. To the left (north) is the **Greenbrier Pinnacle Trail,** a trail that's not maintained by the park; **Ramsey Cascades Trail** continues on through a thicket of rhododendron.

Past this point you find yourself on a trail where roots and rocks are more the norm, so watch your footing. Continue along this trail; it will turn steep, you'll cross the **Ramsey Prong** and a side stream, and you'll know you've arrived when you hear the waterfall. The final approach is rocky and slick, with a lot of scrambling, so use caution. When you've taken in all of the **Ramsey Cascades** you can handle, simply reverse your course to the trailhead.

BRUSHY MOUNTAIN TO MOUNT LECONTE

Distance: 11.8 miles round-trip
Duration: 6-7 hours
Elevation gain: 3,000 feet
Difficulty: moderate
Trailhead: Porters Creek Trailhead on Greenbrier Road, 6 miles east of Gatlinburg off U.S. 321

Directions: From traffic light number 3 in Gatlinburg (junction of U.S. 441 and U.S. 321), travel east on U.S. 321. Drive 6 miles and then turn right on Greenbrier Road, which becomes a gravel road. At the fork in the road 3.1 miles in, continue straight 1 mile to the Porters Creek Trailhead.

The first mile or so of this trail follows an old gravel road, the **Porters Creek Trail.** In the spring, trilliums are profuse here. You'll pass a **cemetery** and several stone walls and then cross a **footbridge** at a fork in the road. Turn left at the fork. You'll meet another fork 100 yards or so down the trail, at which you turn right onto **Brushy Mountain Trail.**

The trail continues for 4.5 miles, climbing some 2,500 feet as it does. At 5.5 miles, you'll meet **Trillium Gap Trail.** Go left on the Trillium Gap Trail and you'll reach **Mount LeConte.** Turn right and you can reach the summit of **Brushy Mountain** in 0.6 miles.

GRAPEYARD RIDGE

Distance: 7.6 miles one-way via shuttle
Duration: 4-5 hours
Elevation gain: 3,250 feet
Difficulty: moderate
Trailhead: Grapeyard Ridge Trailhead in Greenbrier, 6 miles east of Gatlinburg off U.S. 321

This beautiful hike reveals some intriguing sights, such as the remains of a Civilian Conservation Corps (CCC) camp, stone walls, a cemetery, and an old steam engine. This route connects the Greenbrier area of the park with Roaring Fork Motor Nature Trail (closed in winter); it's best to do this as an end-to-end shuttle hike (park a car at one end, drive to the other, and hike back to the car you left). Otherwise, you'll have to arrange transport back to your trailhead or hike back.

Begin the hike along **Greenbrier Road** (closed in winter) and plunge right into a forest thick with galax and mountain laurel. You'll climb quickly, gaining nearly 300 feet in little more than 0.5 miles. At 0.1 miles, pass a spur trail to a **cemetery.** At 0.4 miles, the trail begins to descend, and you'll make the first of many crossings of **Rhododendron**

Creek at 0.5 miles. This crossing has no bridge; you'll have to ford the stream without aid, so watch the water levels and only cross if you're confident in your ability and footing. Over the next 1.2 miles, you'll **cross the stream** four more times.

The trail splits from the creek and begins climbing toward James Gap at the 2.1-mile mark, going through a few rhododendron tunnels, which give it an eerie feel. You'll reach **James Gap** at 2.9 miles, then quickly descend to **Injun Creek** and the wreck of an old steam engine. The name of the creek comes from the steam engine, not the native people. The engine was part of a logging operation in the 1920s; the steam-powered tractor slipped into the creek on the way out and stayed there, too heavy to move.

Turning back here makes this a nice little day hike. If you press on, you'll pass **Backcountry Campsite 32** in 0.3 miles. Here begins another steady uphill climb to **Grapeyard Ridge** at the 4-mile mark. Rather than follow the true ridge, the trail traces a path just below it. This path offers better views and a profusion of wildflowers in each little cove you dip into.

The trail descends toward Grapeyard Branch, meeting with **Dudley Creek** at 4.8 miles. Prior to reaching the creek, you'll see fence posts and other signs of habitation; at Dudley Creek there is a low rock wall and evidence of a homestead. The junction with **Big Dudley Trail** at 4.9 miles marks the next point where the trail climbs as it continues on toward Roaring Fork.

A sign for **Roaring Fork** appears at 6.1 miles; at 6.6 miles is the highest point of the trail. Begin your descent into Roaring Fork. At 7.3 miles, a trail leads to Trillium Gap Trail, but continue straight and you'll soon reach Bales Place and **Roaring Fork.**

PORTERS CREEK TRAIL

Distance: 7.2 miles round-trip
Duration: 3.5-4 hours
Elevation gain: 1,500 feet
Difficulty: moderate

Hen Wallow Falls Trail

Trailhead: Greenbrier Road 0.9 miles beyond the Ramsey Cascades Trailhead

From the traffic loop 0.9 miles up the road from the **Ramsey Cascades Trailhead,** begin hiking along a gravel road. Rock walls and evidence of homesites are all around; soon you'll cross a small creek and find an old **cemetery.** Cross a larger stream by wading (if the water's not too high) or using the foot log.

In 1 mile an **old traffic turnaround** indicates the start of the trail. **Porters Creek Trail** is the trail to the far left. (Brushy Mountain Trail is the middle trail, and the far right trail leads to a historic farm site that you can explore on the way back.)

Once you begin Porters Creek Trail, you'll cross Porters Creek in 0.5 miles. If you're hiking in the spring, you'll be treated to a carpet of wildflowers. **Fern Branch Falls** awaits 0.4 miles farther, adding to the beauty of this hike. The waterfall is surprisingly high at 35 feet, and the surrounding area is thick with moss and wildflowers in the spring.

Continue past the waterfall to the end of the hike and **Backcountry Campsite 31** at 3.6 miles. Explore the creek for a little while, then when you're ready, head back downhill to the trailhead.

COSBY

For the first half of the 20th century, Cosby was known as the moonshine capital of the world. The national prohibition on liquor turned many locals to making their own. When scientists and workers began to come to Oak Ridge to work on secret military ventures like the Manhattan Project, they weren't accustomed to Tennessee's dry-county laws, and the demand for moonshine skyrocketed. Today, there isn't much by way of moonshine production in town, and most of the visitors come here for the national park.

Cosby's present reputation is as a friendly town with one of the lesser-used park entrances. That's good for you, because when autumn leaves begin to change and the crowds pack Gatlinburg and clog the easy-to-access trails along Newfound Gap Road, you can head to Cosby. In town you'll find a few restaurants and a handful of cabin rentals, but the park is the real treasure.

Hiking
★ HEN WALLOW FALLS TRAIL
Distance: 4.4 miles round-trip
Duration: 3.5 hours
Elevation gain: 900 feet
Difficulty: moderate

Trailhead: Gabes Mountain Trailhead, across the road from the Cosby Campground picnic area

From the outset, **Gabes Mountain Trail** is a steady climb on a path that's at times rugged. Follow this trail until you see a sign for the **side trail** leading to the waterfall (2.1 miles into the hike). The 0.1-mile side trail is a little steep, but not problematically so.

Hen Wallow Falls tumbles 90 feet into a small pool below, where there are plenty of salamanders to see. The falls themselves are only 2 feet wide at the top, but fan out to 20 feet at the bottom; during dry months, the falls are still pretty, but less wow-inducing.

To get back to the trailhead, just retrace your steps.

MOUNT CAMMERER TRAIL

Distance: 11.2 miles round-trip
Duration: 7-7.5 hours
Elevation gain: 2,740 feet
Difficulty: strenuous
Trailhead: Low Gap Trailhead, just beyond the Cosby Campground amphitheater area

To start, park in the group parking area and walk along the road to where it curves into the B section of the campground. Just before **campsite 92** you'll see a trailhead; follow it for a short distance until it crosses Cosby Creek, then turn right on **Low Gap Trail.** From here, the trail climbs a little less than 3 miles up the mountain via a series of winding switchbacks until you reach the Appalachian Trail.

Turn left to join the **Appalachian Trail** for 2.1 miles. The first mile of this trail is more level, so it gives you a chance to catch your breath or make up some time. You'll know when you reach the junction with the **Mount Cammerer Trail** because the Appalachian Trail descends to the right; you want to stay straight. The **summit** is 0.6 miles from where you leave the Appalachian Trail.

At the summit is a **stone fire tower** built in the 1930s and restored by volunteers throughout the years. The view from the deck here is awe-inspiring—it's one of the best in the park.

ALBRIGHT GROVE TRAIL

Distance: 6.8 miles round-trip
Duration: 3.5-4 hours
Elevation gain: 1,400 feet
Difficulty: moderate
Trailhead: Maddron Bald Trail
Directions: From Gatlinburg, drive 15.5 miles east on U.S. 321. Turn right onto Baxter Road; at 0.3 miles turn right onto a gravel road. Park near (but don't block) the gate at the dirt road.

Begin hiking on **Maddron Bald Trail,** an old wagon road, which climbs immediately uphill. At 0.7 miles, you'll get your first chance for a breather when you reach a one-room **cabin** on the right. Keep climbing and, at 1.2 miles, you'll meet up with **Old Settlers Trail** (continues right) and **Gabes Mountain Trail** (continues left). Stay straight on Maddron Bald Trail, following the old roadbed for another mile before the wagon road ends at a traffic circle. Here the path begins in earnest.

Cross **Indian Camp Creek** 0.5 miles past the old traffic circle, keeping an eye out for **Albright Grove Loop Trail,** which appears in another 0.1 miles. Since Albright Grove is a loop, you can take this entrance, make the loop, and then descend along Maddron Bald Trail. Or you can climb up another 0.3 miles to the upper junction with Albright and take Maddron Bald Trail back.

Many consider Albright Grove to be a great example of old-growth forest in the national park. Though many of the huge hemlocks trees have died from a pest infestation, they've left gaps in the canopy that allows in sunlight. You'll still see many fine and big trees here, evidence of the forest as it once stood.

After you've explored Albright Grove, head back down Maddron Bald Trail to the trailhead.

Fishing

Anglers can bring their gear to **Cosby Creek,** which has several spots where wild trout are abundant. If you find other anglers along the creek and want some isolation, hike upstream

---

1: Hen Wallow Falls **2:** Cosby Campground

into the headwaters, where small brook trout await.

In the spring you'll catch fish along Cosby Creek, but in the summer you'll want to venture into the headwaters. Fall fishing is spectacular, thanks to that distracting and beautiful leaf show, and in the winter you'll catch fish along the stream on all but the coldest days (because you'll be snug and warm somewhere else).

Camping

Cosby Campground (471 Cosby Campground Rd. A, Cosby, TN, 423/487-2683, www.recreation.gov, Apr.-Oct., $17.50) has 157 sites for tents and RVs. Despite being home to the park's third-largest campground, Cosby is known as the quietest of the park's gateways. There are a number of trails that originate from the campground.

At the northern end of Great Smoky Mountains National Park, you're close enough to the **Cherokee National Forest** (www.fs.usda.gov/cherokee, free) to camp in the Pigeon River Recreation Zone. Dispersed camping is allowed provided campers are 100 feet away from water, trails, parking areas, and developed recreation areas.

Accommodations

Cosby has a few accommodations, but selections are limited. Fortunately, a couple of spots stand out.

Creekwalk Inn (166 Middle Creek Rd., 865/453-2000, www.creekwalkinnandcabins.com, $189-209) is a seven-room bed-and-breakfast with inn rooms and several cabins all set on a 50-acre mountain farm. There are hiking trails and creeks to explore, and a killer breakfast is served every morning. Best of all, the individual cabins are separated, providing privacy for guests, and the B&B rooms are so cozy you'll forget anyone else is there. Until breakfast, that is, when everyone shows up for cast-iron skillet cornbread with peach jam, fried potatoes, sausage, and eggs cooked on a wood stove.

For a sample of mountain life, but with electricity, **Garden of Eden Cabins** (467 Laurel Springs Rd., 423/487-2617, www.gardenofedencabins.com, $85-95) has three cabins in the woods near the national park. They are comfortable and homey, but the decor could use a bit of an update (common in B&Bs and cabins in these parts). Two of the cabins have two bedrooms, making them natural choices for couples traveling together, families, or small groups. Each cabin is pet-friendly and has a fire ring and a picnic area with outdoor seating; two cabins overlook the creek, which makes quite the lovely lullaby.

At **Cosby Creek Cabins** (4376 Cosby Hwy., 800/508-8844, www.cosbycreekcabins.com, $135-230 plus cleaning fee), you'll find larger and slightly more luxurious cabins scattered around Cosby, with several closer to Pigeon Forge and Gatlinburg. The three dozen cabins range from one to four bedrooms and include options like game rooms, fireplaces, and hot tubs; some are pet-friendly. Winter rates ($75-180) make exploring the park in the off-season easy and affordable.

Food

Dining options are few, and all are of the country cookin' variety. But the food is both filling and tasty, though vegetarians may have a hard time finding a meatless meal.

For an early breakfast at **Janice's Diner** (2765 Cosby Hwy., 423/613-5515, 6:30am-8:30pm daily, $7-20), skip the front room (it's a little dull) and head straight for the dining area in back, where it's homey and welcoming. The diner-style food includes eggs and hash browns, burgers, sandwiches, and a couple of salads. It opens early and everything is affordable, so stop in to fuel up pre-hike or replenish those post-hike calories.

Magnolia Tree Restaurant & Country Market (4925 Hooper Hwy., 423/487-2519, 11am-8pm Thurs.-Tues., $6-19) is one of those dual-purpose places that feels like the inspiration for Cracker Barrel. You know the type: Eat a home-cooked meal in the dining room, then buy some fudge or whimsical country gift in the shop. While that may sound a little corny, you can pick up some road or trail snacks here and get a decent meal. Try the cheesesteak, the BLT, and the chicken pot pie, though not all at once. That's a lot of food, and you'll have no room for dessert.

Trust me, **Mama's Kitchen** (3066 Cosby Hwy., 423/487-4433, 8am-9pm daily, $3-12) has the simple, filling breakfast you want plus an easy-to-navigate lunch menu and the homey dinner you've been thinking about all day. But breakfast—pancakes, biscuits, beautifully crisp hash browns—is where it's at.

BIG CREEK

Big Creek is the site of a beautiful and seldom-visited front-country campground and has one of the best hikes for beginning day hikers and backpackers. The Big Creek Trail is more of an easy creek-side walk than a hike, but it's long enough to make you feel accomplished when you're done.

For more of a challenge, turn Big Creek into a big overnighter by including a summit of Mount Sterling, or you can take on Mount Sterling from a couple of different routes, all accessible from this region.

Hiking
★ **BIG CREEK TRAIL**
Distance: 10.6 miles round-trip
Duration: 5-6 hours
Elevation gain: 600 feet
Difficulty: easy
Trailhead: Big Creek Campground and Picnic Area off I-40 at Waterville (exit 457)

Big Creek Trail follows an old motor road built by the Civilian Conservation Corps (CCC) in the 1930s, so it's smooth and wide with a very gentle grade for its entire length. The difficult part of this trail is the distance, so be sure to bring plenty of water and something to eat.

Roughly one mile in from the trailhead, you'll see **Rock House,** an impressive rock cliff that has sheltered more than a few loggers, Civilian Conservation Corps workers, hunters, and hikers from a rainstorm. Just beyond Rock House is **Midnight Hole,** where Big Creek flows through a narrow chute in the

rock, then drops 6-7 feet into a deep, dark pool before flowing on.

Two miles in, you'll see **Mouse Creek Falls,** a 35-foot cascade that drops right into Big Creek. It's a fantastic spot to sit, relax, take some pictures, and enjoy the woods. It's also a great spot to turn around if you may not be up for the whole 10-mile trip.

Push on past Mouse Creek Falls and you'll come upon **Brakeshoe Spring.** In another 2.5 miles you'll reach **Walnut Bottoms** and **Campsite 37.** This is one of the best campsites in the park if you're going to make this hike an overnighter. From here, it's time to retrace your steps back to the trailhead.

MOUNT STERLING VIA BAXTER CREEK TRAIL
Distance: 12.2 miles round-trip
Duration: 5-6 hours
Elevation gain: 4,200 feet
Difficulty: strenuous
Trailhead: Big Creek Campground and Picnic Area off I-40 at Waterville (exit 457)

You can reach the summit of Mount Sterling from a number of trails—but this one is perhaps the most direct. This hike is strenuous not because of any technical or steep sections of the trail (it's actually well-maintained), but because it's a steady uphill climb with a 4,200-foot elevation gain until you turn around for the return trip. At the summit, you're rewarded with a fire tower to climb, giving you massive views of this section of the park.

At the trailhead, cross a **footbridge** over Big Creek, which you'll follow for 0.5 miles until the trail begins to climb the lower slopes of Mount Sterling. Before the uphill section, you'll pass an unmarked **spur trail** at 0.3 miles leading to a rock wall and huge stone chimney, the remains of a lodge once owned by a lumber company.

After crossing Baxter Creek (around the 0.7-mile mark), you'll pass through some spectacular forest, including old-growth and one of the largest (if not the largest) tulip trees in the park at more than 175 feet tall. There are several massive trees here, including more champion tulip trees, the largest northern red oak, and the Carolina silver bell.

The hike is straightforward for the length of the trail: Keep climbing, keep passing amazing trees and lovely spring wildflowers until you reach the summit. At the 5,842-foot summit, you'll notice three things: wind, the temperature, and a **fire tower.** It's cooler, and can be quite windy, which makes the thought of climbing the 60-foot fire tower seem daunting. If you climb, do so carefully and remember the view you'll get at the end. On clear days you can see Balsam Mountain to the west, Mount Guyot to the northwest, Max Patch (along the Appalachian Trail on the Tennessee-North Carolina border) to the east, and Cataloochee Valley just below to the south. When you've had your fill of the views, follow the path back to the trailhead.

BIG CREEK TRAIL AND MOUNT STERLING LOOP

Distance: 17.4 miles round-trip
Duration: 10 hours
Elevation gain: 4,200 feet
Difficulty: strenuous
Trailhead: Big Creek Campground and Picnic Area off I-40 at Waterville (exit 457)

You can make this a rewarding day hike, or break it up into a one- or two-night backpacking experience. All three options follow the same route, with access to backcountry campsites.

Begin by following **Big Creek Trail,** which uses a Civilian Conservation Corps motor road to guide hikers to Rock House (an impressive rock cliff), Mouse Creek Falls, and Brakeshoe Springs. From **Brakeshoe Springs,** hike 2.3 miles to the junction with **Swallow Fork Trail.** If you plan to stay overnight, continue 0.2 miles to **Campsite 37** and Walnut Bottoms. Campsite 37 is one of the best backcountry sites in the park, so consider a night here if you're backpacking.

If pressing on, take Swallow Fork Trail and begin a gradual climb, crossing a couple of small streams along the way. You will reach **Swallow Fork** 1 mile in; cross it on a foot log

and you'll reach **McGinty Creek** and the remains of what was once a sawmill. This section is lousy with wildflowers in the spring, so take your time and enjoy it when the blooms are out.

From McGinty Creek, hike approximately 1 mile before making one more stream crossing, then start a steep climb to **Pretty Hollow Gap.** At the gap, the **Mount Sterling Ridge Trail** intersects with Pretty Hollow Gap Trail (which reaches Cataloochee in a few miles); turn left (east) for Mount Sterling.

After turning onto Mount Sterling Ridge Trail, you'll find another steep climb, but it's only 0.5 miles and it eases up once you reach the top of the knob. From the top, it's 0.4 miles to the summit and the **fire tower.** Adjacent to the summit, is **Campsite 38,** for a first or second night in the backcountry. If you're camping, note that it's often windy here and cooler due to the elevation, so pack appropriately sleeping gear.

At the summit, the trail becomes **Baxter Creek Trail,** which you'll follow back to the Big Creek Trailhead. It's a steady downhill with a couple of notable landmarks. The first is a spring 0.2 miles from the summit, which you'll reach in 150 yards or so off the trail. The second landmark is 2 miles from the summit, where the trail makes a hairpin turn and plunges into another section of old-growth forest. Continue through some impressive and thick woods until arriving back at the trailhead.

MOUNT STERLING

Distance: 5.4 miles round-trip
Duration: 5-6 hours
Elevation gain: 1,900 feet
Difficulty: strenuous
Trailhead: Mount Sterling Trailhead at Mount Sterling Gap
Directions: From I-40, take Waterville (exit 457) and cross the Pigeon River. Stay left and follow the road 2 miles to Mount Sterling. Turn left and drive the curvy 6.7 miles to Mount Sterling Gap. The trailhead is on the west side of the road.

This hike starts off steep and it doesn't relent

Big Creek Trail and Mount Sterling Loop

© MOON.COM

for a long time. Begin hiking up the trail to a junction with **Long Bunk Trail** in 0.5 miles. Continue climbing until you reach **Mount Sterling Ridge** at 2.3 miles. You have a little climbing left—0.4 miles—before you reach the **summit.** There's an additional 60-foot climb if you visit the fire tower, which has quite a view. On clear days you can see Balsam Mountain to the west, Mount Guyot to the northwest, Max Patch to the east, and Cataloochee Valley just below to the south. When ready, retrace your steps back to the trailhead.

Camping

The **Big Creek Campground** (off Hwy. 284/ Mt. Sterling Rd., 12 sites, Apr.-Oct., $17.50) is located off Highway 284. Amenities include a ranger station, pay phone, drinking water, restrooms with flush toilets, a picnic area, and a group camp, as well as equestrian sites (reservations at 877/444-6777 or www.recreation. gov, $25). Trailheads to Baxter Creek Trail, Big Creek Trail, and the Chestnut Branch of the Appalachian Trail lead from the campground.

Big Creek is close enough to the **Cherokee National Forest** (www.fs.usda. gov/cherokee, free) to camp in the Pigeon River Recreation Zone. Dispersed camping is allowed provided campers are 100 feet away from water, trails, parking areas, and developed recreation areas. To get there, take I-40 west into Tennessee and the national forest.

It is also possible to drive farther north to the French Broad River Recreation Zone for more camping, hiking, and fishing opportunities. To get there within Tennessee, take Highway 701 north to Highway 107, which leads to several trailheads and recreation opportunities.

CATALOOCHEE VALLEY

Nestled in the folds of the mountains and encircled by 6,000-foot peaks, the Cataloochee Valley was settled in the early 1830s. This isolated valley on the northeastern edge of Great Smoky Mountains National Park was home to two communities—Big and Little Cataloochee—and more than 1,200 people

in 1910. By the 1940s all but a few were gone, having left the valley for hills and hollows nearby. Today, this is one of the more beautiful spots in the national park, and a few historic structures are all that remain of the communities that thrived here, save a few memories and stories that were written down.

Cataloochee Valley is not far from I-40, but it can be a little difficult to find because the signage directing you here is poor at best. From I-40, take exit 20 onto U.S. 276. Take an immediate right onto Cove Creek Road. The condition of the road—it's alternately gravel and paved—and the narrow, winding route will make you doubt you made the right turn, but you did. Zigzag up this road for about 12 miles and suddenly it will open up into the wide, grassy expanse that is Cataloochee Valley. Before you begin your descent into the valley, stop at the overlook just past the intersection with Big Creek Road. From here you can marvel at the valley sweeping away before you, and the mountains rising up all around.

The valley is open to vehicle traffic 8am-sunset daily, so keep that in mind if you're visiting without plans to camp. Though less visited than other areas, like Cades Cove on the western side of the park, Cataloochee sees its fair share of visitors. Most arrive in the evenings shortly before sunset to see the elk grazing in the fields. If you don't plan on camping and you'd rather avoid the crowds, as small as they may be, visit in midday and take a hike to see if you can find the elk in the woods; it's where they go to escape the heat.

★ Cataloochee

There are four prominent structures still standing in Cataloochee Valley: two homes, a school, and a church. A few other structures and ruins, cemeteries, fences, and walls remain throughout the valley as well. The most prominent building is the **Palmer Chapel and Cemetery.** The chapel was built in 1898, and it's been some time since there's been a regular service here. Today the chapel sees sporadic use, the most regular being the annual reunion of the descendants of some of

Cataloochee Valley

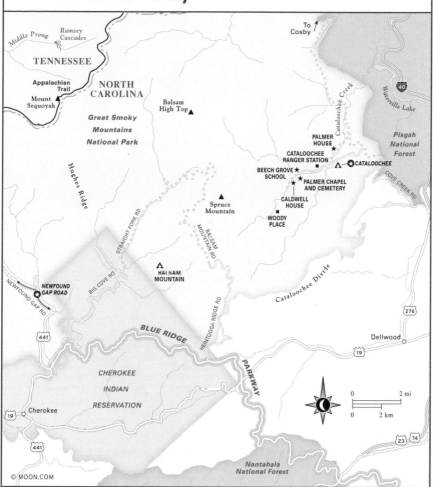

© MOON.COM

the oldest Cataloochee families. Descendants of the Barnes, Bennett, Caldwell, Noland, and Palmer families gather here to eat, hold a short church service, and maintain the cemetery. Throughout the year there are some great opportunities to capture the chapel in all sorts of lighting, weather, and seasonal conditions.

Across the road is the **Beech Grove School,** the last of three schools to serve the children of the valley. It's empty save for a few artifacts. Beech Grove School operated on a very different school schedule than we're familiar with: The only regular school sessions were held November-January, sometimes February and rarely into March. This odd schedule was built around the seasons, which freed children for planting and harvesting, as well as hunting and preserving food—staple activities for many living in the mountains.

Just up the road is the **Caldwell House.** We know from records that the owner, Hiram Caldwell, was prosperous, but you could tell

Boogerman Trail

that just by comparing this 1906 home with the other historic homes in the park, which are, by and large, log cabins. The Caldwell House is frame-built (similar to houses now) with paneling on the interior walls.

The final structure is the **Palmer House,** located off Big Creek Road, not far from the Cataloochee Ranger Station. This was once a log home—two, actually, connected by a covered walkway called a dog trot—but as the owners came into money in the early 1900s, they began making improvements and remodeling the home. They covered the exterior and interior with weatherboarding and began using fancy wallpaper in some rooms; scraps of the wallpaper are there today. When the son inherited the property, he remodeled it, adding rooms to the home and operating it as a boardinghouse. Renters were primarily anglers who came to fish in the three miles of stocked trout stream the family owned.

Hiking
BOOGERMAN TRAIL
Distance: 7.4-mile loop
Duration: 3.5-4 hours
Elevation gain: 1,050 feet
Difficulty: moderate
Trailhead: just past Cataloochee Campground

This trail isn't named for some fearsome and mythical creature from the woods; it's named for Robert "Boogerman" Palmer, the former owner of much of the land along this hike. Palmer is rumored to have earned his nickname in school, where he told his teacher that he wanted to be "the Boogerman" when he grew up. This trail is anything but fearsome, and in the summer you'll likely see a few other hikers; if it's solitude you're seeking, hit the trail during the shoulder seasons.

Start the hike by crossing **Palmer Creek.** Follow Caldwell Fork upstream for nearly a mile and you'll come to **Boogerman Trail.**

Turn left onto the trail and begin a gentle climb. When you reach a lower ridgeline, the path levels out, then descends through a grove of pine trees before ascending again. Soon, the trail makes a steep ascent to another level ridge. This section features some of the largest trees, mostly poplars, that you'll see on this hike.

As you continue on this short ridgeline section, you'll encounter some signs of human settlement, the first of which is a **stone wall.** Continue your descent and cross the stream you're following a few times, passing more rock walls along the way. If the wildflowers aren't too high, you may spot a large, strange piece of metal just off the trail. It's the remnant of some sort of homesteading equipment, perhaps a sluice gate for a water flume, or maybe a piece from a sawmill. Whatever it is, it's alien here.

When you pass the decayed remains of a **cabin,** you're close to the junction with Caldwell Fork Trail. At **Caldwell Fork Trail,** turn right and cross Snake Branch (the stream you've been following), and soon thereafter, Caldwell Fork. You'll cross Caldwell Fork several more times before reaching the junction with **Boogerman Trail** and the path back to the trailhead.

ROUGH FORK TRAIL

Distance: 2 miles round-trip
Duration: 1 hour
Elevation gain: 50 feet
Difficulty: easy
Trailhead: Rough Fork Trailhead at the end of Cataloochee Road

One of the easiest hikes in the whole park, the Rough Fork Trail follows a gravel road for nearly the entire length of the trail. Three stream crossings on foot logs are highlights of the hike, which ends at the Steve Woody House.

The trailhead begins on the other side of a gate that marks the end of the paved road and the start of the gravel road. Follow the wide, flat road as it goes through the woods. The path parallels Rough Fork until it crosses on

a **foot log.** (Foot logs are long logs that have been flattened on the top to create a walkway; they often have hand rails on one side and can be a little bouncy.) The foot logs across Rough Fork are a bit bouncy, but are fun and safe to cross.

Cross Rough Fork twice more via **footbridges,** then continue following the stream on the right as you make your way to the former home and springhouse (a small wooden shed built over a spring) of **Steve Woody.** Be careful around the springhouse because snakes are frequent visitors.

LITTLE CATALOOCHEE TRAIL

Distance: 6 miles one-way
Duration: 3.5-4 hours
Elevation gain: 2,400 feet
Difficulty: moderate
Trailhead: Pretty Hollow Gap/Cataloochee Horse Trail Trailhead, adjacent to Beech Grove School

Little Cataloochee Trail is six miles point-to-point, so you'll need to arrange a car shuttle back to the trailhead. Alternatively, take a shorter hike from the other end of the trail.

Begin at the **Cataloochee Horse Camp** (you may have to park 0.2 miles back down by Cataloochee Entrance Rd.) and follow an old road that parallels Palmer Creek. At 0.8 miles, you'll reach the junction with **Little Cataloochee Trail.** Turn right (northeast) and follow Little Cataloochee to the end at Highway 284.

As you hike, you can look for signs of former homesteads in the form of cultivated flowers like daffodils, yucca plants, and fruit trees. There are many **homestead sites** along the trail, but most are grown over, though you can spot them.

For a while the trail will be steep; at approximately 3 miles, you'll meet up with an old roadbed that makes the hike easier. At 3.3 miles, you'll reach **Dan Cook Place,** a cabin that was reconstructed after the original was destroyed by vandals in the mid-1970s. Continue along the trail to the **Little Cataloochee Baptist Church** and **cemetery.** The original church has been

The Return of Native Elk

Elk are native to the mountains of North Carolina and Tennessee, but overhunting decimated their population across the region. In North Carolina, the last elk was believed to have been killed in the late 1700s; in Tennessee, in the mid-1800s. In 2001, the National Park Service reintroduced elk to the park by bringing 25 elk to Great Smoky Mountains National Park from Land Between the Lakes National Recreation Area in Kentucky. The next year they brought in another 27 animals. Today, they believe somewhere between 150 and 200 elk live in the park.

The majority of the elk can be seen in the **Cataloochee Valley,** though a small herd lives near the **Oconaluftee Visitor Center** and **Smokemont Campground** and can be seen wading across the river and grazing in the fields and forest there.

Adult males, called bulls, weigh 600-700 pounds, while females, referred to as cows, weigh around 500 pounds. Some bulls have antlers that are five feet across. They're territorial, and bulls sometimes see humans as a threat and may charge. It's best to watch the elk from a safe distance. In Great Smoky Mountains National Park it is illegal to approach elk within 50 yards (150 feet) or any distance that disturbs or displaces the animals.

At certain times of the year, you may see calves walking close by their mothers. Never approach or touch a calf. If an elk calf feels threatened and its mother is not nearby, its natural defense is to lie down and be still. It may look orphaned, but mom is within earshot, so back away slowly.

Elk are most active in the early morning and evening, much like deer. Also like deer, their diet is primarily grass, bark, leaves, and acorns. There are no natural predators of elk in the Smokies today, though sick, injured, and young elk are sometimes targets of opportunity for black bears, coyotes, or even the boldest of bobcats.

maintained and is the site of occasional services.

From the church, the road descends rather steeply, passing the former community of **Ola.** Follow the road to a short side trail leading to **John Hackson Hannah Cabin,** then a junction with **Long Bunk Trail.** It's another 1.1 miles to the end of the trail at Highway 284. Use a car shuttle, or hike back along the road (which adds another 3 miles or so), or backtrack to make this a big 12-mile day.

For a shorter hike that sees a few historic structures, drive to the end of the trail on Highway 284 (the trailhead is marked) and hike to the Little Cataloochee Baptist Church and Dan Cook Place (6 miles round-trip).

Fishing

Fishing is plentiful off **Cataloochee Creek** and its tributaries, with the main quarry being wild trout.

Camping

The ★ **Cataloochee Campground** (campground 828/497-9270, reservations 877/444-6777, www.recreation.gov, mid-Apr.-Oct., reservations required, $25) has 27 tent and RV sites. There is a horse camp with seven sites not far up the valley; down the valley there's a group campground with three sites and room for much larger parties. This highly recommended campsite is one of the most secluded you'll find in the front-country.

BALSAM MOUNTAIN ROAD

Since most of the crowds who visit Great Smoky Mountains National Park use Newfound Gap Road exclusively, it's nice to find a route that's less traveled and possibly more beautiful. One such route is **Balsam**

1: elk grazing in a field in Cataloochee Valley
2: Palmer Chapel 3: Caldwell House 4: Rough Fork Trail

Mountain Road (open May-Nov.), a lovely drive where you may be lucky to see 10 other cars.

Accessible only from the Blue Ridge Parkway near Soco Gap, the road traverses 14 miles of ridgeline. To reach Balsam Mountain Road, turn off the Parkway at milepost 458 and follow Heintooga Ridge Road to the Heintooga Overlook and Picnic Area; here the road changes names to Balsam Mountain Road and turns to gravel.

As soon as it turns into Balsam Mountain Road, it becomes one-way, so you're committed to follow it to its end. This will take about 1.5 hours (if you don't stop to hike or take in the scenery), primarily because the gravel road forces you to slow down. It's narrow but well maintained, so you can drive most cars along the route. If you're in doubt of the road's condition or are concerned about your vehicle's clearance, check online (www.nps.gov/grsm) for road closures and advisories.

Balsam Mountain Road is an excellent place to see spring wildflowers, summer rhododendrons, and fall leaves. At these times, traffic may pick up, but the idea of a gravel road discourages enough visitors to keep this road the one less traveled.

When you've driven about 13 miles along Balsam Mountain Road, it becomes two-way again. Here, it begins to follow Straight Fork, which will lead you right onto Straight Fork Road (closed in winter), which cuts through the Eastern Cherokee Reservation to U.S. 441.

Hiking
FLAT CREEK TRAIL
Distance: 5.2 miles round-trip
Duration: 3.5-4 hours
Elevation gain: 900 feet
Difficulty: moderate
Trailhead: Heintooga Overlook and Picnic Area
You can hike Flat Creek Trail as a 5.2-mile out-and-back trail or do it as a 6.2-mile loop. If following the loop, note that the last 3.6 miles are along Heintooga Ridge Road (closed May-Nov.).

From the picnic area, walk out to **Heintooga Overlook** for a great view. Just past the overlook, the trail forks; go right and follow **Flat Creek Trail** as it descends, crossing the creek and entering a rhododendron thicket. Soon the forest opens up and becomes grassy, a sign of previous logging activity.

At 1.9 miles, you'll reach a path (right) that leads to Flat Creek Falls, but don't bother— the views aren't good and it's difficult (and dangerous) to try. Stay on Flat Creek Trail as the trail enters a thick forest, descends, and then crosses a fork of **Bunches Creek.** Shortly after Bunches Creek, you'll climb up to **Heintooga Ridge Road.** Turn around and head back, or continue hiking up the road for a 6-mile hike.

BALSAM MOUNTAIN TRAIL
Distance: 8.2 miles round-trip
Duration: 6 hours
Elevation gain: 3,000 feet
Difficulty: strenuous
Trailhead: Balsam Mountain Road, 8.2 miles from the end of Heintooga Ridge Road at Pin Oak Gap
You have two choices for this hike: a long day hike or an overnighter with a stay at Laurel Gap Shelter. The route is the same no matter which you hike. Laurel Gap Shelter is only 4.1 miles from the trailhead, so if you chose to stay, you'll either have two easy days or one long day if you decide to hike to the summit of Balsam High Top then on to the shelter for water and rest.

The straightforward trail climbs aggressively uphill for 1.9 miles, where you'll reach the now-overgrown **Ledge Bald** and begin to ascend. In 0.4 miles is the junction with **Beech Gap Trail,** which comes in from the left (west) and leads back to Balsam Mountain Road after a 2.5-mile hike. Ignore the trail and press on, ascending again until you reach the ridge. Follow the ridge through a hardwood forest to a grove of fir trees, the mountain's namesake balsam trees. These trees mark **Balsam High Top,** the 3.5-mile mark on the trail. To visit the summit (no views, just do it if you're a peak bagger), you'll have to go off-trail. Otherwise, keep hiking another 0.6 miles to **Laurel Gap Shelter** and the spring there. Make camp or get a little water, have a snack, and rest up. When you're ready, hike out by backtracking the trail.

Camping

The front-country campground at **Balsam Mountain** (46 sites, first-come first-served, May-Oct., $17.50) is located off Balsam Mountain Road at Heintooga Ridge Road. Amenities include an amphitheater, a small

section for tents only, restrooms, and a ranger station with nearby access to Round Bottom Picnic Area and the Flat Creek trailhead.

An equestrian-friendly campground at **Round Bottom Horse Camp** (Round Bottom-Straight Fork Rd., 865/436-1261 or 877/444-6777, www.recreation.gov, Apr.-Oct., $23) has five campsites, pit toilets, stalls, and bedding for horses. Its location north of Cherokee, just inside the park and far up narrow Big Cove Road, makes it perfect for long rides with larger groups.

Western Smokies

The western Smokies are a bit wilder than the eastern Smokies. As pioneers moved in from the east, they first settled the coves and hollows there, then found passes through the Smokies and settled there. The mountains are tall and steep, and the valleys deep, and where there are coves and meadows, they're broad, rich-soiled places that, before the national park, were home to several small communities.

LITTLE RIVER ROAD
Elkmont

At the **Elkmont Campground,** only eight miles from Gatlinburg, drifts of male fireflies rise up from the grass to flash their mating signal, but they don't do so as individuals— they blink in coordinated ways that still baffle researchers. For a two-week window every summer (often **early to mid-July,** but it depends on a variety of factors), their nightly light show delights crowds. It starts slowly, with only a few of these insects showing off. Then more join in, and more, until they reach a crescendo. Slowly, they begin to synchronize until, at the peak, whole fields may flash all at once, giving you a sudden and startling blink of light and just as sudden darkness. Or they may flash in waves moving around the fields and hillsides. Or large groups may appear to flash their lights at one another and wait in

the darkness for a response. Whatever the reason for their display, the synchronous fireflies are amazing little creatures. Nineteen species of fireflies live in Great Smoky Mountains National Park, but these are the only fireflies in the park to synchronize their flashing.

The synchronous fireflies may have been one of the reasons the Wonderland Park Hotel was built here in Elkmont. In 1908, the little logging town of Elkmont was born, and in 1912, the Wonderland Park Hotel was built. Cottages dotted the hillsides and bottoms. Once the park was established, cottage owners were granted lifetime leases on their property, and family members continued to renew the leases at 20-year intervals until the early 1990s. The Wonderland Park Hotel and the cottages were at one time slated for demolition, but the **Elkmont Historic District** is now listed in the National Register of Historic Places. The hotel collapsed in the early 2000s, and the Park Service has visions of restoring a few of the remaining cottages, but work has yet to begin in earnest.

Other properties include the **Appalachian Clubhouse** (500 Elkmont Rd., 877/444-6777, www.recreation.gov, Apr.-Oct., venue rental $250 daily), which has been restored to its 1930s glory. The clubhouse hosts a number of special events every year. The enormous meeting space is anchored by a stone fireplace at

The Firefly Lottery

Viewing the synchronous fireflies at Elkmont is deservedly popular—so much so that in 2016 the park instituted a lottery system to control access and limit traffic congestion. The new lottery assigns parking passes and provides shuttle transportation during the eight days of the synchronous fireflies mating season (late May-early June). Hopeful visitors can apply online during the three days the **lottery** (877/444-6777, www.recreation.gov, 1 pass per household, free, application fee $1) is open; applicants will have two dates to choose from. Once the lottery closes, results become available about a week later. Up to 1,800 parking passes will be made available for about 225 cars per day. The lucky winners will receive a parking pass for Sugarlands Visitor Center; after parking at your assigned arrival time, you'll board the shuttle to Elkmont and back.

one end; doors along the east side open to a large covered porch. A sizable caterer's kitchen (it's bare-bones: outlets and counters only, no appliances or refrigerators) means the building can easily house a large meeting, wedding reception, or get-together of any kind.

The **Spence Cabin** (500 Elkmont Rd., 877/444-6777, www.recreation.gov, Apr.-Oct., venue rental $150 daily), also called River Lodge, is a restored historic Elkmont building that serves as a base for special events and gatherings. Smaller than the Appalachian Clubhouse, this restored cabin shows off what it was like to vacation here in the 1920s and 1930s. Meeting rooms are smaller, with no large central gathering place.

Neither the Appalachian Clubhouse nor Spence Cabin lack for charm, but these are not overnight accommodations; rather, they are event spaces ideal for day-long events like family reunions, Scout Troop meetings, and corporate retreats.

Hiking
LAUREL FALLS TRAIL
Distance: 2.5 miles round-trip
Duration: 1.5-2 hours
Elevation gain: 400 feet
Difficulty: easy to moderate
Trailhead: parking area 3.9 miles west of Sugarlands Visitor Center on Little River Road

As the shortest and possibly easiest waterfall hike in Great Smoky Mountains National Park, Laurel Falls is the most popular of such hikes. The trail is paved and the grade is gentle (after you get past a short, steep section at the start of the trail), and the falls are a little over 1.3 miles from the trailhead.

Prepare to be dazzled when you reach the falls. Laurel Falls drops 75 feet in a wide, picture-perfect cascade. It's a gorgeous spot to photograph, but you have to be there early in the day to get a shot of the falls without people in it.

SUGARLAND MOUNTAIN
Distance: 12.3 miles one-way
Duration: 6 hours
Elevation gain: 5,308 feet
Difficulty: easy
Trailhead: Fork Ridge Trailhead 3.5 miles west on Clingmans Dome Road

This is a long hike at 12.3 miles, so you'll need to arrange for a car shuttle system at one end of the trail. Fortunately, the hiking is all downhill—which can be just as taxing as uphill, so watch your footing and hike at a sustainable pace. There have been numerous bear sightings around this trail, so keep your eyes and ears open.

From the Fighting Creek Gap Trailhead, drive up to Clingmans Dome Road (closed in winter) and begin the hike downhill. The trail begins by taking a short access trail to the Appalachian Trail. Turn left on the **Appalachian Trail** and hike 0.3 miles to a junction with Sugarland Mountain Trail. Turn right and take **Sugarland Mountain Trail,** your path for the next 12 miles.

The first mile is a rocky trail through a spruce-fir forest that is somewhat reminiscent of the Forest Moon of Endor from *Return of the Jedi.* About 0.3 miles after start is the **Mount Collins backcountry shelter**—other than that, it's just wildflowers and songbirds. After 1 mile, you'll begin to climb. Views open up here and there, giving you a glimpse of Mount LeConte and the Chimneys, and, in the distance, Pigeon Forge and Gatlinburg.

The trail passes below the summit of **Sugarland Mountain** (5,494 feet) at 2.3 miles. It's an off-trail scramble to reach the true top, so it's best to stick to the trail.

From here the trail descends, then, at the 3.5-mile point, begins to climb slightly, and makes a sharp western turn. At this point, you should have a good view of Gatlinburg and the Chimneys (if the weather's clear). Continue downhill; the trail becomes easier as the woods change from fir-dominant to a hardwood forest. At 8.3 miles is what was once **Campground 21.** You'll reach **Huskey Gap Trail** in 9.3 miles and a view of Mount LeConte that may be overgrown.

At 11 miles is **Mids Gap** and an 0.5-mile-long uphill stretch. After a downhill day, it will feel big. Once you top out, begin a steep descent down to the trailhead and your shuttle car.

LITTLE RIVER TRAIL

Distance: 12.3 miles round-trip
Duration: 4.5 hours
Elevation gain: 1,100 feet
Difficulty: easy
Trailhead: Elkmont Campground

This hike looks long, and it can be if you hike the whole length. Or you can follow as much of it as you want for a hike of 1, 2, or 10 miles. In the spring, the trail is filled with wildflowers; in October, it's a fall-color extravaganza; and year-round you'll see anglers fly-fishing in the water by the path. But in **late spring,**

this is the place to be to see the **synchronous fireflies.** The path here was once used for logging, and you'll see evidence of this all along the route—look around and you'll notice there's no old growth as in some sections of the park.

The first mile passes through the homeland of the synchronous fireflies, those curious fireflies that blink in unison during their spring mating season; the rest of the hike is a trek alongside the **Little River.** At times the path is a bit more like a trail than a road, but it always follows the logging roadbed.

Most hikers turn around at the 3.7-mile mark, the point where Little River Trail meets **Goshen Prong Trail.** I recommend pressing on a little farther, only 0.2 miles or so to a **bridge** over the river, which is quite scenic.

CUCUMBER GAP AND LITTLE RIVER LOOP

Distance: 5.5 miles round-trip
Duration: 2.5-3 hours
Elevation gain: 800 feet
Difficulty: easy to moderate
Trailhead: Elkmont Campground

This hike makes a loop using Cucumber Gap Trail and a portion of Little River Trail. It's a lovely hike for wildflowers in spring and fall color in October. The trails are easy; the railroad bed of Little River Trail and the typical forest trail of Cucumber Gap make a good combination, and the length is just about perfect for a day hike.

Just past the **Little River Trailhead** is a second parking area to the right of the gate; park here to start the trail on the gravel road past the gate on **Jakes Creek Trail.** There's a steep but short climb to the junction with Cucumber Gap. **Cucumber Gap** will give you a break from climbing—it's a long, gentle ascent through the tulip tree-dominated forest. Cross **Huskey Branch** just a little ways above the waterfall, which you'll see in a few moments. After reaching the junction with Little River Trail, turn left and cross Huskey Branch again, this time right at **Huskey Branch Falls.** From here it is two easy miles back to the Little River trailhead and parking area.

Backpacking

The **Great Smoky Mountains Institute at Tremont** (9275 Tremont Rd., Townsend, TN, 865/448-6709, www.gsmit.org) offers a range of outdoor and Smoky-centric educational opportunities. Classrooms and offices are located just off Hwy. 73/Little River Road (0.2 miles beyond the intersection to Townsend). At the end of this road is a long but excellent hike that will get you on the Appalachian Trail and provide some of the best photo opportunities the park has to offer.

LYNN CAMP PRONG

Distance: 21 miles round-trip
Duration: 12 hours or 1-2 days
Elevation gain: 3,650 feet
Difficulty: strenuous
Trailhead: Road near the Great Smoky Mountains Institute at Tremont

This hike is picture-postcard perfect (seriously, you'll see shots from this trail on park postcards and calendars)—and brutal. If you want to get deep in the Smokies and experience the rugged, wild nature of this place, this hike is for you. If you'd rather get some trail miles in and see some beautiful scenery, you can do that too, but the hike will be considerably shorter and take much less time.

At first, this trail seems easy as it follows a gravel road and old railroad grade for the first 0.5 miles. At 0.5 miles, you'll see a photographer's dream: **Lynn Camp Prong,** a large set of cascades on the stream. For the next 0.2 miles or so, you'll have plenty of chances for some great photos—don't be surprised if you see a number of other photo hounds out here.

After passing the cascades, the trail continues to follow the creek for 3 more miles, where a bridge crosses **Indian Flats Prong.** Now the trail begins to grow steep. If you're thinking of cutting the hike short, push on through this steep section to **Indian Flats Falls** (4 miles), then turn around.

Continue on and turn left (north) on

Lynn Camp Prong Trail. Campsite 28 is another 1.5 miles up the trail. To stay the night, reserve a campsite in advance through the **Backcountry Information Office** (Sugarlands Visitor Center, 865/436-1297, 8am-5pm daily, https://smokiespermits.nps. gov, $4 per night). You can also push on to Derrick Knob Shelter along the Appalachian Trail, another 6 miles or so up the trail.

From Campsite 28, it's a nonstop 2.2-mile climb to the ridgeline and the junction with **Miry Ridge Trail.** Turn right at the junction and continue 2.5 miles to a junction with the **Appalachian Trail.** Turn right and face the steepest climb of the hike as you ascend **Cold Spring Knob.** Finally, descend to a junction with **Greenbrier Ridge Trail.** (If you're staying at Derrick Knob Shelter, it's another 0.3 miles down the trail.) To continue, turn right and hike northeast down Greenbrier Ridge Trail.

As you descend, you'll encounter a pair of lovely stream crossings that may distract you with their beauty, but pay attention, especially in high water, as the footing can be tricky and the water strong. After passing the second creek crossing, you're now within 0.5 miles of **Indian Flats Falls** and the easy hike alongside Lynn Camp Prong back to the trailhead.

Fishing

Anglers take note: this area of the park offers some fantastic fishing. Along the east prong of **Little River** and all along Little River proper you can reel in trout, smallmouth bass, and rock bass. The formation of the bottom along the East Prong and along Little River is right for smallmouth and rock bass: rocky, heavy with roots and some debris, filled with plenty of nooks and crannies to hide, but with plenty of deep pools and slow currents where the feeding is good. In the headwaters you can find places that trout love.

Camping

The **Elkmont Campground** (434 Elkmont Rd., Gatlinburg, TN, 877/444-6777, www. recreation.gov, early Mar.-late Nov., $25-27)

Cades Cove and Fontana Lake Area

has 220 campsites, 55 of them along the Little River, with front-row seats to the firefly light show for those here at the right time. This is the largest of the campgrounds in Great Smoky Mountains National Park, and one of the most visited. In addition to the firefly show and the attraction of Little River, this site also serves as a good base for exploring the area.

Elkmont Campground Concessions (4pm-8pm daily Mar. 8-May, 9am-9pm daily June-Aug. 15, 4pm-8pm daily Aug. 16-Oct., 4pm-6pm daily Nov.) has a handful of snack foods and beverages as well as firewood, ice, and a few camping items.

CADES COVE

Easily the most popular auto tour loop in Great Smoky Mountains National Park, Cades Cove receives around two million visitors a year. They come for the scenery—a long, wide, grassy-bottomed valley surrounded by

© MOON.COM

Black Bears

Biologists estimate there are more than 1,500 black bears living in Great Smoky Mountains National Park, and if you know where and when to look, your chances of seeing one in the wild are quite good. Even if you don't know where to look, if you're in the park in spring or early summer, odds are you're going to spot one as you drive through the park.

Though I've seen bears in a number of spots, one of the most reliable places to see them is **Cades Cove.** Here, in the early morning and as dusk settles, the bears are more active, prowling the forest's edge and even eating apples that have fallen from the trees.

As awesome as it is to see a bear, they can present a problem to park visitors, just as we can present a problem to them. With the great number of visitors to Great Smoky Mountains National Park, many bears have grown accustomed to seeing people and have lost their natural fear of humans, automobiles, and horses. As they grow more used to people, we decide to give them "treats" to lure them closer to our cars and our campsites with food. Bears that are too accustomed to people, especially bears that have been fed a few times, can grow bold, even aggressive, searching campsites and open cars for food or even approaching open car windows or picnic tables. Now, with the rise of Instagram and the ease of sharing photos and video, a few visitors put themselves into dangerous spots just to get something to post online, and that puts park visitors in danger from the bear, and it places the bear in danger of being put down for aggressive behavior.

Fortunately, serious incidents with black bears are rare, but they do occur. In 2000, a mother bear and her cub attacked and killed a camper near the Elkmont Campground. Every year, campsites and trails are closed due to bear activity and the potential for interaction between bears and visitors.

Park staff and volunteers do their best to educate visitors on proper human-bear interaction. Throughout the park you'll see signs and placards advising you on how to properly store and dispose of food and reminding you not to approach bears. Remember that bears are wild animals and unpredictable, and keep these tips in mind:

undulating mountains—to see the handful of preserved homesteads and historic structures, and because it's one of the park's best, and most reliable, spots to see wildlife.

TOP EXPERIENCE

★ Cades Cove Loop

The **Cades Cove Loop** is approximately 11 miles long, but in the summer and especially in the fall when the leaves are at their best, expect to spend two hours or more on this one-way road through the valley floor—and that's if you don't stop to photograph the wildlife or explore the historic structures. If you're the curious type or find the light is perfect for taking pictures, you can easily double the amount of time you spend here. When you do stop, be sure to pull off the road and leave enough room for traffic to pass. One source of traffic jams in Cades Cove is visitors who stop in

the middle of the road to ooh and aah at the wildlife and scenery.

The popularity of this drive is well deserved. In the hours around dawn and dusk, wildlife is especially active. Vast herds of white-tailed deer are the most common sight (I once tallied 50 in a field before I quit counting), but black bears are also frequently spotted. The bears like to cozy up to the apple trees that dot the cove, and you'll occasionally spot them and their cubs napping or eating in the branches.

You may notice that the fields look especially manicured. They are, to an extent. Far from being mown and maintained like a golf course, the fields in Cades Cove are allowed to run wild, but only so wild. The National Park Service maintains the fields and fences, mowing, repairing, and reseeding as necessary to keep the valley looking much like it did when settlers lived here.

- **Do not approach** within 50 yards or any distance that disturbs a bear, and do not allow a bear to approach you. For a good view, invest in a pair of binoculars.

- **Never feed bears.** It only gets them used to humans and causes them to think of us as a source of food.

- **Store food** in appropriate containers and in the proper places when camping. If you're not sure of the proper procedure, ask a ranger.

- **Dispose of garbage** in bear-proof receptacles.

- **Report** nuisance bear behavior or visitors breaking these rules to park officials.

In the unlikely event that **a bear approaches you,** stand tall, wave your arms, and make as much noise as possible. If you need to, throw sticks or rocks at the bear. In most cases, this will intimidate the bear and deter it from coming any closer. If the bear charges, don't run—

black bear

they can sprint 30 miles per hour, so you don't stand a chance. Instead, keep making noise and back away slowly, never turning your back to the bear. Often, bears will make bluff charges, so this is likely what you're seeing. If a black bear actually makes contact, fight back with anything and everything available to you; with a loud-enough and fierce-enough fight, the bear may see you as too much to deal with and leave you alone.

To take this lovely in any-season drive, follow Little River Road west from the Sugarlands Visitor Center for 17.2 miles, there it will turn into Laurel Creek Road and lead you into Cades Cove in another 7.4 miles. You can also access Cades Cove by entering the park at Townsend on Highway 73, then turning right on Laurel Creek Road, following it for 16 miles to the entrance to the cove. Cades Cove is closed to vehicle traffic every Saturday and Wednesday morning May-late September. On those days, the loop is open exclusively to bicycle and foot traffic until 10am. The rest of the year the road is open to motor vehicles from sunrise to sunset daily, weather permitting.

Sights

According to some historians, long before European settlers pushed west through the Smokies, the Cherokee people had hunting camps and possibly even a small settlement established in Cades Cove. In fact, the name Cades Cove is believed to have come from Chief Kade, a little-known Cherokee leader. By the early 1820s, the first Europeans were here, building cabins and barns and carving homesteads out of the forest. More settlers arrived having heard of the rich, fertile bottomland in Cades Cove, and by 1850 nearly 700 people called the valley home. As the collection of cabins and homesteads grew into a community, buildings like churches and schools were constructed. Families lived here even after the National Park Service began purchasing land. The last remaining school in Cades Cove closed in 1944, and the post office closed in 1947.

Today, a number of historic structures remain standing along the valley floor. Among them is the most photographed structure in the park, the **Methodist Church.** From time to time a wedding is held here, though it's more common for visitors to leave hand-written prayers on scraps of paper at the altar.

The **Cable Mill Area** is the busiest section of the loop. Here you can see an actual mill in operation, and can even buy cornmeal or flour ground on-site. In addition to the mill and Methodist Church, the area contains two other churches, a few barns and log houses, and a number of smaller structures.

Halfway around the loop, you'll find the **Cades Cove Visitor Center** (Cades Cove Loop Rd., Townsend, TN, 865/448-2472, 9am-4:30pm daily Dec.-Jan., except Dec. 25, 9am-5pm daily Feb., 9am-6:30pm daily Mar. and Sept.-Oct., 9am-7pm daily Apr.-Aug., 9am-5:30pm daily Nov.), which has a good book-store and gift shop, and, most important, the only public restroom you'll find on the tour.

Hiking
★ ABRAMS FALLS TRAIL

Distance: 5 miles round-trip
Duration: 3 hours
Elevation gain: 350 feet
Difficulty: moderate
Trailhead: Turn right onto a gravel road 4.9 miles from the start of the Cades Cove Loop; at 0.4 miles in is a parking area and the trailhead.

Several trails lead off into the woods from this parking area, but it's obvious which route to take—the most well-worn trail you see. If you're in doubt, follow the group in front of you, as Abrams Falls is the destination for most hikers who set off from this lot. Only a few steps from the trailhead is a **kiosk** that will set you on the right path.

The trail is pretty straightforward—it follows **Abrams Creek** all the way to the water-fall. The only real elevation gains come when you thrice leave the creek to climb up and around a ridge, crossing a feeder stream in the process. The first stream is Arbutus Branch, then Stony Branch, then Wilson Branch, which is very close to the falls.

After you cross Wilson Branch on a **log bridge,** you'll follow the trail downstream,

cross Wilson Branch once again, and arrive at the falls.

Abrams Falls is pretty, and in wet weather can be downright thunderous. Slick, mossy rocks make up the wall where the 20-foot wa-terfall, which has the largest volume of water of any waterfall in the park, tumbles into the pool below. Tempted as you may be to take a dip after a sweaty hike, don't do it; the cur-rents are strong, and a few folks have drowned here.

ROCKY TOP AND THUNDERHEAD MOUNTAINS TRAIL

Distance: 13.9 miles round-trip
Duration: 7-8 hours
Elevation gain: 3,665 feet
Difficulty: strenuous
Trailhead: Anthony Creek Trailhead at the Cades Cove picnic area

Hiking to the famed Rocky Top is border-line brutal—you gain more than 3,500 feet in elevation, and on the trail's first few miles you share the path with horses, so it can get quite muddy and slippery. However, this ex-ceptional hike is worth it. Time your hike for mid-June to see the rhododendrons and mountain laurels in full bloom.

Shortly after starting the **Anthony Creek Trail,** you'll reach Crib Trail Junction, then **Anthony Creek Horse Camp** (reservations required, 877/444-6777, www.recreation.gov, $20). Follow Anthony Creek Trail 3.5 miles to the **Bote Mountain Trail,** where hikers will turn right.

Climbing Bote Mountain Trail, you'll enter a long series of rhododendron "tunnels" and at 5.1 miles in, and you'll reach **Spence Field** and the **Appalachian Trail.** Turn left and you'll get some stunning views of North Carolina and equally stunning views of hill-sides and meadows covered in mountain lau-rels. Continue east along the Appalachian Trail to reach Rocky Top and Thunderhead Mountain.

1: taking a break at Cable Mill in Cades Cove
2: Abrams Falls

Rich Mountain Loop

© MOON.COM

Thunderhead Mountain is made up of three distinct summits. The first summit is **Rocky Top,** 1.2 miles from the Bote Mountain-Appalachian Trail junction and arguably the best view in the park. Next is the middle peak, sometimes called **Rocky Top Two,** just 0.3 miles beyond Rocky Top. Finally, another 0.3 miles on, is the unremarkable summit of **Thunderhead.** Many hikers turn around at Rocky Top, never summiting Thunderhead.

RICH MOUNTAIN LOOP

Distance: 8.5-mile loop

Duration: 4-4.5 hours

Elevation gain: 1,740 feet

Difficulty: moderate

Trailhead: Park at the entrance gate to Cades Cove; the trail begins in the opposite parking lot.

The first part of this hike passes one of the meadows that make Cades Cove such a fabulous place. For 1.4 miles you'll walk through the woods and along the edge of the meadow until you reach the **John Oliver Cabin.**

The trail continues behind the cabin and soon meets up with **Martha's Branch** and begins to climb. As you climb, you'll cross the branch a number of times. At mile 3, you'll find a place where you have a tight view of Cades Cove; don't sweat it, as better views are coming.

Continue 0.3 miles to **Indian Grave Gap Trail** and turn right. In 0.8 miles is **Campsite 5** (for backpackers) and the junction with Rich Mountain Trail. The saddle here has nice views.

Avoid the junction and follow Indian Grave Gap Trail 0.3 miles to a side trail. This path is only about 100 yards long and takes you to the highest point on Rich Mountain, **Cerulean Knob,** and the foundation of the former fire tower. Views are okay, but not fantastic. Get back to the main trail and continue east, where you'll find a much better view than on the top.

When you reach a power-line clearance, you're almost at **Scott Mountain Trail** and **Campsite 4.** From the junction of these trails, continue straight ahead on **Crooked Arm Ridge Trail** (it's what Indian Grave Gap Trail turns into). This trail is steep and rutted and littered with the evidence of horses, so watch your step—that horse evidence can be slippery.

This trail leads back to **Rich Mountain Loop Trail,** 0.5 miles from the parking area.

CHESTNUT TOP TRAIL

Distance: 5.4 miles one-way
Duration: 4 hours
Elevation gain: 1,950 feet
Difficulty: strenuous
Trailhead: Chestnut Top trailhead, 100 yards north of the Townsend "Y" where Little River Road meets Highway 73

Chestnut Top Trail can be tackled two ways: As an end-to-end hike with a shuttle vehicle at either end, or as an out-and-back, which makes for a longer hike. Either way, this hike is filled with wildflowers in the spring and is quite lovely.

After parking across Hwy. 73 from the **trailhead,** lace up and get ready to go. The first 0.6 miles is a steady climb. In the spring, the forest is carpeted with wildflowers; the first flowers appear in early March, and flowers will continue to bloom for the next two months.

As soon as you wrap up this strenuous climb, the trail levels out a little. That soon ends as you begin climbing again toward **Schoolhouse Gap** along **Chestnut Top Lead. Tuckaleechee Cove** is to the right of the trail; you'll catch glimpses of it through summer foliage and have good views of it the rest of the year.

At 4.3 miles you'll reach a junction with **Schoolhouse Gap Trail.** Turn around here for an out-and-back hike of 8.6 miles (which is almost all downhill), or turn left on Schoolhouse Gap Trail and continue hiking 1.1 miles to the **Schoolhouse Gap Trailhead** on Little River Road (requires a shuttle car).

Biking

The **Cades Cove Store** (near Cades Cove Campground, 865/448-9034, www.cadescovetrading.com) rents bicycles in summer and fall (adult bikes $7.50 per hour, kids' bikes $4.50 per hour). Plan to get there early—well before the campground store opens. (I showed up 30 minutes before the store opened and took my place 40 deep in line. I did not rent a bike that day.)

The park closes off the loop road through Caves Cove sunrise-10am Wednesday and Saturday mornings from the second week in May until the second-to-last Saturday in September so that cyclists and hikers can enjoy the cove without having to worry about automobile traffic.

Camping

The **Cades Cove Campground** (10042 Campground Dr., Townsend, TN, 877/444-6777, www.recreation.gov, Jan.-Oct., $25) is a popular spot where you'll definitely want to reserve a campsite. Although the occupancy is a little lower in the dead of winter, you'll still find a few intrepid visitors taking refuge from the cold in one of the 159 campsites here. Hikers, take note: There are several backcountry campsites off the trails in Cades Cove, making it a good base for overnight trips.

At the **Cades Cove Campground Store** (865/448-9034, www.cadescovetrading.com, 9am-5pm daily Mar.-late May, 9am-9pm daily late May-Sept., 9am-7pm daily Sept.-Nov., 9am-5pm Nov.-early Dec.) you can grab a light bite for breakfast, a sandwich or wrap, pizza, and other snack-bar items as well as a very limited selection of groceries and camping supplies.

Parsons Branch Road

Parsons Branch Road (closed in winter) is a

great drive when it's open; deferred maintenance and sporadic tree falls make it difficult to predict, but you can call 865/436-1200, ext. 631, for road closures and conditions. Take a right turn just beyond the Cades Cove Visitor Center parking area and you'll find yourself on a 10-mile-long one-way gravel road leading to U.S. 129 and Deals Gap on the extreme southwestern edge of the park. At times pothole-riddled and crossing 18 or so small streams along the way, the road is a slow one, taking around an hour to drive. If you're careful, the drive is doable in a sedan, but you may feel more comfortable in a vehicle with a little more clearance.

The road passes **Henry Whitehead Place,** an odd-looking pair of conjoined cabins with an interesting backstory. Henry Whitehead, a widower with three daughters, married Matilda Shields Gregory after she and her small child had been abandoned by her husband. During the crisis, the community rallied and built her the small cabin, which is in back of the main structure that Whitehead built after they married.

You'll cross the same stream several times before climbing to the crest of the drive. Here you'll find the trailhead for **Gregory Bald Trail.** This is the halfway mark of the road and it is, as they say, all downhill from here.

GREGORY BALD TRAIL

Distance: 11.4 miles round-trip
Duration: 6-7 hours
Elevation gain: 3,370 feet
Difficulty: strenuous
Trailhead: Cades Cove, 2 miles down Parsons Branch Road

The hike to Gregory Bald is a tough one. The trail is steep, you gain more than 3,000 feet, and to finish in a reasonable amount of time your pace has to be quick and constant. Tackle this trail if you're confident in your endurance or if you have a little extra time to spare in case it takes longer to complete. Note that Parsons Branch Road may close seasonally.

Start off with an easy uphill—think of it as a warm-up—to the top of a short knob before

the trail levels off. Cross **Forge Creek,** then enter an old-growth forest thick with rhododendrons. How thick? So thick that even though you'll be close to the creek for a little ways, you won't often see or hear it. Follow this trail and cross the creek twice more.

Soon you'll pass **Campsite 12** and begin to climb a steep ridge via a set of switchbacks. The rhododendron gives way to galax and mountain laurel, even blueberry bushes, as you climb. Moderate your pace because it's all uphill until you're within 0.2 miles of **Rich Gap.**

At Rich Gap you'll find a four-way intersection. Straight ahead leads to Moore Spring; left leads to the Appalachian Trail at Doe Knob (2.1 miles). Turn west (right) on **Gregory Bald Trail** and follow the ridgeline to Gregory Bald.

From Gregory Bald, you'll have some great views—provided it's not too foggy in the valley. To the northeast you can see Cades Cove; to the southwest are the Unicoi Mountains and Joyce Kilmer-Slickrock Wilderness; to the south is Fontana Lake and Shuckstack Tower. Unfortunately you can't see anything to the west because of the trees. Turn back and retrace your steps to return to the trailhead.

ABRAMS CREEK

Abrams Creek is in the southwestern corner of the park, 20 miles west of Townsend via the Foothills Parkway and 33 miles north of Fontana Dam (via Hwy. 28 and Happy Valley Rd.). Getting here is easy considering the remoteness of the area and the relatively few visitors.

Look Rock is a concrete observation tower that offers a good look at the Smokies. A short hike (just under one mile) leads to the tower, and if you're in this part of the park, it's worth the trip.

Hiking
RABBIT AND ABRAMS CREEKS LOOP TRAIL

Distance: 15.2 miles round-trip
Duration: 7-8 hours

Elevation gain: 4,000 feet
Difficulty: strenuous
Trailhead: Abrams Creek Campground near the ranger station
Directions: From the Abrams Creek Campground, turn right on Happy Valley Road and drive 2.3 miles; turn right onto Flats Road and continue for 0.6 miles. Turn left at the Foothills Parkway sign and follow the signs to the parking area.

Though the mountains are rugged and this hike gains 4,000 feet in elevation, it's a gentle if long hike that has earned a strenuous reputation due its length. Begin the hike by following Rabbit Creek, where wildflowers are plentiful in spring. After 2.5 miles you meet Hannah Mountain Trail; ignore it and keep straight on **Rabbit Creek Trail,** which leads to Cades Cove and the Abrams Falls Trailhead.

At the **Abrams Falls Trailhead,** follow this path to the popular waterfall. You'll reach **Abrams Falls** in 2.5 miles and will have some great photo opportunities. After you've had your fill of waterfalls, continue along the trail as it ascends to **Hannah Mountain Trail.** Turn left to cross the creek and follow Hannah Mountain Trail 1.8 miles to an intersection with Rabbit Creek Trail. Turn right onto **Rabbit Creek Trail** to return to where you started.

LITTLE BOTTOMS TRAIL
Distance: 6.2 miles round-trip
Duration: 3 hours
Elevation gain: 930 feet
Difficulty: moderate
Trailhead: Cooper Road Trail Trailhead at Abrams Creek Campground

Little Bottoms Trail follows Abrams Creek, then descends into Cades Cove near Abrams Falls. As with many trails in the Abrams Creek Campground area, you can use this hike to access Cades Cove, or you can hike it as an out-and-back hike of easy length. This creek-side hike is amazing during the spring wildflower bloom and offers several great opportunities for leaf-peeping and fall photography.

Start off on **Cooper Road Trail,** another trail that leads into Cades Cove. Follow the trail 0.9 miles to where **Little Bottoms Trail** branches off to the right. Turn right and follow Little Bottoms up a moderate ascent as you crest a ridge, then begin a steep descent down into the valley to follow the course of Abrams Creek. There are **five crossings** of feeder streams along this hike; shortly after the fifth crossing, you'll reach a junction with **Hatcher Mountain Trail.** Turn around and return to the campground.

Camping
Abrams Creek Campground (Abrams Creek Campground Rd., Tallassee, TN, 865/436-1200, late Apr.-late Oct., $17.50) sits in the southwestern corner of the park just off the Foothills Parkway. Though this campground is at a pretty low elevation of only 1,125 feet, the mountains here are quite rugged and the woods thick. Not many people visit this section of the park, so if you want a little solitude and a sound night's sleep, put this campground on your to-do list.

There are 16 primitive sites that are first-come, first served. The only real amenity is a restroom. Backpackers and backcountry campers take note. The trail system branching out from Abrams Creek Campground offers access to several **backcountry campsites,** including Campsite 1, 17, 15, and 16.

DEEP CREEK
Just south of Cherokee and just north of Bryson City, Deep Creek is a spot that may be more popular with locals and Bryson City day trippers than most park visitors, but that shouldn't be the case. Deep Creek is relatively placid, aside from a couple of waterfalls a ways upstream. If you're not into wading or tubing, don't worry—this is a lovely place to picnic and hike or even camp away from the crowds found in some of the more popular spots in the park. Two of the trails here, Indian Creek Falls Trail and Deep Creek Loop, are among the only trails in the park to allow bicycles, so

if you're up for a leisurely ride (don't expect as rugged a ride as some of the hikes in the park), you're in for a treat.

Hiking

There are two nice waterfalls to see here. Juney Whank Falls (what a name, right?) is less than 0.5 miles from the Deep Creek Campground and cuts an impressive figure as it drops a total of 90 feet in two stages. Indian Creek Falls is a stunning 60-foot-high set of falls and cascades located 1 mile from the campground.

JUNEY WHANK FALLS TRAIL

Distance: 0.6-mile loop
Duration: 30 minutes
Elevation gain: 120 feet
Difficulty: moderate
Trailhead: parking area at the end of Deep Creek Road across from the campground

Juney Whank Falls supposedly got its name from Junaluska "Juney" Whank, a Cherokee leader said to have been buried near the falls. The path here is pretty straightforward: it's short, at times steep, and at the end, a little slick. You'll walk across a log bridge to get a look at the tall, skinny falls, which actually descend in two stages. The first stage drops 40 feet to a stone outcropping, then flows beneath the log bridge to fall and cascade another 50 feet.

INDIAN CREEK FALLS TRAIL

Distance: 2 miles round-trip
Duration: 1 hour
Elevation gain: 160 feet
Difficulty: easy to moderate
Trailhead: parking area at the end of Deep Creek Road across from the campground

This easier but longer hike takes you past a smaller waterfall, Tom's Branch Falls, on your way to Indian Creek Falls. For about a mile, you'll follow a gently graded roadbed, and soon you'll arrive at the falls. Really, Indian Creek Falls is more of a steep, long, slick cascade of water than an actual waterfall, but it's quite serene.

DEEP CREEK LOOP TRAIL

Distance: 4.9 miles round-trip
Duration: 2.5-3 hours
Elevation gain: 900 feet
Difficulty: easy
Trailhead: Deep Creek Campground

This short hike is excellent for new hikers; the trail is easy and in good shape, plus you'll hike past Tom Branch Falls and Indian Creek Falls. The trail starts on a gravel road. Almost immediately, you'll pass **Tom Branch Falls,** which you can see well in autumn and winter. After crossing a **bridge** at the junction with **Indian Creek Trail** (to the right), pass **Indian Creek Falls,** which is more of a long cascade but no less attractive. Continue hiking along Indian Creek Trail, then pass **Stone Pile Gap Trail.** Staying on Indian Creek Trail, you'll pass a junction with **Sunkota Ridge Trail** and begin to descend to **Deep Creek Trail.** Turn left on Deep Creek Trail and follow it back to the start of the trail.

Fishing

Along **Deep Creek** you'll find some primo trout fishing. Bring a fly rod and get ready to reel in a few brown, rainbow, and brook trout. Anywhere along the creek is fine to cast a line, but some of the best spots are in the places where people aren't. This means hiking up **Deep Creek Trail,** a 14.2-mile trail that follows the creek back to Newfound Gap Road. The trail is straightforward as it follows an old roadbed that turns into a true trail, but it is beside the creek for nearly the entire length.

Camping

At the end of Deep Creek Road are the trailheads leading to the waterfalls. You'll also find the **Deep Creek Campground** (877/444-6777, www.recreation.gov, Apr.-Oct., $17.50). There are nearly 100 campsites here, many of

---

1: Juney Whank Falls Trail 2: Deep Creek Loop Trail
3: Tom Branch Falls

which fill up with locals. If you want to camp here, arrive early or reserve well in advance.

A hundred yards or so outside the park, there's **Deep Creek Tube Center and Campground** (1090 W. Deep Creek Rd., Bryson City, NC, 828/488-6055, www. deepcreekcamping.com, camping $27-55, cabins $79-195), a charming collection of tent and RV campsites and cabins for rent. As the name implies, they rent tubes (all-day $6) for use on Deep Creek. Rentals are cheap, so you can play in the water as long as you like.

Road to Nowhere

An odd place to visit is the so-called **Road to Nowhere.** Just south of the Deep Creek entrance outside Bryson City is a short stretch of highway leading north into Great Smoky Mountains National Park. Lonely, even spooky, the road is all that remains of a parkway planned to trace a path through the Smokies along Fontana Lake. Construction was started on the parkway before being abandoned. Today, the road stops quite abruptly about six miles inside the park, at a stone tunnel. Though hard feelings over the failed parkway have softened, many families still hold a grudge against government officials who vowed to build a road along the lake to provide access to old family cemeteries there.

Cars are prohibited from using the tunnel at the end of the Road to Nowhere, but visitors on foot are welcome to stroll right through. After passing through the tunnel, there's a hike waiting for you that clocks in at 36.5 miles. Fortunately, it follows the northern bank of Fontana Lake, giving you a little reward for the effort.

The Road to Nowhere is accessible from Bryson City. To get here, drive north on Everett Street, which becomes Fontana Road, then Lakeview Drive, before arriving at a parking area in about nine miles. A tunnel marks the end of the road. Be sure you have a flashlight, headlamp, or your phone with you because you'll need a light as you walk through the tunnel.

GOLDMINE LOOP TRAIL

Distance: 3.1 miles round-trip
Duration: 2.5-3 hours
Elevation gain: 400 feet
Difficulty: easy
Trailhead: Lakeview Drive Tunnel at the end of The Road to Nowhere

Though this hike actually begins on the far side of the tunnel, it really begins when you walk through the tunnel and emerge on the other side to find the two-lane road just ends. As you step off the road, walk a short way on a roadbed to follow the proper trail. In a little less than 0.2 miles you'll meet **Tunnel Bypass Trail,** and soon after that you'll reach **Goldmine Loop Trail.** To follow the trail, turn left and begin a steep descent as it traces a path along a ridge, then heads down to a minuscule stream.

Cross the stream and take a look around—you'll see a chimney in a field, evidence of the homes that once stood here. There are many such signs along the trail, so keep a keen eye on the woods for other signs of the former homes.

Drawing closer to the lakeshore, pass a short trail to **Campsite 67** (on the left); pass this and continue along Goldmine Loop. After a short hike you'll reach the shores of **Fontana Lake,** deep in a little cove, which makes for some excellent fall photos. The trail climbs back up alongside **Tunnel Branch,** a small creek that feeds the lake. The ascent grows steep until you meet the other end of **Tunnel Bypass Trail.** Continue along the trail, and in 0.4 miles you'll be back at the tunnel.

LAKESHORE TRAIL

Distance: 35.6 miles one-way
Duration: 2.5-3 hours or multiple days
Elevation change: 1,100 feet
Difficulty: easy
Trailhead: Lakeview Drive Tunnel at the end of The Road to Nowhere

The Lakeshore Trail runs along the northern shoreline of Fontana Lake. The 36.5-mile route is doable as a day hike in sections, but it best done as a multiple-night backpacking trip.

The total elevation gain for this hike is nearly 11,000 feet as you climb up and down, up and down as you crest 10 ridges and knobs in excess of 2,250 feet, with lots of elevation variance along the way. Whether you take this on as a legendary day hike or an overnight backpacking trip, arrange for transportation before you set out. This means a car shuttle at the end of the trail, or parking your own shuttle cars at opposite ends.

The trail begins at the tunnel at the end of The Road to Nowhere. After passing through the tunnel, follow a short bit of road to the point where it turns into a trail. You'll reach your first potential campsite, **Campsite 74,** in just over 2 miles at **Forney Creek Trail.** (Skip it unless you plan on making this a weeklong backpacking trip.)

In 6.6 miles, you'll reach Anthony Branch and Chambers Creek; just after crossing Chambers Creek, approach the lakeshore to find a 0.1-mile trail to **Campsite 98.** This can be a good stopping point if this is a two-night trip. **Campsite 77** is just over 15 miles in, making it a good stopping point if you're aiming for a one-night trip. Or you can press on to **Campsite 76,** at the 11-mile mark.

From Campsite 77, it is 4.2 miles to **Campsite 81** on the south side of the trail. (The trail is lakeside, but the campsite is still 0.2 miles from the water; don't expect a lake view.) Continue on 3.6 more miles to the junction with Hazel Creek Trail and **Campsite 86. Campsite 85** is 2 miles up Hazel Creek Trail, and **Campsites 84 and 83** are 4.5 and 5.3 miles up the trail, respectively. This is a good place to stop for a two-night trip, but Campsite 86 can see a good bit of traffic. You may want to press on another 1.4 miles to **Campsite 88.**

All along the trail, spur trails lead to the coves and shoreline. These vary in length, but feel free to follow them at your leisure. **Hazel Creek Trail** is one of the larger trails in this region of the park; it forms part of a larger network of trails on which you could have a 100-mile, 10-night campout if you wanted. There's plenty to see and do if you're a hard-core hiker, and one trip here will certainly lead to another—this is a beautiful part of the park.

From Campsite 88, it is 3 miles to Flint Gap and Eagle Creek Trail (**Campsites 89 and 96** are a couple of miles up the trail). Another 0.5 miles leads to **Campsite 90** on the banks of Eagle Creek. A small spur trail leads down to the cove, if you want to see the water. In another 0.4 miles, you'll reach the intersection with Lost Cove Trail (**Campsite 91** is 1 mile down the trail). Lost Cove leads 2.7 miles to the Appalachian Trail at Sassafras Gap, just north of Shuckstack; from there it's 3.7 miles south to the trailhead at Lakeview Drive West.

Continue along **Lakeshore Trail** and you'll be on the final leg of the hike, a winding 5.2-mile trek that crosses more than a dozen creeks and streams before it reaches Lakeview Drive West and the parking area. On the off chance Fontana Dam is closed for repairs or security reasons, you may have to hike down Lakeview Drive and cross the dam to get to your car on the other side, adding almost 2 miles to the hike.

BACKCOUNTRY PERMITS

Because so many trails branch off Lakeshore Trail, this region is a hotbed of backcountry campsites. There are eight backcountry campsites—72, 73, 76, 77, 78, 81, 87, and 98—on or near Lakeshore Trail; four of those (72, 73, 78, and 87) are boat-access only. There are another eight campsites within a day hike of Lakeshore.

Recently there has been increased bear activity in this section of the park. One camper was injured when a bear pulled him from his hammock in 2015, leading to the temporary closure of several backcountry campsites and a shelter along the Appalachian Trail. At that time, bears were spotted in a number of locations including campsites, picnic areas, and crossing the road. Usually bears aren't aggressive, just curious, but be wary in bear country, and be sure to check with rangers for bear activity and trail closures. Review proper etiquette regarding bears and proper handling of food in and around your campsite.

To camp backcountry, you'll need a permit from the **Backcountry Information Office** (Sugarlands Visitor Center, 865/436-1297, https://smokiespermits.nps.gov, 8am-5pm daily, $4 per night). They can also answer any questions you have about the campsites, and they're quite helpful—don't be shy.

FONTANA LAKE AREA

At the southern edge of Great Smoky Mountains National Park lies Fontana Lake, a 10,230-acre reservoir created in the 1940s as part of the Tennessee Valley Authority's (TVA) efforts to supply electricity to the various communities and government and industrial facilities in the region.

Fontana Dam

At the southern edge of GSMNP lies Fontana Lake. The 480-foot tall, 2,365-foot wide Fontana Dam, complete with three hydroelectric generators, was completed in 1944, providing much-needed electricity to the factories churning out materials for World War II, including in Oak Ridge, Tennessee, where research leading to the atomic bomb was conducted.

To build Fontana Dam, the TVA purchased more than 1,000 tracts of land and relocated around 600 families in five communities. Those folks left behind homes, schools, churches, and barns, all of which were covered by the lake. This displacement of so many families and elimination of these small communities was part of the tradeoff that resulted in the modernization of the region, when electric power became cheap and readily available and many jobs were required to complete the project. The dam also provides much-needed flood control to a region that receives between 55 and 82 inches of rainfall each year. Today, the TVA can regulate the depth of the lake by releasing water as they anticipate flood events, and the water level of Fontana Lake can vary by as much as 50 feet.

Fontana Dam is the highest concrete dam east of the Mississippi, and it provides great recreational opportunities. The Appalachian Trail crosses the dam itself, and thousands of boaters and anglers take to the lake each year. There are more than 238 miles of shoreline along Fontana Lake and over 10,000 acres of water surface. If you have your own boat, you can launch it from the **Fontana Marina** (40 Fontana Dam Rd., 828/498-2129, www.fontanavillage.com), or you can rent a kayak,

Fontana Lake

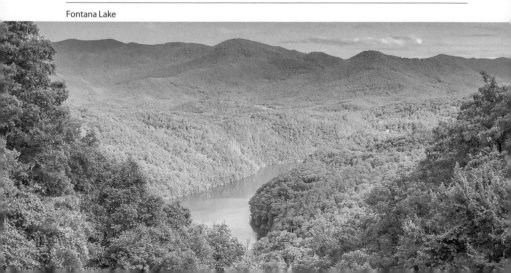

canoe, or paddleboard ($10 per hour, $60 per day) as well as a pontoon or fishing boat ($50 per hour, $350 per day). Fishing guide services and seasonal tours of the lake are also available.

The exhibits at the **Fontana Dam Visitor Center** (Fontana Dam Rd., off Hwy. 28 near the state line, www.tva.com, 9am-6pm daily May-Oct., free) tell the story of the region and the construction of the dam. There's also a small gift shop and a viewing platform overlooking the dam. Hikers take note: They sell backcountry camping permits and have showers in the back.

FISHING AND BOATING

Fishing is big on Fontana Lake. Trout love the feeder streams and headwaters that flow into the lake, and largemouth, smallmouth, and rock bass are all throughout. You'll even find walleye and muskies in the deep water (and it gets deeper than 400 feet deep in some points). On any given day, you'll spot anglers on boats and kayaks and more than a few fly rods strapped to the backpacks of hikers headed out to try the streams along the north banks of the lake.

At the **Fontana Marina** (40 Fontana Dam Rd., 828/498-2129, www.fontanavillage.com), you can rent a kayak, canoe, or paddleboard ($20 per hour, $60 per day) or a pontoon or fishing boat ($50 per hour, $350 per day). Fishing guide services and seasonal tours of the lake are also available.

Fontana Lake is partially in the national park, and partially outside it—which makes fishing here a little more complicated. If you plan on fishing in the lake, you have two options: Get a **North Carolina fishing license** (www.ncwildlife.org) and review the guidelines (to be on the safe side), or rely on a fishing guide to supply a license and understand the rules (most do).

GUIDES

Fontana Guide Service (3336 Balltown Rd., Bryson City, 828/736-2318, www.fontanaguides.com, full-day trips $200-500,

depending on group size) has a number of options that vary by season, interest, and skill level, including options to fish in the national park. In addition to fly-fishing excursions, they also offer kayak fishing, bass and lake fishing, as well as night fishing in select spots.

Fly Fishing the Smokies (Bryson City, 828/488-7665, www.flyfishingthesmokies. net) has a number of guides and options for a day or more of fly-fishing the streams on the north shore of the lake and other trout waters. Wade the streams with them for a half-day (1 person $200, 2 people $250) or full-day (1 person $275, 2 people $325) outing, try a float trip (half-day $225 per boat, full-day $325 per boat), or go backcountry camping and fly-fishing in the Great Smoky Mountains National Park ($500-850 pp).

A top fishing guide in the area, **Steve Claxton's Smoky Mountain Adventures** (828/736-7501, http://steveclaxton.com) specializes in leaving civilization behind in favor of camping, catching wild mountain trout, and getting a true taste of the wilderness. Three-day, two-night camping trips for 5-7 people run around $400 pp, and four-day, three-night trips are $575-700 pp. They also offer half day (1 person $150, 2 people $200, 3 people $250) and full-day fishing trips (1 person $225, 2 people $275, 3 people $325).

Root Hog Fishing Guide Service (828/862-7958, www.fontanafishingguide. com) runs fishing charters (4-hour trip for 1 person $180, $55 per additional person, 6-hour trip $240, $55 per additional person, 8-hour trip $275, $75 per additional person) on Lake Fontana and fly-fishing trips (4-hour trip for 1 person $160, $65 per additional person, 8-hour trip $225, $75 per additional person). Owner and guide Dwight Pigman has been fishing here for decades, so he knows where to find the fish.

Accommodations and Food

Just outside the park, **Fontana Village Resort** (300 Woods Rd., Fontana Dam, 828/498-2211 or 800/849-2258, www.fontanavillage.com, lodge $113-173, cabins

$113-353, camping $15-40) offers a place to lay your head in your choice of accommodations: tent or RV camping, one- to three-bedroom cabins, and lodge rooms. There are 100 lodge rooms, 110 cabins, and 20 campsites. At the lodge you'll find complimentary wireless internet in the public areas; other amenities include an outdoor pool and lazy river, as well as a fitness center and small day spa.

The complex contains two restaurants, a snack bar, an ice cream shop, and a general store. **Mountainview Restaurant** (828/498-2211, 8am-11am daily, 5pm-9pm Thurs.-Sat., breakfast $4-9, dinner $14-28) serves steaks, chicken, and a nice selection of seafood that includes several preparations of trout. Reservations are recommended during weekends and in peak season. **Wildwood Grill** (828/498-2211, 11:30am-9pm daily Apr.-Oct., $8-19) serves pizza, burgers, and an array of fried appetizers. In the summer, concerts on the deck give visitors a little listening enjoyment to go with dinner.

TWENTYMILE

One of the remotest sections of the park, Twentymile is on the southern end, just past Fontana Lake and Dam and alongside the smaller Cheoah Lake. Despite the name, Twentymile Trail only goes 5 miles into Great Smoky Mountains National Park, but you can make it into a 20-mile journey by combining it with other trails, or you can keep it to a manageable day hike of around 8 miles by doing a smaller loop. Though this part of the park is out of the way, Twentymile is a popular hike, so expect to see some fellow hikers, especially on weekends and through the week on beautiful days in summer and autumn. There is a trio of **backcountry campsites** (reserve at www.smokiespermits.nps.gov) at Twentymile Trail: campsites 13, 92, and 93.

Hiking
TWENTYMILE LOOP TRAIL
Distance: 7.6-mile loop
Duration: 3.5-4 hours
Elevation gain: 1,200 feet

Difficulty: easy
Trailhead: Twentymile Ranger Station
Directions: Twentymile Ranger Station is 6 miles west from Fontana Dam on Highway 28. Turn at the sign for Twentymile.

This hike is very easy, following a roadbed and a well-maintained trail along Twentymile Trail, Twentymile Loop Trail, and Wolf Ridge Trail. There are a number of stream crossings along this route, and though there are log bridges spanning Moore Springs Branch and Twentymile Creek, floods may wash them away. If you're there before repair crews can fix the bridges, you may have to wade across.

From the trailhead, go 0.5 miles to where **Wolf Ridge Trail** branches off to the left. Follow Wolf Ridge Trail for 1.1 miles to **Twentymile Loop Trail.** Along Wolf Ridge, you'll cross Moore Springs Branch five times as you climb. Along the way, there are abundant wildflowers, including bloodroot, fire pink, and trilliums, and the opportunity to see bears, deer, and other wildlife.

After following Wolf Ridge just over 1 mile, you'll see Twentymile Loop Trail branching off to the right. Cross Moore Springs Branch and follow the trail 2.9 miles along an easy grade before descending to a crossing of Twentymile Creek and the junction with **Twentymile Trail.**

Turn right on Twentymile Trail to descend back along the creek and to the trailhead. From here, it's just over 3 miles back to your car.

GREGORY BALD VIA TWENTYMILE TRAIL
Distance: 15.7-mile loop
Duration: 9 hours
Elevation gain: 3,650 feet
Difficulty: strenuous
Trailhead: Twentymile Ranger Station
Directions: Twentymile Ranger Station is 6 miles west from Fontana Dam on Highway 28. Turn at the sign for Twentymile.

This hike makes Twentymile live up to its name, even though it's a mere 15.7 miles. It's doable in a day, but it's a long, hard day, so camping for a night in the backcountry is recommended.

From the trailhead, follow **Twentymile Trail** for 0.5 miles until it intersects with **Wolf Ridge Trail**. Turn here and follow Wolf Ridge Trail 6.3 miles to **Gregory Bald Trail**. The grade of Wolf Ridge Trail is somewhat steep, but more than that, it's a relentless uphill climb all the way to where you crest the ridge before reaching **Parson Bald**. As you approach the ridge and Parson Bald, you'll find copious amounts of blueberry bushes, and, if they're in season, a fair number of bears enjoying blueberries. The same holds true at Parson Bald, just over the ridge. If you're on the trail in August, when the blueberries tend to ripen, be cautious.

When you reach Parson Bald, it's a short, easy walk to Sheep Pen Gap, where you'll find **Campsite 13** (reservations and information 865/436-1297, www.smokiespermits.nps.gov) and the end of Wolf Ridge Trail. Turn right

on Gregory Bald Trail and climb just under 0.5 miles to **Gregory Bald**. There are azaleas in great abundance and during midsummer the bald is a riot of blooms. But even if you come when there's not a bloom to be found, the views make the hike worth it.

From here, keep heading east to **Rich Gap,** where you'll come upon a four-way trail junction. Follow **Long Hungry Ridge Trail** to the right, heading south. This trail is pretty flat for the first mile, then it begins to descend, and the descent becomes increasingly noticeable as you move down the trail. You'll find **Campsite 92** at 3.4 miles from Rich Gap. Once you've reached the campsite, you've left the steepest part of the hike behind you.

Continue down Long Hungry Ridge Trail to the place where it meets Twentymile Trail, following Twentymile Creek 2.6 miles back to the junction with Wolf Ridge Trail. At this point, you're only 0.5 miles from the trailhead.

Transportation and Services

CAR
The 33-mile-long Newfound Gap Road (U.S. 441) bisects the park from north to south. It's the most heavily traveled route in the park and provides a good introduction for first-time visitors. Newfound Gap Road starts at the southern terminus of the Blue Ridge Parkway, just outside Cherokee, North Carolina, and ends in Knoxville, Tennessee, 70 miles to the northwest through Great Smoky Mountains National Park.

From Cherokee, you can head straight to the eastern entrance of Great Smoky Mountains National Park via Newfound Gap Road. Take U.S. 441/Highway 71 north through Great Smoky Mountains National Park to Gatlinburg, Tennessee. It's easy to make the trip from one end to the other in an afternoon, though it may take a little longer in peak seasons. Knoxville, Tennessee, is 36 miles northwest of Great Smoky Mountains National Park along U.S. 441 and Highway 71.

There are **no gas stations** along Newfound Gap Road. You'll need to fuel up and buy snacks in Cherokee.

AIR
Asheville Regional Airport (AVL, 61 Terminal Dr., Asheville, NC, 828/684-2226, www.flyavl.com) is about one hour east of Cherokee. **McGhee Tyson Airport** (TYS, 2055 Alcoa Hwy., Alcoa, TN, 865/342-3000, www.tys.org) is about one hour west of Gatlinburg.

SERVICES
Groceries and camping supplies are limited in Great Smoky Mountains National Park. Food is virtually nonexistent, so bring snacks. The Sugarlands and Oconaluftee Visitor Centers have a small selection of vending-machine beverages and a few convenience items (batteries, memory cards), but little else.

Calendar of Events

- **Wildflower Pilgrimage** (Apr.): Hikes, talks, and photography sessions explore the park's abundant and diverse wildflowers (www.springwildflowerpilgrimage.org).

- **Music of the Mountains** (mid-Apr.): This three-day festival celebrates the musical traditions of the Appalachians with demonstrations and concerts at the Sugarlands Visitor Center, as well as locations in Cosby and Townsend.

- **Junior Ranger Day** (late Apr.): Get the kids started on their Junior Ranger Badge with this park-wide celebration of youthful discovery—then keep it going with the weekly Junior Ranger programs throughout the year.

- **Cosby in the Park** (mid-May): Hikes, music, and demonstrations of domestic life create a deeper connection with the park during this one-day event.

- **Women's Work Festival** (mid-June): At Mountain Farm Museum, learn about the role women played in the making and maintaining of a mountain home and farm.

- **Mountain Life Festival** (mid-Sept.): Mountain Farm Museum comes alive with demonstrations of domestic and cultural life—from music to demonstrations of domestic chores such as soap-making and cooking.

- **Festival of Christmas Past** (mid-Dec.): Get a taste of the holidays in the Smokies with demonstrations of arts and crafts (spinning, weaving, and quilting); music, singing, and storytelling; and children's activities like games and toy-making.

Medical

If you find yourself in an emergency situation in the park, dial 911 if you have cell access. When speaking with the 911 operator, inform the operator that you are in Great Smoky Mountains National Park, and give your location as best you can (if you're in the backcountry, that means the trail name and the nearest campsite or shelter to you). The operator will send rangers and emergency responders. If you don't have cell service, send another hiker or driver for help.

The nearest hospitals are **LeConte Medical Center** (742 Middle Creek Rd., Sevierville, TN, 865/446-7000, www.lecontemedicalcenter.com), about 25 minutes from the west park entrance; **Blount Memorial Hospital** (907 E. Lamar Alexander Pkwy., Maryville, TN, 865/983-7211, www.blountmemorial.org), an hour away from the west park entrance; and **Swain County Hospital** (45 Plateau St., Bryson City, NC, 828/488-2155, www.myswaincommunity.org), a little less than 30 minutes from the eastern park entrance in Cherokee.

RANGER PROGRAMS

Few of us will ever have the opportunity to get to know a park as well as a park ranger. Every day they're immersed in the landscape, the culture, the history, and the beauty of their respective park and they work with a legion of volunteers to create enrichment programs that will expand the use and appreciation of parks (and the outdoors as a whole) in the public. Great Smoky Mountains National Park has some mighty fine park rangers, and they work hard to introduce every visitor to the beauty, the stories, and the flora and fauna of the park. Through the **Junior Ranger Program,** they get kids ages 5-15 excited about the Smokies; through their Not-So-Junior Ranger Program they get everyone ages 13-130 involved too.

Rangers lead daily hikes along nature trails and creek-side paths, take visitors on nighttime hikes of Cades Cove, host campfires and storytelling sessions, lead hayrides and history lessons, introduce us to the animals—from furry to slimy—of the park, and celebrate the history and culture here. A full schedule of seasonal programs is available online (www.nps.gov/grsm).

Guided Hikes

Hiking in the Smokies is as simple as picking up a map, choosing a trail, and heading into the woods; however, some people prefer to hike with a group and a guide. Fortunately the park trail system accommodates both styles. Several organizations lead outings and excursions—from day hikes to trip planning assistance to overnight backpacking trips.

FRIENDS OF THE SMOKIES

Friends of the Smokies (North Carolina office 828/452-0720, Tennessee office 865/932-4794, www.friendsofthesmokies.com) is one of my favorite groups; they provide support to the Trails Forever program and help with trail repairs and maintenance. The group leads hikes (Mar.-Dec., members $20, non-members $35) along some of the classic trails in the park. Hikes include spots like Little Cataloochee Trail and Grotto Falls, overnighters to places like Mount LeConte, and trips to Mount Sterling. Each hike highlights one of the programs supported by Friends of the Smokies. Look at their schedule for upcoming trips and registration information.

SMOKY MOUNTAINS HIKING CLUB

Smoky Mountains Hiking Club (www.smhclub.org) runs weekly outings in the Smokies and in east Tennessee, though their primary mission is to assist with the maintenance of the Appalachian Trail within the park. They've been around since 1924 and currently have more than 600 members, so these hikes are always with a group of experienced and knowledgeable outdoors enthusiasts. The weekly outings are free and open to anyone who wants to participate; trips include on- and off-trail hikes as well as workdays. Check the website for the schedule and to register.

A WALK IN THE WOODS

Several commercial outfitters lead walks, hikes, and overnight trips in the park in addition to providing trip planning assistance and hiker shuttles. **A Walk In The Woods** (865/436-8283, www.awalkinthewoods.com) is a guide company offering nature walks ($28-160), hikes ($105-275 for 1 hiker, $50 per additional hiker), backpacking trips ($285-500, discounts if supplying your own equipment), hiker shuttles (cost varies depending on trailhead and time of day), and trip planning ($50 plus $7 pp per night, including your Backcountry Permit Fee).

WILDLAND TREKKING

Wildland Trekking (800/715-4453, www.wildlandtrekking.com) offers trips that include multiday backpacking trips ($440-1,540), inn-based hikes that include overnight accommodations ($1,220-2,200), day hikes ($130-355), and a Fontana Lake Paddle and Hiking expedition ($280-795).

Appalachian Trail

From Georgia to Maine, the Appalachian Trail's nearly 2,200 miles traverse some rugged, lonesome, and picturesque landscapes, cresting ridges and summiting peaks, crossing streams and rivers, passing through bogs and marshes, climbing near-vertical peaks, and even following city streets.

Cutting through the heart of Great Smoky Mountains National Park, the Appalachian Trail runs along the high ridgeline that forms the border between North Carolina and Tennessee. There are 71.6 miles of the Appalachian Trail in Great Smoky Mountains National Park, and it's a highlight for thru-hikers (those taking the Appalachian Trail north to Maine or south to Georgia, all in one enormous hike), segment hikers (those hiking the whole thing one piece at a time), and day hikers (the rest of us).

This guide to the Appalachian Trail within Great Smoky Mountains National Park doesn't cover the trail mile by mile but includes enough to get you out for a multiday backpacking trip. For the lowdown on the Appalachian Trail, contact the **Appalachian Trail Conservancy** (www.appalachiantrail.org) or visit the **National Park Service** (www.nps.gov/appa), where you'll find trip planning information, maps, trail reports, and more.

Most people hike the Great Smoky Mountains National Park section as a sevenday trek, though you can tailor this trek to suit your hiking style and the time you have—stretching it out to 10 or 12 days with a little planning, or pushing the pace to complete it in 3 brutal days.

Permits

Though there are no fees required to hike the Appalachian Trail, there are requirements when hiking the Appalachian Trail in Great Smoky Mountains National Park. Thru-hikers are eligible for a **thru-hiker permit** (www.smokiespermits.nps.gov, $20); thru-hikers must begin and end their hike at least 50 miles from the border of the park and only travel on the Appalachian Trail while in the park.

Segment hikers and backpackers need a permit from the **Backcountry Information Office** (Sugarlands Visitor Center, 865/436-1297, https://smokiespermits.nps.gov, 8am-5pm daily, $4 pp per night). A permit is not required for day hikers.

Trail Shelters

For Appalachian Trail thru-hikers, there's only one choice for where to stay in Great Smoky Mountains National Park: **Appalachian Trail shelters.** Of the 12 sites at each shelter, four spots are reserved for thru-hikers only, and they're first-come, first-served. If you're thru-hiking and find a shelter full, you are permitted to pitch your tent next to the shelters.

Segment hikers and backpackers can reserve spots in these Appalachian Trail shelters, or at any of the numerous backcountry campsites along and near the Appalachian Trail.

There are too many backcountry campsites near the Appalachian Trail, as well as other backcountry shelters, to list here. For a complete list, consult a **park trail map** (www.nps.gov/grsm).

There are a dozen shelters located along the Appalachian Trail in the park. South to north:

the Appalachian Trail

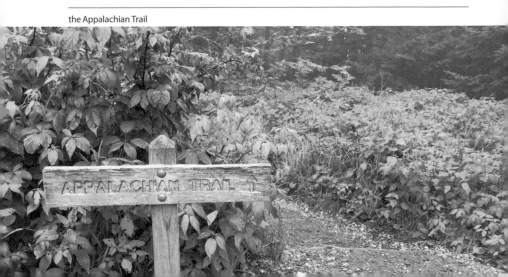

- Mollies Ridge at 4,570 feet, 10.3 miles
- Russell Field at 4,360 feet, 13.1 miles
- Spence Field at 4,900 feet, 15.9 miles, has a privy nearby
- Derrick Knob at 4,890 feet, 22 miles
- Silers Bald at 5,460 feet, 28 miles
- Double Spring Gap at 5,507 feet, 29.5 miles, has a privy nearby
- Mount Collins at 5,870 feet, 35.8 miles, has a privy nearby
- Icewater Spring at 5,920 feet, 43.3 miles, has a privy nearby
- Pecks Corner at 5,280 feet, 53.7 miles
- TriCorner at 5,920 feet, 55.9 miles, has a privy nearby
- Cosby Knob at 4,700 feet, 63.6 miles, has a privy nearby
- Davenport Gap at 2,600 feet, 70.7 miles

DAY HIKING

Day hikers are drawn to the Appalachian Trail's fantastic balds (high natural and agricultural meadows), like Andrews Bald and Silers Bald; peaks like Mount Cammerer and Rocky Top (yes, the one from the song); and just to say they've hiked part of the Appalachian Trail. The route through the park is always high and at times rocky, at other times steep, at times both, but the views are worth it.

Day hikers who want to log a few miles of the Appalachian Trail will find a few opportunities to get their boots muddy. Notable day hikes include:

- **Charlies Bunion** (8.1 miles round-trip): Access the Appalachian Trail north from the trailhead at the Newfound Gap Road Overlook.
- **Mount Cammerer** (11.2 miles round-trip): Take the Low Gap Trail at the Cosby Campground to the Appalachian Trail, then proceed to the summit and a stone fire tower. Note: Only 4.2 miles are on the Appalachian Trail.

- **Rocky Top** (13.9 miles round-trip): Follow the Anthony Creek Trailhead from the Cades Cove picnic area to Bote Mountain Trail. At Spence Field, you'll meet up with the Appalachian Trail; follow it to Rocky Top and spectacular views. Note: Only the last portion is on the Appalachian Trail.

THRU-HIKING

From Fontana Dam to Davenport Gap, the Appalachian Trail brushes past peaks surpassing 5,000 feet in elevation, including the highest point along the entire trail, the 6,643-foot Clingmans Dome. Gaps (low points in the mountains) along this stretch top out at nearly 4,000 feet.

Most thru-hikers begin in Georgia in the spring and hike north to Maine. These hike descriptions follow that northbound flow of foot traffic. The Appalachian Trail is broken down into two hikes: one from Fontana Dam to Newfound Gap, the other from Newfound Gap to Davenport Gap. Notations and mileage markers are given for the Appalachian Trail shelters, as well as points where other trails connect with or cross the Appalachian Trail.

Western Smokies
FONTANA DAM TO NEWFOUND GAP
Distance: 40.3 miles one way
Duration: Multiple days
Elevation gain: 4,900 feet
Difficulty: strenuous
Trailhead: Fontana Dam

This section of the Appalachian Trail hits the highest peak in the Smokies, Clingmans Dome, which is also the highest point along the entire length of the trail. There are seven **shelters** along this route: Mollies Ridge (mile 10.3), Russell Field (mile 13.1), Spence Field (mile 16), Derrick Knob (mile 22.3), Silers Bald (mile 27.8), Double Spring Gap (mile 29.5), and Mount Collins (mile 35.8).

Begin the hike at **Fontana Dam** and get ready for a big uphill push; you'll gain 3,035 feet in the first 11 miles. After crossing Fontana Dam, you'll leave the paved road at 0.6 miles and begin to climb **Shuckstack**

Fontana Dam to Newfound Gap

© MOON.COM

Mountain. At 3.2 miles, you'll reach the gap between Shuckstack and Little Shuckstack, then at 3.8 miles you'll hit a viewpoint that offers a great look at Fontana Lake.

When you reach 4 miles, there is a road on the east side of the trail that leads to a fire tower at the top of Shuckstack Mountain. Make the side trip if you want; otherwise keep hiking and descend to Sassafras Gap and the intersection with Lost Cove Trail to the east and Twentymile Trail to the west.

You'll continue up and down as you follow the terrain, and at 7.5 miles reach the summit of Doe Knob (4,520 feet), then descend some steep 300 feet to Mud Gap at 7.9 miles, only to climb again to Ekaneetlee Gap (3,842 feet) at 8.9 miles. Keep climbing and you'll reach **Mollies Ridge Shelter** at 10.3 miles. Depending on your pace, the time allotted for your hike, and your reservations (if necessary), make camp here.

At 10.9 miles you'll reach Devil's Tater Patch (4,775 feet) and begin a long section of what's often referred to as a "roller-coaster" section, meaning it's up and down as the trail follows the undulating ridgeline. You'll have frequent and steep ascents and descents, but little overall change in elevation between here and the 25-mile mark at Buckeye Gap.

From Devil's Tater Patch, descend to Little Abrams Gap (4,120 feet) then to Big Abrams Gap (4,080 feet) at 12.7 miles. At 13.1 miles you'll reach **Russell Field Shelter** and a spring. At 13.8 miles you'll reach McCampbell Gap (4,328 feet).

When you hit the 15.9 mile mark you've reached the south end of **Spence Field;** the shelter is 0.1 miles on, then 250 yards down Eagle Creek Trail on the east side of the Appalachian Trail. Bote Mountain Trail intersects with the Appalachian Trail at 16.4 miles, where you meet Jenkins Ridge Trail, marking the north end of Spence Field.

As the trail begins to climb from Spence Field, you might as well start humming "Rocky Top" as you're approaching the summit of the mountain made famous in song. Rocky Top's 5,441-foot peak awaits at 17.2

miles, then the summit of Thunderhead (5,527 feet) 0.6 miles further. The views from Rocky Top are great but absolutely nonexistent from Thunderhead.

From here to Derrick Knob you'll pass through five additional gaps, then, at 22 miles, reach Chestnut Bald; **Derrick Knob Shelter** is 0.3 miles ahead on the west side of the trail.

At 25.1 miles you'll find yourself at the 4,817-foot Buckeye Gap and begin a 7.3-mile, 1800-foot ascent to Clingmans Dome. Along the way you'll hit **Silers Bald** (5,607 feet) at 28 miles, where the views are quite good; Jenkins Knob at 29 miles; and **Double Spring Gap** shelter (5,570 feet) at 29.5 miles. Begin a steep ascent, pass Goshen Prong Trail to the west at 30.1 miles, summit Mount Buckley (6,582 feet) at 31.9 miles, then reach Clingmans Dome Bypass Trail at 32 miles.

If you want to top out on the 6,643 foot Clingmans Dome and hike to the top of the observation platform (recommended, especially if the weather is good), take a detour on a side trail to the east; head to the top, then back to the trail. You're now at 32.4 miles and are less than 8 miles from Newfound Gap, the end of this section of the Appalachian Trail.

Continue descending to the summit of Mount Love (6,446 feet) and Collins Gap (5,886 feet). At 35.8 miles you'll reach Sugarland Mountain Trail and **Mount Collins Shelter** (0.5 miles west). The Appalachian Trail joins North Carolina's Mountains-to-Sea Trail at the 36.2-mile mark.

Indian Gap (5,317 feet) and the intersection of Road Prong Trail await at 38.6 miles. At 39.4 miles, a few openings in the trees provide views of Mount LeConte to the west. Ascend a graded trail to **Newfound Gap** (5,045 feet) and the overlook there.

Eastern Smokies
NEWFOUND GAP TO DAVENPORT GAP
Distance: 31.3 miles one-way
Duration: Multiple days
Elevation gain: 4,380 feet

Newfound Gap to Davenport Gap

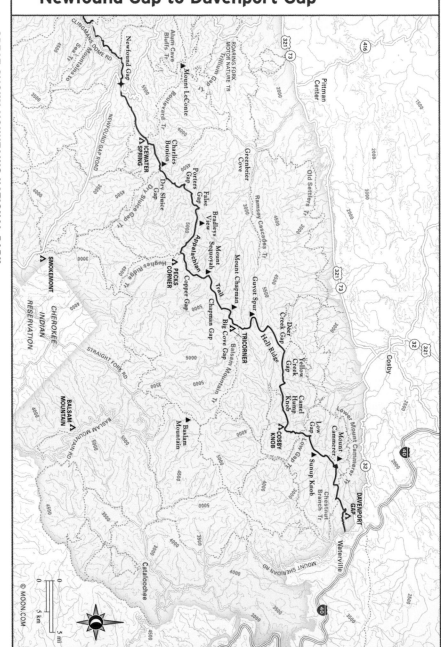

© MOON.COM

Difficulty: strenuous
Trailhead: Newfound Gap

Along this section you'll have 11 major climbs and descents like Mount Cammerer, Cosby Knob, Mount Guyot, Charlies Bunion, and Mount Kephart. There are five **shelters** here: Icewater Spring (mile 3), Pecks Corner (mile 10.4), TriCorner Knob (mile 15.6), Cosby Knob (mile 23.3), and Davenport Gap (mile 30.4).

Begin at **Newfound Gap,** taking a wide trail past the rock overlook and into the woods. You'll reach a viewpoint at 1.9 miles, then reach a junction with Boulevard Trail at 2.7 miles. The Boulevard leads to Mount LeConte, and from LeConte a day hiker can descend to Roaring Fork Motor Nature Trail via Trillium Gap Trail or descend to Newfound Gap Road via Alum Cave Bluffs Trail. Appalachian Trail hikers should proceed past the junction and reach **Icewater Spring Shelter** at the 3-mile mark.

The trail passes east around Charlies Bunion at 3.9 miles and then Dry Sluice Gap (5,375 feet) at 4.1 miles. Pass Dry Sluice Gap Trail (leading to Smokemont Campground) at 4.2 miles. Porters Gap (5,500 feet) is the next landmark at 5.8 miles, then False Gap (5,400 feet) at 6.5 miles. At the 9.1-mile mark you'll be at Bradleys View, where you'll have some of the best views of North Carolina that you'll find.

At 10.4 miles you'll reach a junction with Hughes Ridge Trail, which will take you to **Pecks Corner Shelter** to the east. There is another outstanding view at 11.3 miles where you'll be looking down into the headwaters of Eagle Rocks Creek. Begin climbing at Copper Gap (5,478 feet), 12.1 miles in, and head on to the summit of Mount Sequoyah (6,003 feet) at 13.1 miles.

Descend to Chapman Gap (5,801 feet) at 13.8 miles, then climb again to Mount Chapman (6,218 feet) at 14.6 miles. You'll cross Big Cove Gap (5,825 feet) at 15.5 miles, and 0.1 miles further on, the trail to **TriCorner Knob Shelter.**

The junction with Balsam Mountain Trail lies at the 15.8-mile mark, and a sharp ridge at 16.2 miles. The next landmarks are Guyot Spur (6,360 feet) at 16.8 miles, Guyot Spring at 17.4 miles, and the so-called "Hell Ridge" section at 17.9 miles. The 4-mile Hell Ridge earned its name not from the tough trail but from a forest fire that raged here after prepark logging left it particularly vulnerable; you'll notice the absence of the larger and old-growth trees seen elsewhere along the trail.

Deer Creek Gap (6,020 feet) at 18.5 miles and Yellow Creek Gap at 19.1 miles are the next two landmarks before you reach Camel Hump Knob (5,250 feet) at 20.8 miles. At 22.7 miles you'll be at the north end of Hell Ridge and pass back into a lovely deciduous forest.

Cosby Knob Shelter awaits at 23.3 miles, then Low Gap (4,242 feet) and the interaction with Low Gap Trail at 24 miles. The Appalachian Trail brushes past Sunup Knob at 25 miles, then crests the ridge and the North Carolina-Tennessee border on the slopes of Mount Cammerer at 25.9 miles. If you want to summit Cammerer and the stone fire tower there, you'll find the 0.6-mile spur trail at 26.1 miles.

There's a great view at 26.9 miles, and a spring east of the Appalachian Trail at 28.2 miles. Lower Mount Cammerer Trail comes in at 28.5 miles, then Chestnut Branch Trail at 29.4 miles. Davenport Gap Trail waits at the 30.4-mile mark; it's 200 yards or so off the west side of the trail. From here it's 0.9 miles to the **Davenport Gap Shelter.** Here you'll find State Route 1397, the Pigeon River, and I-40.

And, of course, the end of the Appalachian Trail passes out of Great Smoky Mountains National Park and turns northwest into North Carolina and toward Maine.

Tennessee Gateways

There was a time when this was the frontier, when the Smoky Mountains stood too high and too rough to pass.

But settlers made their way across this a huge green wall with what few supplies they could carry to carve out an existence in the virgin wilderness, not to mention the threat—or perceived threat—of hostile natives. They found coves of rich bottomland around which to settle outposts. Eventually these outposts turned into communities, which turned into towns and cities, and something like what we see today was carved out of the wild—Gatlinburg at the foot of the Smokies, Pigeon Forge on the river just a few miles distant, and Knoxville growing large on the bluffs of the deep, wide Tennessee River.

Today the setup is the same, but the inherent risks of frontier life are

Look for ★ to find recommended sights, activities, dining, and lodging.

★ **Sample Moonshine Distilleries:** Moonshiners were rampant in these hills during Prohibition, celebrated in songs like "Rocky Top," but now you can sample a little legal 'shine in Gatlinburg (page 110).

★ **Shop at Great Smoky Arts and Crafts Community:** Interact with more than 120 traditional Appalachian artists, artisans, and craftspeople (page 112).

★ **Go for a Ride at Dollywood:** At this theme park owned by the country music legend, roller coasters go hand in hand with Appalachian music, culture, and history (page 118).

★ **Uncover the Past at East Tennessee History Center:** This landmark tells the story of the Tennessee foothills through surprising exhibits (page 126).

★ **Explore the Knoxville Museum of Art:** Enjoy an impressive collection of contemporary pieces, including works by artists native to the city and the region (page 127).

★ **Step Back in Time at the Tennessee Theatre:** The official state theater is an architectural marvel offering a glimpse of Gilded Age opulence (page 128).

Tennessee Gateways

gone. In their place, Gatlinburg and Pigeon Forge are tourist hot spots, or even tourist traps. (I mean that in the most flattering, fun, kitsch-filled sense of the term.) Gatlinburg is, proudly, the gateway to the Smokies, and Great Smoky Mountains National Park rubs shoulders with the town limits. Not to be outdone, Pigeon Forge is the home of Dollywood—an amusement park that's part rides, part Appalachian culture, and part homage to Dolly Parton's childhood.

The two towns are bright dots of light connected by a glittering ribbon—a sharp contrast to their next-door neighbor, the most-visited

national park in the United States. Some 30 miles west of the park, Knoxville is the nearest city of any size, and it's as pretty and proper a Southern city as there ever has been. It offers a cosmopolitan respite from the wildness of the Smokies and the country kitsch of Gatlinburg and Pigeon Forge, all while maintaining its own identity as an intellectual and creative urban center that's grown up but has never forgotten its roots.

PLANNING YOUR TIME

To get a true sense of this complex place and a real taste of the cultures at work here, plan

Previous: Gatlinburg Sky Lift; Sugarlands Distilling Company; Dollywood to spend at least **four days.** Split your time evenly between Gatlinburg and Pigeon Forge, with two days in each. (The in-your-face faux-hillbilly attractions are so silly that you can't help but embrace them.) Pay a visit to the Great Smoky Arts and Crafts Community, where more than 120 artists, artisans, and craftspeople practice traditional Appalachian arts. Head to Dollywood for a sense of the area's history while waiting in line for a roller coaster. Taste some traditional food—from barbecue to country-kitchen standards—and clear the slate for an evening of moonshine tasting, as most distilleries use versions of old family recipes likely made in the nearby hills. After that, head to Knoxville for **two days**

and soak in the contemporary, creative vibe of the city. You'll likely hear some traditional or bluegrass musicians, but listen close and you'll find the ways they're making these old styles current. At the Knoxville Museum of Art, and throughout downtown, the art here is certainly of the place, and seeing how it blends old with new gives you an idea of how these worlds come together. Visit the Ijams Nature Center, one of the premier urban wilderness areas in the nation, and see why several magazines have called this city one of the top outdoor towns in the South. If you're here on a weekend, Market Square is a happening spot with outdoor concerts, plenty of alfresco dining options, and a lovely farmers market.

Gatlinburg

On a typical Saturday night, when 40,000 people pack the restaurants and sidewalks of Gatlinburg, you would never know that only about 4,000 people live here. As the unofficial capital of the Smokies and gateway to the national park, Gatlinburg benefits greatly from the 10 million visitors drawn here for the views, the wildlife, the hikes, and the kitsch. And if there's anything Gatlinburg has in abundance, it's kitsch.

Gatlinburg is unabashedly a tourist town, and owning up to that fact makes it all the more charming. On Parkway, the cheekily named main drag, there are T-shirt shops, candy stores and fudgeries, taffy pullers, more than one Ripley's attraction, novelties both racy (in that family-friendly, double-entendre way) and tame, knife shops, mini golf, ice cream parlors, restaurants, and more odd little art, craft, and gift shops than you can count. Don't let that deter you from staying (and even enjoying yourself) here. The Ripley's Aquarium is quite nice, and at Great Smoky Arts and Crafts Community and the Arrowcraft Shop, you'll find modern interpretations of traditional mountain arts that were handmade nearby.

SIGHTS
Space Needle
All of downtown Gatlinburg is a sight to behold. The mountains rise all around you, that namesake Smoky mist rising from them, and the street glitters and twinkles like a sort of vacationland Milky Way. One of the best ways to take it all in is from the **Space Needle** (115 Historic Nature Trail, 865/436-4629, www.gatlinburgspaceneedle.com, 10am-11pm Sun.-Thurs., 10am-midnight Fri.-Sat., adults $13, seniors and military $10, ages 4-11 $8, under age 4 free). I know what you're thinking: "But the Space Needle is in Seattle." Yeah, it is; this is the other one. From the observation deck 407 feet above Gatlinburg, you have truly stellar views. For the best views, get to the top shortly before sundown and watch as the mountains darken and the strip of downtown comes alive with lights. At the foot of the tower, there's a two-level, 25,000-square-foot arcade with games galore, laser tag, a gift shop, a snack bar, and restrooms.

Gatlinburg Sky Lift
The **Gatlinburg Sky Lift** (765 Parkway, 865/436-4307, www.gatlinburgskylift.com,

Gatlinburg

© MOON.COM

9am-9pm daily Apr.-May, 9am-11pm daily May 24-Labor Day, 9am-10pm daily Sept.-Dec., 9am-10pm Fri.-Sun., 10am-5pm Mon.-Thurs. Jan.-Feb., 9am-10pm daily Mar.-May 23, adults $24, over ages 64 $21, ages 4-11 $18, under age 3 free) is a ski lift that carries you 1,800 feet up the side of a mountain to a gift shop, a snack bar, decks overlooking downtown, and the 680-foot SkyBridge. The SkyBridge spans a deep valley and at its highest is 140 feet over the ground below. At that point the bridge's normal planking gives way to a trio of glass panels, giving you a dizzying view. On my visits to the SkyBridge, I've seen

people take selfies on the glass panels, take a death grip on the handrail and shuffle across, giggle, cry, go pale, and be thrilled by the experience. You have pretty views of Gatlinburg on the way up and back down, and even better views from the top. Nighttime tends to be the best time to ride the Sky Lift. The Sky Lift was built in the early 1950s and was the first chairlift in the region, seeing more than 100,000 visitors by its third season in operation. You'll

1: Space Needle **2:** Gatlinburg Sky Lift **3:** Ripley's Aquarium of the Smokies **4:** Ole Smoky Moonshine distillery

find the lift in the heart of downtown; it's impossible to miss.

★ Moonshine Distilleries

Moonshine is a high-octane corn liquor made in the hills, hollows, and coves all throughout and around the national park, especially in Gatlinburg. Today, moonshine is brewed legally and there are a few distilleries right in Gatlinburg, the best of which is **Sugarlands Distilling Company** (805 Parkway, 865/325-1355, www.sugarlands.com, 10am-10:30pm daily, except Dec. 25). Sugarlands has their whole distilling process on display, and free tours are offered, but if you want to really get into it, the Blended Cocktails Tour ($12) provides a tasting with a private tour and mixology class; the Meet the Distiller workshop ($40) is a hands-on experience that sends you home with a full jar; and Distiller for the Day ($250) guides you through the process from start to finish. There are sampling stations (ID required), a gift shop, and the chance to buy a quart or two. The Back Porch is the performance space, where musicians and storytellers come to sing songs and spin yarns; check to see who's there when you visit.

In the middle of Gatlinburg is yet another moonshine distillery, **Ole Smoky Moonshine** (www.olesmoky.com), which has several locations. There's **The Holler** (903 Parkway, Suite 128, 865/436-6995, 10am-11pm daily) and **The Barrelhouse** (650 Parkway, 865/325-1111 10am-11pm daily) in Gatlinburg, and **The Barn** (131 The Island Dr., 865/436-6995, 10am-11pm daily) at The Island in Pigeon Forge. At each you'll find plenty of shine to sample, as well as shirts and glasses and mixers for sale alongside shirts and other Ole Smoky merchandise.

At the other end of downtown from Sugarlands is **Doc Collier Moonshine** (519 Parkway, 865/325-1468 or 800/398-5132, https://doccollier.co, 10am-10pm Mon.-Sat., noon-7pm Sun.). Using the recipe of locally famous Doc Collier, his ancestors continue the tradition of making some of the finest 'shine in Tennessee and selling it to the thirsty public

at their Gatlinburg storefront. According to the family, Doc's moonshine was in such high demand that he needed a better way to distribute it, so he bought a mercantile and sold straight goods to some customers and jars of white lightning to those in the know. In the store, you can see some great photos and even pieces of Doc's equipment while you sample some moonshine before grabbing a bottle and going on your way.

Ripley's Aquarium of the Smokies

Ripley's Aquarium of the Smokies (traffic light no. 5, 88 River Rd., 865/430-8808, www.ripleyaquariums.com/gatlinburg, 9am-8pm Mon.-Thurs., 9am-10pm Fri.-Sun. Jan.-Feb., 9am-9pm Mon.-Thurs., 9am-10pm Fri.-Sun. Mar.-Memorial Day and Labor Day-New Year's Day, 9am-10pm Mon.-Thurs., 9am-11pm Fri.-Sun. Memorial Day-Labor Day, adults $33, ages 6-11 $18, ages 2-5 $8) is one of countless Ripley's attractions in Gatlinburg and Pigeon Forge. The other attractions are skippable unless you have kids in tow, but the aquarium is another story. Ripley's Aquarium is the largest in the state, with more than 1.4 million gallons of water. Exhibits include the Touch a Ray Bay, where you can touch a stingray; the Penguin Playhouse, where tunnels lead you through the exhibit, putting you eye to eye with penguins as they do their thing; and Shark Lagoon, where a 340-foot-long glide path takes you under the lagoon, where sand tiger and nurse sharks swim with sea turtles and moray eels.

Arrowmont School of Arts and Crafts

Gatlinburg has a surprising artistic side. The artists and craftspeople here take their work very seriously. Many of them are carrying on mountain traditions, while others are finding new modes and media to express the inspiration they draw from the landscape here. Artists go to the **Arrowmont School of Arts and Crafts** (556 Parkway, 865/436-5860, www.arrowmont.org, 8:30am-5pm Mon.-Fri.,

Wedding Fever

To say that Gatlinburg is a popular place to get married is a gross understatement. This tiny town is second in the nation only to Las Vegas in the number of weddings held each year. On average, around 20,000 couples tie the knot here (that's 55 ceremonies a day) and the number of witnesses and guests they bring pushes the number of people in town for weddings north of 600,000. Guess that explains why Gatlinburg is called the "wedding capital of the South."

What makes Gatlinburg such a hot spot for weddings, even for celebrities (Billy Ray Cyrus, Patty Loveless, and others)? It could be that Tennessee makes it easy. No blood tests or waiting periods are required before getting married. It could be the abundance of wedding venues both natural and artificial. It could be the fact that there are plenty of romantic spots where one can retreat with their betrothed.

If being here has you in the mood for marriage, it's easy to find a place. In Gatlinburg alone there are more than a dozen chapels and more officiants than you can count. You can find all the information you'll ever need for planning a Smoky Mountain wedding at the website of the **Smoky Mountain Wedding Association** (www.smwba.com).

10am-4pm Sat., workshops $325-1,100) to hone their techniques. Founded in 1912 as a philanthropic project by the Pi Beta Phi women's fraternity, the Pi Beta Phi Settlement School sought to deliver basic education and health services to the children of the area. The schoolchildren brought the school staff homemade gifts—baskets, weavings, wood carvings—made by their parents. Recognizing the talent here, the school brought in a weaving teacher and began some vocational education. Then in 1926, the school opened the Arrowcraft Shop, a market selling crafts and wares made by the people of the region. As this gained popularity, the idea of summer craft workshops came about. In 1945, the first of many summer workshops saw 50 students attend. Today the school holds weekend and one- and two-week workshops for adults every spring, summer, and fall. Classes include traditional and contemporary takes on weaving and fiber arts, pottery, metal and jewelry, painting, and drawing. Three galleries in the school display rotating and permanent exhibitions and are open year-round.

ENTERTAINMENT AND EVENTS

Nightlife

One spot to grab a drink other than moonshine is **Smoky Mountain Brewery** (1004 Parkway, 865/436-4200, www.smoky-mtn-brewery.com, 11:30am-1am daily), a microbrewery with close to a dozen handcrafted beers brewed here or at one of the three nearby sister breweries. Mainstay beers include a light beer, red ale, pilsner, porter, and pale ale; they also brew seasonal and specialty beers, like the creamy Winter Warmer Ale and the Brown Trout Stout. Stop in and grab a hot pretzel (or some wings or a pizza) and a sampler flight of beers.

Performing Arts

There are a number of stage shows going on nightly throughout Gatlinburg. The **Iris Theatre** (115 Historic Nature Trail, 888/482-3330, www.iristheater.com, showtimes vary, adults $28, military and seniors $20, ages 4-11 $13) is home to a rotating slate of performers. Expect to see family-friendly comedy and magic shows, hypnotists, and the like. Shows go on most nights except Monday; check the schedule for times and current performers.

Then there's the **Sweet Fanny Adams Theatre** (461 Parkway, 865/436-4039, www.sweetfannyadams.com, box office 10am-10pm show days, adults $25, under age 12 $9), home to a musical comedy review and "outrageous humor and hilarious fun" since 1977. Shows vary by the theater season but typically include an improv showcase, a vaudeville-type revue, a holiday show, and other original musical comedies.

Festivals and Events

Throughout the year, several events draw attention to the things that make Gatlinburg the place it is. The **Spring Wildflower Pilgrimage** (www.springwildflowerpilgrimage.org, adults $75-100, students $30, under age 12 $5), usually during mid-April, is a five-day event with around 150 guided walks and presentations that celebrate the spring blooms, a photography contest, and more. From the end of September to early November, celebrate **Oktoberfest at Ober Gatlinburg** (865/436-5423, www.obergatlinburg.com) with a beer hall, sing-alongs, yodeling, and authentic German food. **Gatlinburg Winter Magic** (800/588-1817) is a 120-day celebration of all things winter and holiday. From early November through February, the city is a riot of millions of LED bulbs strung up in trees and lining elaborate displays. There's a chili cook-off, carolers, a Christmas parade, and more.

SHOPPING

Gatlinburg's touristy side has a big personality, and there are plenty of shops selling T-shirts and the expected souvenirs, but for something that truly speaks to the heritage of this place, you'll need to do a little looking around.

★ Great Smoky Arts and Crafts Community

Your first stop should be the **Great Smoky Arts and Crafts Community** (turn right at traffic light no. 3 and go 3 miles to Glades Rd., www.gatlinburgcrafts.com, most studios and shops open 10am-5pm Mon.-Sat., call ahead for Sunday and holiday hours). Founded in 1937, it is among the largest group of independent artisans in the United States. There are more than 100 shops, studios, and galleries along this eight-mile loop consisting of Glades Road, Buckhorn Road, and U.S. 321. Look for the logo denoting membership in the community so you know that wares you're seeing and buying are from genuine local and regional artisans. One thing that sets this community apart is the fact that you can interact with the artists in their studios and galleries. You can watch them work, ask questions, maybe even lend a hand (if asked). With 100 stops here, you can easily spend a day if you want to take a peek into each and every gallery, shop, and studio.

The shop artisans include candle makers, watercolor artists, photographers, leatherworkers, and the creators of traditional mountain crafts. **Ogle's Broom Shop** (670 Glades Rd., 865/430-4402, www.oglesbroomshop.com) is one such traditional crafts shop, with third-generation broom makers. The owner carries on the tradition today, making brooms from broom straw and hand-carving canes and walking sticks.

Otto Preske, Artist in Wood (535 Buckhorn Rd., 865/436-5339, www.ottopreskeartistinwood.com) is a superb wood-carver. He carves and turns Christmas ornaments, hiking staffs, fireplace mantels, religious carvings, and highly detailed figures and relief carvings. The work is stunning, and to watch him carve is simply amazing. Another woodworker is **Tim Weberding Woodworking** (600 Glades Rd., Unit 5, 865/430-8811, www.timweberding.com), where the eponymous owner, a fourth-generation woodworker, makes religious signs and placards, wooden baskets, ornaments, boxes, and more.

Throughout the community there are several basket weavers, but nothing like what you'll find at **Licklog Hollow Baskets** (1360 E. Parkway, 865/436-3823). Not only do they have the strangest name, the work here is superb. Whether you're buying for form or function, you'll find a basket that fits your style and probably your budget.

At **Woodland Tiles** (220 Buckhorn Rd., 865/640-9089), they create tiles and functional pottery pieces inspired by the leaves on the trees surrounding Gatlinburg. Custom glazes capture the jewel green of summer and the blazing colors of fall, and the sizes and shapes are spot on as the tiles mirror the leaves that inspired them.

The Village

In downtown Gatlinburg, you'll find **The Village Shops** (634 Parkway, 865/436-3995, www.thevillageshops.com, 10am-5pm daily Jan.-Feb., 10am-6pm daily Mar., 10am-8pm Sun.-Fri., 10am-10pm Sat. Apr.-May and Nov., 10am-10pm daily June-Oct., hours vary Dec.), a collection of 27 shops centered around a courtyard in a Bavarian-style structure. Among the shops here is **Cartoons & Toys** (865/430-8666), a kid-centric shop loaded with toys and games. They also sell wool socks, dress socks, and more—as long as it goes on your feet. **The Day Hiker** (865/430-0970, www.thedayhiker.com) provides the basic gear you need to take day and short overnight hikes in the national park. **The Silver Tree** (865/430-3573) is a silver lover's paradise with plenty of silver jewelry and accessories to peruse. Guess what you'll find at **The Sock Shop** (www.sockshoptn.com, 865/325-6000)? That's right, fun and funky socks. Last but not least is **The Donut Friar** (865/436-7306, from 5am daily), an amazing bakery making doughnuts, cinnamon bread, and other pastries; they also have the requisite coffee to go with your doughnut.

Other Shops

For a unique shop-museum (there is only one other place in the world like this, and it's in Spain), stop in at **The Salt and Pepper Shaker Museum** (461 Brookside Village Way, 865/430-5515, www.thesaltandpeppershakermuseum.com, 10am-2pm daily, adults $3, under age 13 free). The name tells you what you'll find here, but it doesn't prepare you for the more than 20,000 salt and pepper shakers from around the world and the growing collection of pepper mills. The collection began on a lark, growing from one pepper mill into this massive assembly of the most banal of kitchen accessories.

It's weird, so it's worth the cost of admission, especially when you can apply your admission fee to any gift shop purchase—and who doesn't want a salt and pepper set shaped like outhouses?

RECREATION

There is no end to the outdoor recreation opportunities near Gatlinburg. At **Nantahala Outdoor Center Gatlinburg** (1138 Parkway, 865/277-8209, www.noc.com, 10am-6pm Sun.-Thurs., 10am-9pm Fri.-Sat.), you'll find a huge retail store selling everything you'd ever need to gear up for an outdoor adventure. NOC is the region's leader in outdoor guide services, providing white-water rafting, float trips, and kayaking on several rivers across the region; guided hikes and fly-fishing trips; and more. Their trips vary by season, so check the website or ask someone at the store about current trips and activities.

Rafting in the Smokies (813 E. Parkway, 800/776-7238, www.raftingthesmokies.com, 8am-8pm daily Memorial Day-Labor Day) is another white-water rafting outfitter in the area. Trips ($35-42) depend on the weather and water levels, so it's a good idea to call ahead or check online for current trips and reservations. Once you've gotten it nailed down, check in at the rafting outpost in Hartford (I-40, exit 447). They also have a zip line ($39), a high ropes course ($33), and a climbing wall ($20).

At **CLIMB works** (155 Branam Hollow Rd., 865/325-8116, www.climbworks.com, Mon.-Sat. year round, reservations required), they brag that "your feet won't touch the ground for two and a half hours." And it's true, no matter whether you take their impressive mountaintop zip-line tour ($99) or treetop tour ($89), ride their intermediate- to expert-level mountain biking trails ($59 with a rental bike, $25 with your own bike), or take one of their mountain e-bikes ($59) for a spin; mountain e-bikes are electrical assist bikes that are otherwise regular rugged mountain bikes, they just take some of the burn out of long uphill climbs.

One of the newest things to do in Gatlinburg is at **Anakeesta** (576 Parkway, at traffic light no. 5, 865/325-2400, www.anakeesta.com, hours vary, generally 9am-9pm daily, adults $22, ages 4-11 $17, over age 59 $20), a mountaintop theme park where you'll find an 880-foot treetop sky bridge, a treehouse adventure village, dueling zip lines (adults $30, ages 4-11 $25, over age 59 $30), a single-rail mountain coaster ($13-15), gem mining, live music, and several places to relax and take in the view. If you purchase a ticket after 6pm, you have free admission the next day. At Firefly Village, the collection of shops and stands at the top of the hill, there's a coffee shop, the restaurant and bar **Cliff Top** (11am-close Mon.-Sat., noon-close Sun., $6-12), an ice cream shop, and **Anakeesta Smokehouse** (open park hours, $5-10) where you'll find plenty of pork and brisket to eat. If you're a frequent visitor to Gatlinburg and the Smokies, it may be worth your while to buy an annual pass (adults $44, ages 4-11 $36, over age 59 $40).

Ober Gatlinburg

Ober Gatlinburg (1001 Parkway, 865/436-5423, www.obergatlinburg.com, hours vary by activity, generally 9:30am-9pm daily spring-fall, 10am-7pm daily winter, $4-15, activity pass adults $29-34, ages 5-11 $29-39), the mountaintop resort that looks out over Gatlinburg, is a ski resort in winter and a mountain playground the rest of the year. There are eight ski and snowboard trails, and Ober Gatlinburg is equipped with plenty of snowmaking equipment to make up for what Mother Nature doesn't supply. Warm-weather activities include the awesome Alpine Slide, a sort of luge that follows one of the ski slopes down the hill; a pair of raft-based waterslides; a maze; and year-round indoor ice skating. There's also a Wildlife Encounter where you can see many of the native species found in the area. If you're hungry, there are several places to grab a bite, ranging from a slice of pizza to a steak.

The resort is a little dated and leans toward the campy end of the spectrum, and many people skip it if it's not ski season. Others think it's worth the little bit of time and money to ride the tram to the top of the hill and ride the Alpine Slide one more time.

FOOD

Dining in Gatlinburg, especially for foodies, can be tricky. In a town where, literally, millions of people pass through, you get a lot of restaurants that have stopped caring about repeat customers and seek only to provide a heaping plate of food and mediocre service at premium prices, knowing their diners will be in for one, maybe two meals during their visit. And there are plenty of major chains ready to take your dining dollars. That said, it is possible to find a good, even great, meal here.

Mama's Chicken Kitchen (1244 E. Parkway, 865/412-1333, www.mamaschickenkitchen.com, 11am-10pm daily, $8-25) might be a tongue twister of a name, but the fried chicken they serve is a delight the minute it hits your lips. Whether you get a plate or bucket, and whether you eat there or make a picnic of it (nothing like a cold fried chicken picnic in Cades Cove), you'll love every bite.

A totally unexpected treat is ★ **Red Oak Bistro and Caffe** (669 Glades Rd., 865/325-1717, www.redoakbistro.net, 4pm-10pm Thurs.-Sun., $12-30), a tapas, wine, and European beer spot. The food is exceptional and unlike anything else you'll find in Gatlinburg. Thoughtfully composed cheese and charcuterie boards, fresh hummus and other spreads, bruschetta, dolmas, *banitza*, *kebarche* (a Bulgarian pork sausage), and beet napoleon complement a wine list that may just be the best in town. There's outdoor seating, a fire pit and fire place, couches and places to relax, no wonder you need a reservation. It's a must-visit if you take food seriously and want to escape the cookie-cutter restaurants on the strip.

★ **Buckhorn Inn** (2140 Tudor Mountain Rd., 865/436-4668, www.buckhorninn.com, 7pm-late daily, $35) serves a four-course prix-fixe meal nightly to inn guests and visitors. The food makes creative use of regional ingredients, with dishes that at times span Southern, East Tennessee, and international cuisine pantheons. Expect to find dishes like pan-seared trout or tandoori salmon, flank steak, or pork tenderloin with soy-citrus sauce, all served with a soup, salad, and dessert.

Gatlinburg favorite **Alamo Steakhouse and Saloon** (705 E. Parkway, 865/436-9998, www.alamosteakhouse.com, 11am-10pm Sun.-Thurs., 11am-11pm Fri.-Sat., $14-31), which earns "Best Steak" accolades year after year, was lost during the 2016 wildfire but reopened in 2017. If you're not in the mood for steak, there are a number of pork, chicken, and seafood dishes. The service is generally very good, but, like all restaurants in a busy vacation town, can get bogged down in the high season.

Another longtime Gatlinburg eatery, **The Peddler Steakhouse** (820 River Rd., 865/436-5794, www.peddlergatlinburg.com, from 5pm Sun.-Fri., from 4:30pm Sat., $23-37), has a reputation for making a fantastic steak. The dining room overlooks the river, making it a nice spot to eat. The menu is steak-heavy, but they also have shrimp, chicken, and trout, and every entrée comes with a pretty robust salad bar.

Big Daddy's Pizzeria (714 River Rd., 865/436-5455, www.bigdaddyspizzeria.net, 11am-10pm Sun.-Thurs., 11am-11pm Fri.-Sat., $9-23) has locations in Gatlinburg, Pigeon Forge, and Sevierville. Their claim to fame is a wood-fired brick oven and a creative flair in the creation of their pies. Get the tried-and-true pepperoni and cheese, or go wild with the Smoky Mountain Cheesesteak (with shaved prime rib, caramelized onions, gorgonzola cheese, and potato slices), the Herbivore (a veggie-packed delight), or one of their other signature pizzas. They also have salads, meatballs, and sandwiches prepared on house-made focaccia.

Gatlinburg has pancake houses in spades. The oldest pancake house in town opened in 1960, and it also happens to be the first of its kind in Tennessee. ★ **Pancake Pantry** (628 Parkway, 865/436-4724, www.pancakepantry. com, 7am-4pm daily June-Oct., 7am-3pm daily Nov.-May, $6-10) still puts out a great spread of flapjacks. There are 24 varieties of pancakes and crepes, as well as a half-dozen waffles, omelets, and french toast. Breakfast is served all day, but if you feel like a burger or sandwich for lunch, they have a few of those too, and if you're going for a hike, go easy on the pancakes—they sit a little heavy—but you can get a to-go boxed lunch made just for hikers and day-trippers into the park.

Near the entrance to the park, **Crockett's Breakfast Camp** (1103 Parkway, 865/325-1403, www.crockettsbreakfastcamp.com, 8am-1pm Mon.-Fri., 7am-1pm Sat.-Sun., $2-15) serves, predictably, breakfast. A giant cast-iron skillet outside marks the restaurant but doesn't accurately predict how fun the menu is. Fried cinnamon rolls (think french toast plus cinnamon roll), the Waffle of Insane Greatness, and the Thick Aretha Frankensteins Pancakes (great pancakes, funny name), as well as biscuits and breakfast burritos, are only part of the menu.

Wild Plum Tea Room (555 Buckhorn Rd., 865/436-3808, www.wildplumtearoom. com, 11am-3pm Thurs.-Sat., $10-19) is a lunch-only restaurant inspired by Austrian teahouses. They serve the Southern classic tomato pie, but the real stars of the menu are the chef's specials. The specials vary daily, but in the past have included lobster pie, a salmon burger, smoked salmon sandwiches, and yellowfin tuna. Unless you want to wait for a while, make a reservation so you can sit down and enjoy your meal, not devour it while you're hangry.

ACCOMMODATIONS

Something about being in Gatlinburg makes me want to stay in a cabin. Fortunately, there are plenty of options whether you're traveling solo, as a pair, or with even the largest of groups. ★ **Mountain Laurel Chalets** (440 Ski Mountain Rd., 865/436-5277, www.

mtnlaurelchalets.com, 2-4-person cabin $139-239, 6-10-person cabin $179-409, 10-24-person lodge $499-1,120) has several lodges and large houses sleeping anywhere from 10 to 24 people if you're traveling with your extended family, or smaller cabins that sleep a couple or small group on a getaway. The cabins are spread out over a huge property, so they're private in addition to being cozy. Some of the cabins, the last ones in line for a refresh, are dated, but others are quite nice inside, so check cabin descriptions online if this matters to you.

Located between Gatlinburg and Pigeon Forge, **Autumn Ridge** (505 Crest Rd., 865/436-4111 or 800/397-4343, www. autumnridgerentals.com, $105-165) has five cabins, each with a two-night minimum and a view you'll come back for. King beds are the norm, as are whirlpool tubs or hot tubs and wood-burning fireplaces (firewood provided). This is a romantic spot and a popular one for honeymoons, so make your reservation sooner rather than later.

Lovely, comfortable, and highly regarded **Laurel Springs Lodge Bed and Breakfast** (204 Hill St., 888/430-9211, www. laurelspringslodge.com, $145-185) has five rooms, all well decorated and comfortable, and a gourmet breakfast is served every morning. Downtown is a short walk away, but even though you're close, you're away from the buzz of Gatlinburg's main drag and can relax when you come back to your room.

★ **The Foxtrot Bed and Breakfast** (1520 Garrett Lane, 865/436-3033, www. thefoxtrot.com, $190-230) is a little different than most B&Bs in that an actual chef prepares breakfast. That's just one thing that sets it apart. The Foxtrot is high on the hill, well above the noise, traffic, and bustle of downtown Gatlinburg, making it a true retreat. There are several packages you can add to your room, like spa packages, honeymoon and anniversary packages, cooking schools, and more.

Camp LeConte Luxury Outdoor Resort (1739 E. Parkway, 865/436-8831, www.

campleconte.com) has a variety of accommodations that include luxury tree houses (from $149), safari tents (from $89), retro campers (from $99), and RV (from $39) and tent (from $29) sites. The open-air tree houses offer views of Mount LeConte and can sleep up to four guests. The safari tents are tents on pads, similar to a "glamping" experience, while the cool retro campers are replica 1961 Shasta Airflytes. There's a pool and small general store on-site as well.

Throughout Gatlinburg, there are a number of chain hotels with prices ranging from budget to mid-range. **Courtyard by Marriott Gatlinburg** (315 Historic Nature Trail, 865/436-2008, www.marriott.com, $189-259) is in a good location for exploring Gatlinburg. The **Gatlinburg Inn** (755 Parkway, 865/436-5133, www.gatlinburginn. com, $129-299) sits one block back from the main drag and is within walking distance to most everything you want to do in Gatlinburg. Finally, the **Hilton Garden Inn** (635 River Rd., 865/436-0048, www.hilton. com, $179-220) is also walkable to downtown and has free parking.

TRANSPORTATION AND SERVICES
Car

Most visitors arrive in Gatlinburg via Newfound Gap Road (U.S. 441) heading west from Cherokee, North Carolina, through Great Smoky Mountains National Park. From Cherokee it's approximately 45 minutes' drive through the park. Gatlinburg is easy to find: one minute you're in the park, the next minute you're in Gatlinburg.

For those driving from the north or west, I-40 is the most convenient road into town. From I-40, take exit 407 onto U.S. 66 south; this road feeds into U.S. 441 and leads past Sevierville and Pigeon Forge to Gatlinburg. This is the easiest and most heavily traveled route into town from I-40. You can avoid the peak-season crowds by taking exit 435 near Knoxville (an hour away) and following U.S. 321 south to Gatlinburg.

Coming from the east on I-40, the best bet is to take exit 443 and drive along the beautiful Foothills Parkway to U.S. 321 south, from which you cruise right into town.

PARKING

Finding parking in Gatlinburg can be quite tough. There are a number of public and private parking lots and garages where you can park your car if you're not staying at a hotel nearby. Parking rates vary depending on public or private ownership, so for affordability, it's often best to stick to the public parking garages at **Ripley's Aquarium of the Smokies** (88 River Rd., 1st hour $1.75, additional hours $1, $6 per day, cash only) and the **McMahan Parking Garage** (520 Parkway, at traffic light no. 3, 1st hour $1.75, additional hours $1, $6 per day).

Air

The **McGhee-Tyson Airport** (TYS, 2055 Alcoa Hwy., Alcoa, TN, 865/342-3000, www.tys.org) outside Knoxville is 42 miles from Gatlinburg. From the airport, head south to Maryville on U.S. 129. Once you're in Maryville, take U.S. 321 north to Pigeon Forge, then turn right and take U.S. 441 to Gatlinburg.

Public Transit

Gatlinburg has a great trolley system that can get you to and from every attraction in

Gatlinburg and nearby Pigeon Forge, including Dollywood. The **Gatlinburg Trolley** (88 River Rd., Suite 101, 865/436-3897, www.gatlinburgtrolley.org, 10:30am-10pm daily Mar.-Apr., 8:30am-midnight daily May-Oct., 10:30am-6pm Sun.-Thurs., 10:30am-10pm Fri.-Sat. Nov.-Feb., extended hours some holiday and event dates) has more than 100 stops in Gatlinburg alone. It's cheap, with most rides only $0.50, but your best bet is to pick up an All Day Trolley Pass ($2) from the **Gatlinburg Welcome Center** (1011 Banner Rd., 865/436-0519, www.gatlinburg.com, 8:30am-7pm daily) or the **Aquarium Welcome Center** (88 River Rd., 9am-9pm daily).

Services

There are two visitors centers in Gatlinburg: the **Gatlinburg Welcome Center** (1011 Banner Rd., 865/277-8957, www.gatlinburg.com, 8:30am-7pm daily) and the **Aquarium Welcome Center** (88 River Rd., 9am-9pm daily). On the radio, **WWST** (93.7 FM) plays the Top 40. **WSEV** (105.5 FM) is an adult contemporary station.

LeConte Medical Center (742 Middle Creek Rd., Sevierville, 865/446-7000, www.lecontemedicalcenter.com) is the nearest hospital, just over 20 minutes away. The **Gatlinburg Police** (1230 E. Parkway, 865/436-5181) are available if the need arises.

Pigeon Forge and Sevierville

The dominating presence in Pigeon Forge and Sevierville is that of Dolly Parton. Her namesake amusement park is in Pigeon Forge, and she was born and raised in Sevierville, where a statue of Dolly stands in front of the courthouse. You'll see her face, hear her music, and maybe even meet one of her many cousins everywhere across these two towns.

These towns have grown a lot since Dolly was born, thanks largely to the popularity of Great Smoky Mountains National Park. More

growth came when the amusement park that would become Dollywood opened its doors, and again when nearby Knoxville hosted the World's Fair. But to keep more than 10 million annual visitors coming back year after year, Pigeon Forge and Sevierville had to become destinations unto themselves, and, for the most part, they've succeeded. Pigeon Forge has become one of the biggest "tourist traps" (which I say not with disdain, but astonishment—the place is a wonderland of

Pigeon Forge

To ✪ DOLLYWOOD
Entrance, Dollywood's
Splash Country, and
DreamMore Resort

449

DOLLYWOOD ✪

To Dolly Parton
Statue, *Titanic*
Pigeon Forge, and
WonderWorks

THE POTTERY
HOUSE CAFÉ
AND GRILLE

OLD MILL SQUARE

OLD MILL
RESTAURANT

DOLLYWOOD
SERVICE ENTRANCE

WHISPERING
PINE
CONDOMINIUMS

Gatlinburg

Golf Course

RIVERSTONE
RESORT AND SPA

0   300 yds

0   300 m

DOLLY PARTON'S
DIXIE STAMPEDE

© MOON.COM

vacation delights) on the East Coast. Want to ride go-karts and go bungee jumping at 9pm on a Wednesday? No problem. Midnight mini golf? Got it. Roller coasters, neon signs, and fudge shops? Pigeon Forge has got you covered. But don't be fooled by all the neon, hotels, and attractions: Pigeon Forge remains a small town, with fewer than 7,000 year-round residents.

In the midst of this swirl of touristy flotsam is a surprising center for engaging with the community's culture: Dollywood. This amusement park has been around in some form or another since the 1960s, though in the early days it was kitsch over culture. As the park matured and expanded, so did its attention to the culture of mountain living. Today the park is home to some great bluegrass and country shows and a good deal of shops and exhibits where Appalachian crafters showcase their skills and their wares.

SIGHTS

TOP EXPERIENCE

★ Dollywood

At **Dollywood** (2700 Dollywood Parks Blvd.,

Pigeon Forge, 800/365-5996, www.dollywood. com, Apr.-Dec., $61-74, parking $15, $18 RVs), you might just catch a glimpse of Dolly Parton walking through the park or performing for the crowds at the park's opening. Even if you don't see her, the park has plenty of rides, cultural stops, shows, and nature experiences to keep you busy.

Dollywood started in 1961, when Rebel Railroad, a small attraction with a steam train, a general store, a blacksmith shop, and a saloon, opened. By 1977, the park had grown and changed hands more than once. Renamed Silver Dollar City, the park eventually caught the attention of Dolly Parton. She became a partner and lent the park her name. Since then, it's become Tennessee's most-visited tourist attraction outside the national park and is consistently named among the top theme parks in the world.

Dollywood has a great look: one part Appalachian village, one part small Southern town. There are tree-lined streets and paths, and several streams follow their courses through the park. You don't see the rides until you're right up on them because they're tucked away in the woods. One of the best-known spots in the park is **Showstreet**, where stages and theaters are always busy with musicians, square dances, and storytellers. There's also a bevy of master craftspeople practicing their Appalachian arts for all to see: blacksmiths, basket weavers, candle makers, and woodworkers. On Showstreet, you may see some of Dolly's relatives playing and singing in shows throughout the year. Seasonal shows include a half-dozen Christmas concerts, Harvest Celebration Southern Gospel, and more.

Also on Showstreet is a carriage, sled, and wagon shop called **Valley Carriage Works.** It takes orders from clients from around the world and builds beautiful, fully functional, historically accurate carriages. At the Museum of the Cherokee Indian in Cherokee, North Carolina, you can see a replica Cherokee wagon that they built to commemorate the 165th anniversary of the Trail of Tears.

Given that the park allows nature to be such a prominent feature in its design, it's no surprise to learn that Dollywood has partnered with the American Eagle Foundation and is authorized by the U.S. Fish and Wildlife Service and the Tennessee Wildlife Resources Agency to possess eagles and other birds for education, exhibition, rehabilitation, and breeding. The 30,000-square-foot **aviary** is home to the nation's largest group of non-releasable bald eagles (many of these birds have been injured and wouldn't survive if released into nature). Daily shows put visitors in close proximity to these incredible birds.

Dollywood has more than 40 rides and attractions that range from kid-friendly to thrilling. My favorites were the Blazing Fury, an indoor roller coaster where you're trying to outrun an out-of-control fire; Thunderhead, a great wooden coaster; and Daredevil Falls, an updated version of the log flume ride. Plenty of snack stands and restaurants are located throughout the park.

Dollywood's Splash Country

Water parks abound in Pigeon Forge and Sevierville, but the best is **Dollywood's Splash Country** (2700 Dollywood Parks Blvd., Pigeon Forge, 800/365-5996, www.dollywood.com, May-Sept., $45-50, parking $15, RVs $18). This water park has 30 waterslides, a lazy river, 3 water play areas for kids, a 7,500-square-foot leisure pool, and a 25,000-square-foot wave pool. There are also concessions and a gift shop, stroller rentals, and lockers to rent.

Dolly Parton Statue

Local artist Jim Gray sculpted a **statue** (125 Court Ave.) that shows Dolly with a wide smile and her guitar, as if she's ready to write a song at any moment. Stop by downtown Sevierville to take a picture with the statue, located on the courthouse lawn.

Tennessee Museum of Aviation

Head to the Gatlinburg Pigeon Forge Airport

in Sevierville to brush up on your aviation history at the **Tennessee Museum of Aviation** (135 Air Museum Way, Sevierville, 866/286-8738, www.tnairmuseum.com, 10am-6pm Tues.-Sat. Mar.-Nov., 10am-5pm Tues.-Sat. Dec.-Feb., adults $12.75, seniors $9.75, ages 6-12 $6.75). Housed in a 35,000-square-foot hangar are a number of exhibits and a dozen historic aircraft, including two airworthy P-47 Thunderbolts (that sometimes take to the air), a MiG-21, and F-86 Saberjet. But the best treat is when you visit the museum and one of the historic World War II aircraft is taking flight.

Titanic Pigeon Forge

One somewhat odd attraction is the *Titanic Pigeon Forge* (2134 Parkway, Pigeon Forge, 417/334-9500 or 800/381-7670, www. titanicpigeonforge.com, from 9am daily, adults $27, ages 5-12 $14). This massive museum includes three decks and 20 galleries in its 30,000 square feet. The galleries feature artifacts salvaged from the sunken luxury ship. There are reproductions of the Marconi wireless room, a first-class suite, and a third-class cabin, as well as a full-scale reproduction of the grand staircase. Touring the ship takes about two hours.

WonderWorks

WonderWorks (100 Music Rd., Pigeon Forge, 865/868-1800, www.wonderworksonline. com, 9am-10pm daily, adults $28, children $19) is another weird one. From the outside, the building appears to be upside down, and inside there are more than 100 interactive exhibits. Some, like the Tesla Coil and the Earthquake Café, are strange and seem dangerous, while others challenge you to use your imagination to solve challenges or test your willpower. While it's definitely geared toward kids in the tween range, adults will find plenty to marvel at. There's also the **Wonders**

of Magic ($19), a family-friendly show of illusions and magic tricks.

ENTERTAINMENT

If you want to wet your whistle in Pigeon Forge, your options are exclusively bars in restaurants. The two best bars happen to be at Smoky Mountain Brewery and at Mellow Mushroom at the Island in Pigeon Forge. **Smoky Mountain Brewery** (2530 Parkway, Suite 15, Pigeon Forge, 865/868-1400, www.smoky-mtn-brewery.com, 11am-midnight Sun.-Thurs., 11am-1am Fri.-Sat.) brews every drop of their draft beer in-house or at one of the three sister restaurants, and they serve up some good grub if you want something to munch on or are hungry enough for a full meal. **Mellow Mushroom** (131 Island Dr., Suite 3101, Pigeon Forge, www.mellowmushroom. com, 11am-midnight daily) specializes in the best national and regional craft beer and some very tasty pizza, subs, and salads. **Iron Boar Saloon** (104 Waldens Main St., Pigeon Forge, 865/429-7779, www.ironboarsaloon. com, 11am-late daily) has a bottom-shelf beer selection, but it's the only biker bar in town. Come for the crowd and to hang out with other bikers and bike lovers. Plus, they have good tacos.

Paula Deen's Lumberjack Feud (2530 Parkway, 865/366-3330, www. lumberjackfeud.com, 9am-10pm daily, from adults $30, children $14) is 90 minutes of log-rolling, chainsaw-revving, pole-climbing, ax-throwing, flannel-attired family fun as two teams of world-class lumberjacks compete in more than a dozen contests of skill and lumberjack acumen. The strength and coordination of the lumberjacks is amazing, and there's no shortage of oohs and aahs as they chop, climb, splash, and try to outdo one another. There's also the **Lumberjack Feud Adventure Park** (from $20) that's a combo aerial adventure park and junior lumberjack activity center. You'll get the chance to compete in a log roll (you're harnessed in, so when you fall off you'll only

---

1: amusement park ride at Dollywood
2: Wonderworks in Pigeon Forge

get a little wet) as well as a pair of 80-foot free-fall jumps and a number of aerial elements to take on.

While the **Hatfield & McCoy Dinner Show** (119 Music Rd., 800/985-5495, www.hatfieldmccoydinnerfeud.com, shows 2pm, 5pm, and 8pm daily, adults $47, ages 3-11 $30) is no accurate portrayal of either the Hatfields (who hail from my home county in West Virginia) or the McCoys (just over the border in Kentucky, near where I grew up) or their now legendary feud, it is a good time and there's plenty of food to be had. You'll pick a side when you buy your tickets, so you enter and sit with either the Hatfields or the McCoys, then the show begins. Take in the songs, dances, corny but legitimately funny (and family-friendly) jokes, and a few stunts while your all-you-can-eat country buffet is served. There's fried chicken, pulled pork barbecue, mashed potatoes, corn on the cob, and dessert.

SHOPPING

There's no shortage of touristy shopping around here, but you can find specialty shops, galleries, and decent shopping if you know where to look.

Pigeon Forge earned part of its name from a forge set up in 1820 by Isaac Love (the other part of its name came from the incredible number of passenger pigeons the early settlers found living along the banks of the Little Pigeon River). A decade later, Love's son established a mill, which is now a National Historic Site that you can visit: The **Old Mill Square** (175 Old Mill Ave., Pigeon Forge, 877/653-6455, www.old-mill.com, hours vary by store) is a collection of shops and restaurants in a cute restored and recreated historic area. **The Old Mill General Store** (865/453-4628, 8am-9pm Mon.-Sat., 8:30am-8pm Sun., hours vary off-season) has all sorts of country provisions, including fresh-ground grains milled next door at the Old Mill. **The Old Mill Farmhouse Kitchen** (865/428-2044, 9am-9pm Mon.-Sat., 9am-8pm Sun., hours vary off-season) also sells a variety of

provisions and ingredients that you need to cook your own country meal at home. They also have a nice pottery shop and gift baskets. You can get your fill of candy at **The Old Mill Candy Kitchen** (865/453-7516, 9am-9pm Mon.-Sat., 9am-8pm Sun., hours vary off-season).

Three Bears General Store (2861 Parkway, Pigeon Forge, 865/453-2775, www.threebearsgeneralstore.com, 9am-9pm Sun.-Thurs., 9am-10pm Fri.-Sat.) has candy and fudge, corny gifts and T-shirts, jams and jellies, pocketknives, jewelry, Christmas decor, and just about anything else you might want to bring home.

At **The Apple Barn Cider Mill and General Store** (230 Apple Valley Rd., Sevierville, 800/421-4606, www.applebarncidermill.com, 9am-5:30pm Mon.-Fri.), you can buy fresh cider, a bushel of just-picked apples, a pie hot from the oven, and more. At this great stop, you'll be on a working orchard with more than 4,000 trees, and you can watch the cider presses at work while you munch on an apple doughnut.

In Sevierville, **Tanger Outlets** (1645 Parkway, Sevierville, 865/453-1053, www.tangeroutlet.com, 9am-9pm Mon.-Sat., 9am-7pm Sun.) has dozens of shops, including brand-name outlets like Coach, Levi's, Michael Kors, Polo Ralph Lauren, Samsonite, Vera Bradley, and Banana Republic.

Smoky Mountain Kniveworks (2320 Winfield Dunn Pkwy., Sevierville, 865/453-5871, www.smkw.com, 10am-6pm Sun.-Thurs., 10am-8pm Fri.-Sat.) has long held a reputation for quality pocketknives, hunting knives, and specialty blades. You can pick up a Swiss Army Knife here, a fishing or kitchen knife, even antique and collectors knives that can cost upward of $4,000.

RECREATION

There is plenty to get into when you're in Pigeon Forge and Sevierville. Of course, you can hike in the national park, but you can also white-water raft, ride a crazy alpine coaster, or even try skydiving, but with a twist.

You can try indoor skydiving at **Flyaway Indoor Skydiving** (3106 Parkway, Pigeon Forge, 877/293-0639, www.flyawayindoorskydiving.com, 10am-8pm daily, 1st flight $34, additional flights $22). Indoor skydiving is done in a vertical wind tunnel—think a silo with giant fans in the base—with an experienced skydiving instructor. After a brief ground school, you'll get dressed and be ready to fly. In the wind tunnel, it's disorienting the first time you leave your feet and assume the skydiving position because you're floating a few feet off the net where you were just standing. Relax, follow your instructor's directions, and enjoy the experience. If you're lucky, before or after your session, you'll get to see some experienced indoor skydivers perform amazing acrobatic tricks that look like something out of *The Matrix* as they whirl around the tunnel with precise control.

One of the most interesting outdoor activities is the **Smoky Mountain Alpine Coaster** (867 Wears Valley Rd., Pigeon Forge, 865/365-5000, www.smokymountainalpinecoaster.com, 10am-10pm Sun.-Thurs., 10am-midnight Fri.-Sat., adults $14, ages 7-12 $11, ages 3-6 $4.50). This odd little quasi-roller coaster puts you in a track-mounted sled complete with an automatic speed control and manual brakes, and then sends you down a one-mile track, spiraling through tight turns and down a few steepish drops. It looks scary, maybe even really scary, from the parking lot, but the ride is more thrilling than frightening, so give it a go.

At **Adventure Park Zip Lines** (1628 Parkway, Sevierville, 877/287-6946, www.adventureparkziplines.com, 10am-4pm daily, $75) the zip routes range from a measly 450 feet to a long 2,000-foot ride. Another option is **Legacy Mountain Zip Lines** (800 Legacy Vista Dr., Sevierville, 888/869-0289, www.legacymountainziplines.com, 8am-7pm daily, $100), with 4.5 miles of zip lines and some runs as long as 2,500 feet that will take you 450 feet into the air.

SpeedZone Fun Park (3315 S. River Rd., Pigeon Forge, 888/352-7507, www.speedzonefunpark.com, 9am-midnight daily, 1 track $10, 3 tracks $20) is one of many go-kart places in Pigeon Forge, but what sets this one apart is the quartet of tracks in one spot. The Slick Track is a fast, paved go-kart track where you drift around every turn. The Tennessee Twister is a curve-riddled wooden track. The Coaster Track has a steep downhill drop at the end for big speed. And the Kids Track is slower, easier, and lets little drivers get behind the wheel.

Though most of the golf you've seen has been of the mini variety, the **Gatlinburg Golf Course** (520 Dollywood Lane, Pigeon Forge, 865/453-3912, www.golf.gatlinburg.com, daily, call for hours and tee times, $30-65) offers a full size round on a beautiful course with some dramatic holes. The signature 12th hole, nicknamed "Sky Hi," is 194 yards long and has a 200-foot drop from the tee to the green, making it a puzzling hole for many golfers and a fun one for all. The pro shop here has everything you'll need to play a round, including a full-service restaurant so you can grab a bite and a beer after your round.

The Island in Pigeon Forge (131 Island Dr., 865/286-0119, www.islandpigeonforge.com, 10am-11pm Mon.-Thurs., 10am-midnight Fri.-Sat., 10am-10pm Sun.) is a tourist extravaganza. You'll find a half-dozen restaurants and as many snack shops, 35 or so stores selling everything from jerky to puzzles to gems, and rides galore. Rides and entertainment options include the 200-foot-tall Great Smoky Mountain Wheel, a mirror maze, and a huge arcade.

FOOD

At Old Mill, there's a quaint collection of shops and a pair of restaurants. **The Old Mill Restaurant** (164 Old Mill Ave., Pigeon Forge, 865/429-3463, www.old-mill.com, 8am-8pm daily Jan.-Feb., 8am-9pm daily Mar.-Nov., 8am-8:30pm Sun.-Thurs. Dec., $13-23) is family-friendly and has a small selection for kids. The Pigeon River flows by right outside the dining room, and this is a bigger draw than the food, which is traditional country fare, though breakfast is pretty good.

★ **The Pottery House Café and Grill** (3341 Old Mill St., Pigeon Forge, 865/453-6002, www.old-mill.com, 11am-9pm daily, brunch 10am-2pm Sat.-Sun., $7-19) is known for its delicious quiche and outstanding desserts. They serve everything from steaks to fried chicken livers (served with Buffalo sauce and blue-cheese dressing) and sandwiches. Rather than trout, which is served by many area eateries, they serve catfish here, which is just as good. If you like what you get for dessert, it's likely you can get a whole cake or pie to take home with you.

A favorite for their German beer and crispy schnitzel is **Wild Bear Tavern** (4236 Parkway, 865/868-0737, www.resort.to, 8am-10pm daily, breakfast $8-12, lunch and dinner $10-18). It doesn't hurt that their breakfast has Corn Flakes-breaded french toast and some pretty tasty breakfast sandwiches, but for me, it's all about lunch and dinner when you can sit on the deck, enjoy a Radler or pilsner, and chow down on a Bavarian bratwurst or traditional schnitzel (pro tip: get it without the sauce).

Poynor's Pommes Frites (131 The Island Dr., Suite 3107, Pigeon Forge, 865/774-7744, 11am-10pm daily, $5-10) may not look like much from the outside, but the food is great. The specialty is the pommes frites (french fries). Done in a Belgian style (fried, cooled, then fried again), they're crispy on the outside and fluffy inside, and served plain, with your choice of sauce or even topped with cheese, bacon, onions, and jalapeños. You can't make a meal of french fries, so Poynor's serves a short menu of German bratwurst served on a German hard roll.

With tasty, relatively inexpensive dishes served at breakfast, lunch, and dinner (and even rare late-night dining), you can't go wrong at **Mel's Diner** (119 Wears Valley Rd., Pigeon Forge, 865/429-2184, www.melsdinerpf.com, 7am-midnight daily, $6-10), serving classic diner food with a side of 1950s

flair. The breakfast plates are quite hearty, and the burgers and sandwiches piled high with toppings, but save room for dessert and order a whopping six-scoop banana split or a more reasonable shake or malt.

All throughout the Smokies, pancake houses rule the breakfast world. A good option to get your fix of pancakes, french toast, waffles, and the like is **Sawyer's Farmhouse Restaurant** (2831 Parkway, 865/366-1090, www.sawyersbreakfast.com, 8am-2pm daily, $4-12). It's breakfast and lunch only, but that works because there are only so many times you can eat pancakes in a day.

For the best burger in town, go to ★ **Local Goat New American Restaurant** (2167 Parkway, 865/366-3035, www.localgoatpf. com, 11am-10pm Mon.-Thurs., 11am-11pm Fri.-Sat., 11am-10pm Sun., $8-26), where the beef is ground fresh and the buns are baked daily. This place is a rarity in Pigeon Forge and Gatlinburg: It's dedicated to staying as local as possible. That means 22 of their 24 draft beers are from regional brewers, and they make almost everything in-house. Expect a good burger, a great entrée salad, and fresh flavors on every plate.

Ready to eat all the catfish you can? That's one thing you can do at **Huck Finn's Catfish** (3330 Parkway, 865/429-3353, www. huckfinnsrestaurant.com, 11:30am-9pm daily Mar.-Dec., 11:30ap-8pm daily Jan.-Feb., closed Thanksgiving Day and Dec. 25, lunch $9-10, buffet $18-20, dinner $11-18). They serve an à la carte menu and have an all-you-can-eat dinner that also includes bottomless "vittles" (read: sides), so you're covered if you want to eat a normal meal or put on a clinic in buffet dining. You'll find fried chicken and catfish, grilled pork and shrimp, chicken livers, even frog legs and alligator tail. If you're a repeat visitor to the Smokies and you're into Huck Finn's menu, it's worth your while to pick up a T-shirt while you're here because they have a little Wall of Fame showing proud Huck Finn's Catfish T-shirt wearers, each of whom received a free meal for playing along.

ACCOMMODATIONS

There are several chain hotels in Pigeon Forge and Sevierville, and for the most part, they're all the same. The **Courtyard Pigeon Forge** (120 Community Center Dr., 865/366-3201, www.marriott.com, $109-269) is convenient to anything you'll want to do in Pigeon Forge. **Wild Bear Inn** (4236 Parkway, 865/453-3530, www.westgateresorts.com, from $77) is at the southeastern edge of Pigeon Forge, making it a breeze to get to Great Smoky Mountains National Park. It's inexpensive and convenient to the park, the shopping, mini golf, and go-karts in Pigeon Forge. Gatlinburg is just a few minutes away.

Whispering Pines Condominiums (205 Ogle Dr., Pigeon Forge, 800/429-4361, www.whisperingpinescondos.com, $150-300) has a great location if you want a front-row seat on the action of Pigeon Forge, or you can opt for mountain views and unwind a little. The condos are large, so they're ideal for families or small groups traveling together, especially if you don't want to break the bank.

An outstanding place to stay is **The Inn at Christmas Place** (119 Christmas Tree Lane, Pigeon Forge, 888/465-9644, www.innatchristmasplace.com, $150-329). Given that the place is permanently festooned with Christmas decorations (they are somewhat subdued January-October) and they play Christmas music on a constant loop, I was surprised at how great this property is. Impeccable landscaping, a robust breakfast, an indoor and outdoor pool complete with a 95-foot waterslide, and a game room are only a few of the reasons this inn is such a find.

The Inn on the River (2492 Parkway, Pigeon Forge, 800/388-1727, www.myinnontheriver.com, $139-240) has 128 rooms, many with a fireplace, in configurations perfect for solo, duo, or family travelers. On the property, you'll find an outdoor pool, a fire pit, covered patio seating, and a riverside walkway.

Inspired by Dolly's own family-filled front porch, ★ **Dollywood's DreamMore Resort** (2525 DreamMore Way, Pigeon Forge, 865/365-1900 or 800/365-5996, www.dollywood.com, from $189) gives guests that same experience, or pretty close. In addition to its 307 rooms, indoor and outdoor pools, restaurants, and views of the Smokies, there are storytelling stations, seasonal and holiday activities, fire pits, a small and homey outdoor movie pavilion, and plenty of things for the kids to do. It's the first hotel on Dollywood property, and staying here has its privileges, like a complimentary shuttle to the park, early Saturday entry to Dollywood, and a complimentary TimeSaver pass, which gives you priority spots in line on 10 different rides and attractions. There are also ticket and room packages available, making it more affordable to go to Dollywood and the water park to have a great stay.

TRANSPORTATION AND SERVICES

Car

If you've followed the Blue Ridge Parkway to this point, you'll be coming into Gatlinburg along U.S. 441 through the national park; on this route, one minute you're in the park, and the next revolution of the wheels you're in Gatlinburg.

For those arriving from the north or west, I-40 is the most convenient road into town. Leave the interstate at exit 407 and hop on U.S. 66 south, a road that feeds into U.S. 441 and leads into Gatlinburg. This is the easiest and most heavily traveled route into town from I-40. You can avoid the peak-season crowds by taking exit 435 near Knoxville (an hour away) and following U.S. 321 south into Gatlinburg.

From the east on I-40, the best bet is to take exit 443 and drive along the beautiful Foothills Parkway to U.S. 321 south, and cruise right into town.

Air

The **McGhee Tyson Airport** (TYS, 2055 Alcoa Hwy., Alcoa, 865/342-3000, www.tys.org), outside Knoxville, is 42 miles from Gatlinburg. From the airport, head south to Maryville on U.S. 129. Once you're in

Maryville, take U.S. 321 north to Pigeon Forge, then turn right and take U.S. 441 to Gatlinburg.

Public Transportation

Gatlinburg has a great trolley system that can get you to and from every attraction in Gatlinburg and nearby Pigeon Forge, including Dollywood. The **Gatlinburg Trolley** (865/436-3897, www.gatlinburgtrolley.org, 10:30am-10pm daily Mar.-Apr., 8:30am-midnight daily May-Oct., 10:30am-6pm Sun.-Thurs., 10:30am-10pm Fri.-Sat. Nov.-Feb.) has more than 100 stops in Gatlinburg alone and will get you to where you need to go. Most routes cost $0.50 per ride; a few cost $1-2. There's also a $2 day pass.

Services

The **Pigeon Forge Welcome Center** (1950 Parkway, 800/251-9100, www.mypigeonforge. com, 8:30am-5pm Mon.-Sat., 1pm-5pm Sun.)

is located at traffic light no. 0 on Parkway. Here, and at the **Pigeon Forge Information Center** (3107 Parkway, 865/453-8574, 8:30am-5pm Mon.-Fri.), you can find all the information on the area and volunteers ready to help you plan your time here.

The folks at the **Sevierville Chamber of Commerce Visitors Center** (110 Gary Wade Blvd., 865/453-6411 or 888/738-4378, www.visitsevierville.com, 8:30am-5:30pm Mon.-Sat., 9am-6pm Sun.) are ready to help with trip planning or simply pointing you in the right direction and helping you enjoy your vacation.

If you need a hospital, **LeConte Medical Center** (742 Middle Creek Rd., Sevierville, 865/446-7000, www.lecontemedicalcenter. com) is your best bet. There are two police departments here: the **Sevier County Sheriff's Office** (106 W. Bruce St., 865/453-4668) and the **Pigeon Forge Police Department** (225 Pine Mountain Rd., 865/453-9063).

Knoxville

Perhaps best known among college football fans, Knoxville is the biggest city in East Tennessee and a major travel hub granting access to Great Smoky Mountains National Park and, beyond that, the Blue Ridge Parkway. Unlike Nashville and Memphis, which have national reputations as music towns, Knoxville's comes from the University of Tennessee Volunteers athletics, but the city is also home to the historic Tennessee Theatre and the Bijou Theatre, and has a very lively music scene of its own.

In 1982, the World's Fair came along and ignited Knoxville's hometown pride, and many residents and business owners saw what Knoxville could become. By the early 2000s, downtown Knoxville resonated with business owners. Restaurants and shops opened in spruced-up buildings from yesteryear. Bars followed, and boutiques flourished. Soon, downtown had turned into what it is today—a fun cultural center for the city.

SIGHTS
★ East Tennessee History Center

In the heart of downtown, there's a great little museum telling the story of more than 200 years of East Tennessee's history. The **East Tennessee History Center** (601 S. Gay St., 865/215-8830, www.easttnhistory.org, 9am-4pm Mon.-Fri., 10am-4pm Sat., 1pm-5pm Sun., adults $5, seniors $4, under age 17 free, free Sun.) has exhibits on the Cherokee people, the local involvement in skirmishes and battles during the Civil War, notable enslaved people and formerly enslaved people from the region, the origins of country music, and many displays and scenes showing Knoxville throughout the years. There are also displays on logging and mining, two vocations important to the region, as well as Oak Ridge National Laboratory, where important work on World War II's Manhattan Project went on.

Downtown Knoxville

To Fountain City ↑ 33 441

0   0.25 mi
0   0.25 km

To Knoxville
Hostel, Cook Loft
and Old City

KNOXVILLE ★ VISITORS CENTER
STOCK & BARREL
MARKET SQUARE
NOT WATSON'S KITCHEN + BAR
THE TOMATO HEAD
THE FRENCH MARKET
CAFE 4
KRUTCH PARK
TENNESSEE THEATRE
CIVIC AUDITORIUM AND COLISEUM
WOMEN'S BASKETBALL HALL OF FAME ★
KNOXVILLE MUSEUM OF ART ✪ ★
THE OLIVER HOTEL
EAST TENNESSEE HISTORY CENTER
JAMES WHITE FORT ★
SUNSPHERE
HILTON KNOXVILLE
BIJOU THEATRE
FEDERAL COURTHOUSE
World's Fair Park
CITY/COUNTY BUILDING
BLOUNT MANSION
FORT SANDERS
JAMES AGEE PARK
THREE RIVERS RAMBLER
VOLUNTEER LANDING
UNIVERSITY CENTER
MAPLEHURST INN
LOWER
NEYLAND STADIUM
River
FRANK H. McClung MUSEUM
FORT DICKERSON
THOMPSON-BOLING ARENA
Tennessee River
To South Knoxville ↓

UNIVERSITY OF TENNESSEE

© MOON.COM

KNOXVILLE

TENNESSEE GATEWAYS

The museum itself is great, but also note the wonderful neoclassical Italianate architecture of the building as you walk in. It's Knoxville's old Customs House, built in 1874. Since then, it has served several purposes—as recourthouse, a post office, and the TVA offices. Like many buildings around town, it's built with Tennessee marble.

★ Knoxville Museum of Art

The **Knoxville Museum of Art** (1050 Worlds Fair Park Dr., 865/525-6101, www.knoxart.org, 10am-5pm Tues.-Sat., 1pm-5pm Sun., donation) is a three-story showcase of the art and artists of East Tennessee.

A huge exhibition, *Cycle of Life: Within the Power of Dreams and the Wonder of Infinity,* from renowned glass artist Richard Jolley, hangs on the walls and ceiling of the ground floor, and a colorful, impressive element of it—a nebula of colored glass orbs—can be seen as you walk through the museum doors. On the top level, two galleries show historical and contemporary works created by artists from or inspired by East Tennessee. The main level has another pair of galleries with rotating exhibits of national, international, and regional works as well as single-artist shows and themed collections, like the assembly of more than a dozen pieces of amazing blown and cast glass sculptures.

★ Tennessee Theatre

The **Tennessee Theatre** (604 S. Gay St., 865/684-1200, www.tennesseetheatre.com, box office 10am-5pm Mon.-Fri., 10am-2pm Sat., show times and prices vary) is magnificent. In October 1928, this fabulous space opened its doors to rave reviews. The exterior features a classic marquee, and the inside puts any contemporary movie theater or music hall to shame. The Spanish-Moorish-style interior was painstakingly restored to its original grandeur. Today, when you walk into the lobby, huge chandeliers twinkle high above. The ornate ceiling and walls complement the marble floor. Twin staircases lead to the balcony upstairs, and inside the theater, there's more ornate wood and plasterwork. On stage, there's a gorgeous Wurlitzer organ from the same era as the theater. The best part is the theater actually has someone who knows how to play it, and play it well. Shows here vary from national and international musicians to plays and stage shows to a handful of films.

Sunsphere

When the World's Fair came in 1982, the city was transformed. The most dramatic element is a recognizable symbol of the city. The **Sunsphere** (810 Clinch Ave., 865/215-8160, www.worldsfairpark.org, 9am-10pm daily, free) is a 266-foot-tall tower topped by a huge golden ball. Inside the ball are private offices, a lounge, and a great observation deck that allows a 360-degree view of Knoxville.

Zoo Knoxville

Zoo Knoxville (3500 Knoxville Zoo Dr., 865/637-5331, www.zooknoxville.org, 9am-5pm daily, adults $20, seniors and ages 2-12 $17, parking $5) has more than 900 animals from all over the world, including the expected zoo animals and some surprises. There are a number of red pandas here (the zoo is a breeding facility for them), a giraffe you can feed, and Budgie Landing, an enclosed aviary in Clayton Family Kids Cove that's filled with what seems like a million budgies (a parakeet, a type of small parrot) flying around.

The MUSE

Adjacent to Zoo Knoxville is **The MUSE** (516 N. Beaman St., 865/594-1494, www.themuseknoxville.org, 9am-noon Mon., 9am-5pm Tues.-Fri., 10am-5pm Sat.-Sun., ages 2-64 $8, under age 2 and over age 64 free), Knoxville's kid-centric science museum. There's the only public planetarium in the city, a space exploration play area called the *U.S.S. Muse*, a tinkerer-maker space, and performance and STEM activity areas. It's a well done museum and one of those perfect rainy day things for parents and grandparents to have in the entertainment arsenal.

Women's Basketball Hall of Fame

Given the basketball prowess of the University of Tennessee Lady Vols and famed former coach Pat Summitt, Knoxville is a fitting place for the **Women's Basketball Hall of Fame** (700 Hall of Fame Dr., 865/633-9000, www.wbhof.com, 10am-5pm Mon.-Sat. May-Labor Day, 11am-5pm Tues.-Fri., 10am-5pm Sat. Labor Day-Apr., adults $8, seniors and ages 6-15 $6). This facility, the only one devoted entirely to women's basketball achievements at all levels, opened in 1999 and celebrates the rich history of women's basketball. The exhibits here are more than just a plaque and write-up on Hall of Fame members; there are interactive areas like the basketball court, where you can practice passing and dribbling skills or shoot a few balls at baskets both contemporary and from the earliest days of the game. Other exhibits include displays honoring current NCAA national champions and a set of mannequins dressed in uniforms from over the years. There's also a gift shop where you can pick up basketballs autographed by Hall of Fame members. The building is hard to miss—one end has the world's largest

---

1: Tennessee Theatre **2:** Sunsphere

basketball, which appears to be dropping into a net.

Haunted Knoxville Ghost Tours

Haunted Knoxville Ghost Tours (36 Market Square, 865/377-9677, www. hauntedknoxville.net, adults $40, ages 9-12 $35, tour dates and times vary, reserve online) is more than just a person walking around telling some "scary" stories filled with local color; these guides offer one of the leading historical and investigation-based ghost tours. They've dug up some juicy, and creepy, stories that reveal a hidden side of this friendly city. And they continue to carry out investigations, bringing with them on every tour a host of tools used to gather information on the paranormal.

ENTERTAINMENT AND EVENTS
Nightlife

Hops & Hollers (937 N. Central St., 865/312-5733, www.hopsandhollers.com, 2pm-midnight Mon.-Thurs., 2pm-late Fri., 10am-late Sat., 11am-10pm Sun.) is a good place to start. This fun little craft beer bar has more than 100 bottles and cans ready to go and 32 beers on draft. The bartenders know their brews and can make reliable recommendations (when in doubt, ask for a tasting pour). Musicians stop by on a regular basis, and food trucks are here just about every night of the week.

For a long time, Tennessee lagged behind North Carolina in terms of brewery density and diversity, but the whole state has come a long way. Knoxville's brewery scene in particular has grown a lot. The Knoxville Area Brewers Association has the **Knoxville Ale Trail** (www.knoxvillebrewers.com), with 18 stops in and around the city. The Ale Trail works like this: Pick up a passport at one of several locations (Hops & Hollers is one), grab a pint and get a stamp at the breweries, and redeem your passport for cash and prizes. OK, there's no cash, only prizes, but do you really need a reward for visiting breweries?

One of the stops on the Knoxville Ale Trail is **Crafty Bastard Brewery** (6 Emory Place, 865/755-2358, www.craftybastardbrewery. com, 6pm-10pm Mon., 4pm-midnight Tues.-Fri., 2pm-midnight Sat., 2pm-9pm Sun.), which has a reputation for being one of the more experimental breweries in Knoxville. Their lineup—complete with an extra-roasty Imperial Milk Stout, an Earl Grey Tea pale ale, a dill pickle sour, and even weirder things on deck—puts them on the fringe of most breweries here, but their selection of IPAs and double IPAs makes up for it. They also have food trucks every night of the week (every one features some kind of vegan or vegetarian option), and music most Friday nights.

Hexagon Brewing Company (1002 Dutch Valley Dr., Suite 101, 865/888-5138, www.hexagonbrewing.com, 4pm-9pm Mon.-Thurs., 2pm-11pm Fri., noon-11pm Sat., 2pm-8pm Sun.), also on the Ale Trail, takes their name from the owner's love of a particular hexagonal-shaped fly-fishing rod and beekeeping (yet somehow they don't make a mead). They brew up a half-dozen beers on the regular—a black IPA, dunkelwizen, kolsch, American pale ale, alt bier, and spicy rye IPA—in addition to seasonal brews that include a Mexica lager, spiced sweet potato ale, and a smoked pepper beer. They also have a kitchen ($5-15) serving wings, Frito Pie, and snacks.

Casual Pint (421 Union Ave., 865/951-2160, www.thecasualpint.com, 3pm-11pm Mon.-Thurs., 3pm-2am Fri., noon-2am. Sat., noon-11pm Sun.) brews several beers in-house and always has a deep lineup on draft. Grab your Ale Trail Passport, then go for a sampler flight or the pint of your choice, or fill up a growler to take your brew home with you.

In the historic old city is a chic spot for wine and charcuterie: **Old City Wine Bar** (108 W. Jackson Ave., 865/851-7676, www. oldcitywinebar.com, 5pm-11pm Tues.-Thurs., 5pm-midnight Fri.-Sat., 11am-3pm Sat.-Sun., $4-28) has 48 wines by the glass, 150 bottles,

Tennessee's Unsung Music Town

Knoxville gets short shrift when folks talk about Tennessee music. Ever eclipsed by Nashville and overlooked by bluegrass and mountain string band lovers for spots like Gatlinburg and Pigeon Forge, Knoxville is often forgotten. But no more. The music scene in this hip Southern town is lively and growing livelier by the minute. Bands like The Black Lillies, with their mountain-influenced indie rock, and The Black Cadillacs, who take a more bluesy spin, have made a name for themselves nationally in recent years, playing at Bonnaroo and the Grand Ole Opry.

All across town you'll find buskers playing on the street, bands tucked into restaurants and bars, and free concerts on Market Square during the summer. Jam sessions pop up and musicians flow freely from one impromptu band to another until they find the perfect fit. Two historic venues—The **Tennessee Theatre** (the state's official theater, and a stunning place to see a band) and the **Bijou Theatre**—host concerts with clockwork regularity.

Music festivals, like **Big Ears Festival** (www.bigearsfestival.com), **Smoky Mountain Music Fest** (www.smmfestival.com), and **Rhythm N Blooms Fest** (www.rhythmnbloomsfest.com), celebrate the sounds of the city and bring in visiting bands and music fans from all over.

Make it a point while you're in town to take in one of the daily free shows at **WDVX-FM,** where their noontime Blue Plate Special concert series brings in local and regional acts to play for a live radio broadcast in front of a studio audience.

a lovely cocktail list, and a good assortment of local and regional craft beer. They have drag brunches once a month, do special dinners with their sister restaurant Rebel Kitchen, and hold tastings and classes on wine, whiskey, and beer.

At **The EDGE of Knoxville** (7211 Kingston Pike, 865/602-2094, 5pm-3am daily), you'll find performances of almost any kind. Live music, drag shows, karaoke? They got it. Trivia, comedy, bar games? Got that too. Toss in friendly people and good drinks, and it works.

Peter Kern Library (407 Union Ave., 865/521-0050, www.theoliverhotel.com, 4pm-midnight Mon.-Tues., 4pm-1am Wed.-Fri., 11am-2am Sat., 11am-midnight Sun.), the bar in The Oliver Hotel, names their drinks after literary characters. The bar is modeled after a library: To read the menu, you have to crack open an old book. It's a cozy bar with boozy and flavorful cocktails—what's not to love?

Performing Arts

The **Bijou Theatre** (803 S. Gay St., 865/522-0832, www.knoxbijou.org, ticket prices vary) is one of Knoxville's most important venues

for live musical performances. Everyone from the Marx Brothers and Dolly Parton to The Ramones and Dave Matthews played here, and the audience at one time included President Andrew Jackson. The Bijou (well, the building anyway) dates to 1817 and has been a hotel and tavern, a place for social gatherings, and an object of some consternation for its myriad owners until it finally opened as a theater in 1908. A vaudeville stage for a long time (with a rare-for-the-time policy of admitting black patrons to the gallery seating), the Bijou showed films on occasion, but that stopped when the Tennessee Theatre opened up the street. The builders of the Tennessee bought the Bijou, then sold it with one caveat: the Bijou couldn't be used as a theater for the next five years. After various incarnations, the Bijou reopened as a fully renovated theater in 2006.

The Concourse at The International (944 Blackstock Ave., 865/851-7878, www.concourseknox.com, showtimes and prices vary) brings in musical acts from heavy metal to rap to DJs and more. It's a cool building, once an International Harvester tractor showroom and then home to the Great Atlantic

Shoe Company, now it's a concert and events venue and an example of something that's going on all across Knoxville: people who love their town working to give old buildings a new purpose.

Festivals and Events

Knoxville has several great events throughout the year, and two good ones are March's **Big Ears Festival** (www.bigearsfestival. com, general admission from $65, some individual events ticketed separately), a celebration of music and movies, and the **Tennessee Valley Fair** (3301 E. Magnolia Ave., 865/215-1471, www.tnvalleyfair.org, adults $8, ages 6-11 $6) in mid-September. Big Ears has a robust schedule with screenings going on at more than a dozen venues around town, including some overnight shows that blend ambient, psychedelic, electronic, and live performances with shifting visuals going on simultaneously. At the Tennessee Valley Fair you'll find a traditional agricultural fair, but bigger. And there are concerts, rides, funnel cake and fair food galore, and a good time to be had.

Film is big in Knoxville, and the **Knoxville Film Festival** (www.knoxvillefilmfest.com, festival pass $50, film blocks from $10) takes place in mid-September. In addition to excellent film screenings, there's a student filmmaking competition and a high-stakes seven-minute film competition. The 7-Day Shootout happens in August, when teams of filmmakers gather in Knoxville to develop their scripts and shoot them. The completed films are shown at the festival; the grand prize winner takes home $20,000 to turn their seven-minute film into a full feature.

SHOPPING

Market Square provides a central square (actually, a rectangle) around which people can gather. Just one block off Gay Street, this excellent little shopping and dining district is always busy. Summer concerts, buskers, and a small fountain for the kids to play in draw folks here, and the variety of people walking by and stores to peruse make it easy to kill time while waiting for your table to be ready. There are a half-dozen restaurants on the square, and close to a dozen shops, including the **Mast General Store** (865/546-1336, www.mastgeneralstore.com, 10am-6pm Mon.-Wed., 10am-9pm Thurs.-Fri., 9am-9pm Sat., noon-6pm Sun.), where you can buy everything from camping gear to home goods to penny candy; **Earth to Old City** (865/522-8270, www.earthtooldcity.com, 10am-9pm Sun.-Thurs., 10am-10pm Fri.-Sat.), which carries all sorts of odd and funky home decor, some of which may be more at home in a dorm room than your house; and **Bliss** (865/329-8868, www.shopinbliss.com, 10am-9pm Mon.-Thurs., 10am-10pm Fri.-Sat., 11am-8pm Sun.), which sells home goods and lifestyle accessories. The **Market Square Farmer's Market** (11am-2pm Wed. and 9am-2pm Sat. May-Nov.) shows up in late spring, bringing with it dozens of farmers and craftspeople selling their wares, edible and otherwise.

Nothing Too Fancy (435 Union Ave., 865/951-2916, www.nothingtoofancy.com, 10am-9pm Mon.-Fri., 10am-9pm Sat., 11am-6pm Sun.) has some very cool T-shirts and other silk-screened goods designed by local artists. Reflecting the culture, in-jokes, and vibe of Knoxville in their work, the shirts are fun, even for those not in the know.

Nostalgia (5214 Homberg Dr., 865/584-0832, www.nostalgiaknoxville.com, 11am-6pm daily) calls itself a "vintique market," as they sell both vintage items and antiques. Portmanteau aside, it's a cool shop. Inside, you'll find mid-century modern furniture, vinyl records, vintage clothing, shabby chic furniture, and more, from around 30 vendors with well-stocked spaces.

RECREATION

The star of Knoxville's recreational scene is **Ijams Nature Center** (2915 Island Home Ave., 865/577-4717, www.ijams.org, grounds 8am-dusk daily, visitors center 9am-5pm Mon.-Sat., 11am-5pm Sun.). This 300-acre urban wilderness is laced with hiking and single-track mountain biking trails, and former quarries to explore on foot or even paddle around; it's also dog friendly. This vast, wild space is a strange thing so close to the city, but people love it. At any time of any day, there are walkers, hikers, trail runners, bikers, families, couples, and singles on the trails here. From Ijams Nature Center, you can connect with a larger, nearly contiguous loop some 40 miles long. Grab a map when you come in or download one and plan your route ahead of time, or you could just bring some water and your camera and wander.

World's Fair Park (www.worldsfairpark. org) is the best city park in Knoxville. This 10-acre park has walking paths, a small lake, open grassy spaces, soccer fields, fountains, and a gorgeous stream running right down the middle. It's the home of the Sunsphere and Tennessee Amphitheatre, and at the north end of the park, past a fantastically large fountain, is a 4,200-square-foot playground. The playground and fountain get pretty crowded with kids, but there are other places you can go if you're traveling without a few of your own.

The **University of Tennessee Knoxville** (www.utk.edu) has a loyal (some say rabid) fan base. UT fields more than a dozen varsity-level teams including football (six national championships), men's and women's basketball (eight national championships for the women's team), soccer, rowing, volleyball, and more. If you want to cheer on the UT Volunteers (the Vols, if you want to sound like a local), **tickets** (865/656-1200, www.allvols.com) are available for football season (Sept.-late Nov.), basketball season (Nov.-Mar.), tennis (Sept.-Apr.), soccer and volleyball (Aug.-mid-Nov.), and swimming and diving (Sept.-late Feb.). Men's basketball tickets range $7-45, women's basketball $10-20. Football tickets are both difficult to come by and pricey, as most games sell out or come close; some tickets fetch upward of $1,000 a seat on resale markets, with the only tickets available to some games. The football team plays at **Neyland Stadium** (1300 Phillip Fulmer Way), basketball at **Thompson-Boling Arena** (1600 Phillip Fulmer Way), baseball at **Lindsey Nelson Stadium** (1511 Pat Head Summitt St.), and softball at **Sherri Parker Lee Stadium** (2323 Stephenson Dr.); more information on facilities and teams is available at www.utsports. com.

FOOD

Knoxville Food Tours (865/201-7270, www. knoxvillefoodtours.com, $99) shows off some of the best spots to drink and dine in downtown Knoxville. Tour dates are Friday and Saturday afternoons and evenings, but custom tours are available any day. The walk's not far—generally under a mile—and you get to find a place to have dinner, all while under the tutelage of a local foodie.

★ **Dead End BBQ** (3621 Sutherland Ave., 865/212-5655, www.deadendbbq.com, 11am-9pm Sun.-Thurs., 11am-10pm Fri.-Sat., $8-23) was started by a group of guys who would get together and make barbecue. Turns out they were onto something good. After their neighbors and wives praised them enough, they decided to enter a barbecue competition. This obsession turned into a restaurant, and a good one at that. Everything they do here is top-notch, so unless the brisket or ribs or some other dish catches your eye, get the sampler plate. They have one dish you don't see very often—beef brisket burnt ends. Far from being burnt, these succulent little morsels are trimmings off the brisket, and they go down easy. The sauce here is fantastic, and the sides outstanding. Save room for dessert; the banana pudding is so rich and thick that it's more like cheesecake.

The burgers at **Nick & J's Cafe** (1526 Lovell Rd., 865/766-5453, www.nickandjscafe.com, 7am-4pm daily, $2.50-11) may find a spot on your personal Top Five Burger list. If you're not a burger fan, something on the menu at this diner will find a place on your own "best of" list. Maybe it's the egg sandwich, the stack of buttermilk pancakes, or the breakfast bowl; could be the grilled Reuben or the all-veggie pita. Whatever it is, it'll be good and you'll come back for more.

Rebel Kitchen (108 W. Jackson Ave., 865/851-7676, 5pm-9pm Tues.-Thurs., 5pm-10pm Fri.-Sat., brunch at Old City Wine Bar Sat.-Sun., $13-25) and sister restaurant Old City Wine Bar share a food philosophy and a space in Knoxville's Old City. Philosophically they're both dedicated to providing exceptional experiences and expanding the palate of their guests. A small menu from local providers means high quality and a selection of items that's varied but focused. You'll find duck with sweet potatoes, stinging nettles, and chanterelle mushrooms when they're in season. Trout from North Carolina with squash and purslane provide a seafood fix. And ingredients like veal find they do double duty appearing as a carpaccio starter and a rib-eye main.

If you're looking for soul food or a Knoxville take on Hot Chicken, you need **Jackie's Dream Café** (1008 E. Woodland Ave., 865/219-5789, www.jackiesdreamcafe.com, 11am-8pm Wed.-Sat., from 11am until they sell out Sun., $1.75-13). It's cheap, only $1.75 for a fried chicken leg or tender, and only $2.25 for the same in Hot Chicken. But why buy chicken by the piece when you can get a whole chicken meal, baked spaghetti with corn and a salad, smothered chicken, ribs, ox tail, or a pork-chop meal? And if you're really hungry, go for one of the chicken boxes (regular only, $17-42) that can feed an army.

When you're talking soul food and barbecue, you can't skip the little mom-and-pop spots. Often these are my favorite as they've got their 'cue down pat and a loyal following of locals to prove it. **Chandler's Deli** (3101 Magnolia Ave., 865/595-0212, www.chandlersstore.com, 11am-3pm Mon., 11am-7:30pm Tues.-Thurs., 11am-8:30pm Fri., noon-8:30pm Sat., noon-6pm Sun., $1.15-20) has that loyal following, great soul food, and some tasty barbecue. In a former Taco Bell (you can't miss the distinct shape, even though they've painted it pink), their fried chicken, salmon patties (a dish that spans the soul food and Appalachian cuisine gap), chicken and dumplings, pigs feet (also called trotters), and chitterlings are great. They serve pulled pork barbecue and ribs by the bone, so you know it's legit.

House-made pasta and seasonally-driven Italian food is on order at **Emilia Italian** (16 Market Square, 865/313-2472, www.emiliaknox.com, 5pm-9:30pm Tues.-Thurs., 5pm-10pm Fri.-Sat., 5pm-9pm Sun., $12-34) on Market Square. Genovese-style fisherman's stew, pan-roasted salmon, a pork blade steak, orecchiette with Bolognese ragù, sensational gnocchi, campanelle and even fusilli round out the dinner offerings, but don't forget dessert, where the panna cotta and semifreddo are in a perpetual competition for best way to end your meal.

The French Market (412 Clinch Ave., 865/540-4372, www.thefrenchmarket knoxville.com, 8am-3pm Mon., 8am-9pm Tues.-Thurs., 8am-10pm Fri.-Sat., 9am-3pm Sun., $3-12) has breakfast and lunch daily, and as the city's first authentic crepe restaurant, it's where you have to go if you're a fan of these French staples. Dinner is good too, with a nice array of dishes that will transport you to France with a bite. They have a second location in **West Knoxville** (161 Brooklawn St., 865/288-7912, 9am-3pm Mon., 8am-8pm Tues.-Thurs., 8am-9pm Fri.-Sat., 9am-3pm Sun.)

When you have a hankering for falafel, hummus, or other Mediterranean flavors, look no farther than **Yassin's Falafel House** (706 Walnut St., 865/219-1462, 11am-9pm Mon.-Sat., $5-12). There are only a few things you can get, but I always consider that to be a good sign—it means they are perfecting everything on the small menu, and Yassin's has perfected, or come close to perfecting, the falafel. Whether you get falafel (just go ahead and get falafel), chicken, gyro, or vegetables in a sandwich or salad or on a plate, you'll be hooked and you'll be back.

Café 4 (4 Market Square, 865/544-4144, www.cafe4ms.com, 7am-9:30pm Mon.-Thurs., 7am-10:30pm Fri., 9am-10:30pm Sat., 9am-8:30pm Sun., $11-23) has more than just a great-looking menu for lunch and dinner.

Their bakery makes macarons and other treats for breakfast or snacks; The Mezz—the cocktail lounge—shakes up some excellent drinks; and they've got space to hang out. The black-bean burger is a solid choice, as is the Tomato Duet, a dish that combines fried green tomatoes and tomato jam to make a fine sandwich. If you want something heartier, go for the blackened fish and grits, meatloaf, or fried chicken.

Not Watson's Kitchen + Bar (15 Market Square, 865/766-4848, www.notwatsons.com, 11am-10pm Mon.-Thurs., 11am-11pm Fri.-Sat., 11am-9pm Sun., $9-22), an eatery on Knoxville's Market Square, dishes up plates of tasty favorites like fried green tomatoes, fish-and-chips, beef short ribs, blackened mahimahi, and chicken and waffles. Get a beer off their long list of drafts and bottles, then order something to eat while you watch the people on the Square.

When a former rock musician opens a restaurant, you expect it to have a lot of personality, and ★ **Sweet P's Barbecue & Soul House** (3725 Maryville Pike, 865/247-7748, www.sweetpbbq.com, 11am-8pm Tues.-Thurs., 11am-9pm Fri.-Sat., noon-7pm Sun., $4-22) delivers. Owner and pit master Chris Ford ate in every barbecue joint he could find while on tour with his band and began developing recipes long before he had the idea for a restaurant. When the time came to open Sweet P's, he was ready. This is some fine barbecue, whether it's the ribs, the brisket, or the sides. The potato salad is good and the mac and cheese done just right, but the coleslaw is out of this world. Good news if you're going to stick to downtown Knoxville: **Sweet P's Downtown Dive** (410 W. Jackson Ave., 865/281-1738, www.sweetpbbq.com, 11am-9pm Tues.-Thurs., 11am-10pm Fri.-Sat., noon-9pm Sun., $5-20) lets you get your fix of 'cue without venturing far from the city's heart.

Pete's Coffee Shop (540 Union Ave., 865/523-2860, www.petescoffeeshop.com, 6:30am-2:30pm Mon.-Fri., 7am-2pm Sat., $2-8) is a diner that's dirt-cheap and super tasty. Their french toast is exceptional, as are their pancakes, and for lunch, Pete's Supreme (ham and melted Swiss on a hoagie) is excellent, as is the patty melt.

At **The Tomato Head** (12 Market Square, 865/637-4067, www.thetomatohead.com, 11am-9:30pm Mon.-Thurs., 11am-10:30pm Fri., 10am-10:30pm Sat., 10am-9pm Sun., brunch 10am-3pm Sat.-Sun., $3-28) you can sit outside, weather permitting, and watch the crowds on Market Square while you eat your pizza. The menu here features pizzas, sandwiches, burritos, and salads, but stick to pizza—not because the other stuff is bad, but because the pizza is so good. You can build your own or choose one of their topping combinations. Odd combos like fresh spinach and black beans, lamb sausage and sundried tomatoes, and smoked salmon and pesto actually go down quite easily.

The folks at **SoKno Taco Cantina** (3701 Sevierville Pike, 865/851-8882, www.soknota.co, 11am-1am Sun.-Wed., 11am-2am Thurs.-Sat., late-night menu 10pm-1am Sun.-Wed., 11pm-2am Thurs.-Sat., lunch and dinner $3.25-10, late night $3-8.50) make some bold claims about their food: "People lose their minds" for it, their selection of drinks is "more than you need." I like their attitude, and I like that they back it up. The menu is pretty basic—tacos, tamales, burritos, and quesadillas; chicken cod, shrimp, steak, chorizo, carnitas, and tofu—but they deliver on the plate. And those drinks? True to the boast, there's a great draft, bottle, and can selection of beer.

Stock & Barrel (35 Market Square, 865/766-2075, www.thestockandbarrel.com, 11am-late daily, $7-16) has an unparalleled bourbon selection, a list of burgers that are as tasty as they are creative, to-die-for fries, and a line out the door. Seriously, even if you make a reservation, you'll wait for a seat, but it's worth it because once you get in, you won't want to leave. Get a flight of bourbon and whatever burger pushes your buttons, and enjoy.

The best option for sushi in Knoxville is **Nama Sushi Bar** (506 S. Gay St., 865/633-8539, www.namasushibar.com, 11am-11pm

Tues.-Wed., 11am-midnight Thurs., 11am-1m Fri.-Sat., noon-10pm Sun., $4-24). Their fish is always fresh, and they serve both traditional rolls and rolls that are a little more inventive. The Moon Special Roll and the Orange Crush go pretty far afield from your basic roll and make for a delicious bite. This place gets crowded, especially on weekends or when Knoxville is hopping, so get there early or make a reservation.

Wild Love Bakehouse (1625 N. Central St., 865/200-8078, www.wildlovebakehouse.com, 7am-6pm Mon.-Fri., 8am-6pm Sat.-Sun., $3-12) bakes up fresh breads and pastries every day and keeps a fresh rotating menu to match. Every day the menu is a little different, so you might find a butter croissant one day and a rye reuben open-face croissant the next, or blueberries or strawberries adorning or filling a pastry, even olive oil cake, tarts and pies, or, if you're lucky, kougin amann.

ACCOMMODATIONS

Outstanding boutique hotel ★ **The Oliver Hotel** (407 Union Ave., 865/521-0050, www.theoliverhotel.com, $165-410) has impeccable service and amazing rooms—everything is done to a luxurious, but not ostentatious, level. When you first find the hotel, you'll likely walk right past it as it blends in with the rest of the block almost seamlessly. Originally built in 1876 as a bakery, it was converted into a hotel for the World's Fair. There are 24 guest rooms with wet bars, coffee service, and fabulous bedding.

The Tennessean (531 Henley St., 844/413-0026 or 865/232-1800, www.thetennesseanhotel.com, $209-599) overlooks World's Fair Park and offers rooms that are truly luxurious. Whether you stay in an ordinary room or in the Governor's Suite ($3,000), you'll find sumptuous linens, tasteful decoration, and an attentive staff.

Large rooms where you can spread out and stay affordably for a few days make **Home 2 Suites by Hilton Knoxville West** (380 N. Peters Rd., 865/973-9444, www.hilton.com, $150-190) a good selection for spending some

time in Knoxville and exploring this part of the Smokies and the Tennessee mountains.

Hilton Knoxville (501 W. Church Ave., 865/523-2300, www3.hilton.com, $175-355) is only two blocks off Gay Street and has fantastic rooms. With on-site dining, a Starbucks right in the lobby, and parking next door, it's the best of the name-brand hotels you'll find.

There are a number of other chain hotels in town, including the **Hampton Inn Knoxville North** (5411 Pratt Rd., 865/689-1011, www.hilton.com, $139-170), Hampton Inn Downtown (618 W. Main St., 865/522-5400, www.hilton.com, from $168) and the **Country Inn & Suites Knoxville at Cedar Bluff** (9137 Cross Park Dr., 855/693-4500, www.countryinns.com, $95-180).

TRANSPORTATION AND SERVICES
Car

Driving to Knoxville is easy. If you've followed the Blue Ridge Parkway through Great Smoky Mountains National Park, just stay on U.S. 441, which runs right into downtown. Coming from the east or west via I-40, take exit 388 for Gay Street.

From Asheville, take I-40 west for 116 miles (2 hours) to Knoxville. From Charlotte, where you'll find a major airport, take U.S. 74 west to I-40 west to Knoxville, a four-hour drive. Alternatively, take the same route but leave I-40 toward U.S. 19 and Cherokee, then take U.S. 441/Highway 71 through the national park to Knoxville.

From the south, I-75 offers a direct route to Knoxville from Chattanooga, Tennessee (1 hour and 45 minutes), and Atlanta (3 hours). Likewise, I-40 is a direct route from Nashville to Knoxville (2 hours and 45 minutes). From the north, Knoxville is accessible via I-81.

Air

McGhee Tyson Airport (TYS, 2055 Alcoa Hwy., Alcoa, 865/342-3000, www.tys.org) is 20 minutes south of Knoxville in Alcoa, Tennessee. You can get here on U.S. 129. From I-40, take exit 386-B to U.S. 129 south; it's 12 miles to the airport. Airlines serving McGhee Tyson include Allegiant, American Airlines, Delta, Frontier, and United.

If you need taxi service between the airport and Knoxville, **Discount Taxi** (865/755-5143) and **Knoxville Taxi** (865/691-1900) are two of the car services you can call if you're not using ride-share.

Public Transportation

Once you're in town, there is plenty to walk to. **Knoxville Trolley Lines** (301 Church Ave., 865/215-7800, www.katbus.com, free), operated by Knoxville Area Transit, also run throughout downtown. Check online or call for current schedules and routes.

Services

The **Knoxville Visitors Center** (301 S. Gay St., 865/523-7263 or 800/727-8045, www.

visitknoxville.com, 8:30am-5pm Mon.-Fri., 9am-5pm Sat., noon-4pm Sun.) is what visitors centers should be. They have the expected rack of maps and helpful volunteers on hand to answer questions, but what sets them apart is the gift shop filled with locally made art and foodstuffs, a kids' corner, coffee, and a radio station. This is the only visitors center I know of where you can watch a free concert every day at lunch or listen to it as a live radio broadcast.

If you need medical care, there are more than a half-dozen clinics and hospitals in Knoxville. The **University of Tennessee Medical Center** (1924 Alcoa Hwy., 865/305-9000, www.utmedicalcenter.org) is a 581-bed teaching hospital, and **Fort Sanders Regional Medical Center** (1901 Clinch Ave., 865/541-1111, www.fsregional.com) is conveniently located downtown.

North Carolina Gateways

A sense of otherworldliness and of magic rises

up from these hills like the mist that evokes the Smoky Mountains.

Maybe it's the way the land is folded and rumpled like a quilt at the foot of the bed, or perhaps it's some element of Cherokee mythology come to life. After all, this is the ancestral home of the Cherokee people and the present home of the Eastern Band of the Cherokee Indians; it's possible that something in these hills and hollows remains, imprinted from their collective memories. In towns like Cherokee, the magic is thick, but it's also present in Bryson City, throughout the Nantahala National Forest, and along Maggie Valley, calling to visitors and enchanting them year after year.

The town of Cherokee sits on the Qualla Boundary at the edge of

Highlights

Look for ★ to find recommended sights, activities, dining, and lodging.

★ **Experience Cherokee Culture:** Art, history, and millennia-old culture are on display at a museum, gallery, living history village and long-running outdoor drama in the heart of the Eastern Band of the Cherokee Indian (page 145).

★ **Ride the Great Smoky Mountain Railroad:** Steam and diesel locomotives carry passengers along mountain rivers and lakes on sightseeing tours, moonshine tastings, and more (page 155).

★ **Raft the Nantahala River Gorge:** This steep gorge where Olympic athletes train is an unbeatable place for a day of white-water rafting that will leave you breathless (page 157).

★ **Fly-Fish on the Tuckasegee River:** Several outfitters can hook anglers up for a great

day on the river, which conveniently flows right through Bryson City (page 158).

★ **Hike the Joyce Kilmer Memorial Forest:** This 3,800-acre forest is full of old-growth trees that show what the Smoky Mountains were like a century ago (page 163).

★ **Visit John C. Campbell Folk School:** This light in promoting American craft heritage, nurtures new generations of artists, securing the future of Appalachian traditions (page 164).

★ **Tour the Biltmore Estate:** Asheville's most popular attraction is not only an awe-inspiring palace and symbol of the Gilded Age; it's also a collection of great little restaurants, shops, and a popular winery, all in a beautiful riverside setting (page 168).

North Carolina Gateways

TENNESSEE

NORTH CAROLINA

Blue Ridge

Maryville

Murphy

Brasstown

JOYCE KILMER MEMORIAL FOREST

JOHN C. CAMPBELL FOLK SCHOOL

Blairsville

Andrews

Hiawassee

GEORGIA

Clayton

Fontana Village

Fontana Lake

Nantahala

NANTAHALA RIVER GORGE

TUCKASEGEE RIVER

Dillard

Highlands

Cashiers

Rosman

Pickens

Greenville

SOUTH CAROLINA

Great Smoky Mountains National Park

Townsend

Gatlinburg

ELKMONT

ELKMONT

Spence Field 4,900ft

Shuckstack 4,020ft

Thunderhead Mountain 5,530ft

Silers Bald 5,607ft

Clingmans Dome 6,643ft

GREAT SMOKY MOUNTAIN RAILROAD

DEEP CREEK

Bryson City

Franklin

Sylva

Cherokee Indian R.

Cherokee

CHEROKEE CULTURE

SMOKEMONT

Mt. LeConte 6,593ft

Charlie's Bunion

Newfound Gap 5,048ft

Pigeon Forge

Sevierville

Cosby

Mt. Guyot 6,621ft

Mt. Sterling 5,835ft

CATALOOCHEE

BALSAM MOUNTAIN

Maggie Valley

THE STOMPIN' GROUNDS

WHEELS THROUGH TIME MOTORCYCLE MUSEUM

Waynesville

Blue Ridge Parkway

Brevard

Hendersonville

BILTMORE ESTATE

Fletcher

Asheville

SEE ASHEVILLE AREA MAPS

0 10 mi
0 10 km

© MOON.COM

Great Smoky Mountains National Park. Make no mistake, this isn't a reservation; it's ancestral Cherokee land. They're quite proud of the small group of forefathers who refused relocation and the travesty of the Trail of Tears, choosing instead to hide in these hills, wage a guerilla war, and ultimately win the right to set up a Cherokee government.

Other towns here abut the national park or are just a few miles away, and the Cherokee influence is felt everywhere you go. An altogether lovely place, the mountains are tall, the roads winding, and the streams downright picturesque. It's a place people are proud to call home, whether their family has been here for 10 years or 10,000.

PLANNING YOUR TIME

To make the most of your time, spend **two days** in Cherokee, (one for the casino, one for the cultural sights), set aside at least **one day** to visit the national park, and use **one day** for exploring the small towns. If camping is your thing, there are plenty of campsites in the park and some very good ones on the outskirts; if it's not, there are lovely B&Bs and funky older hotels around. A more luxurious experience can be had at Harrah's Cherokee Casino.

Maggie Valley

Maggie Valley is a vacation town from the bygone era of long family road trips in wood-paneled station wagons. Coming down the mountain toward Maggie Valley, you'll pass an overlook that, on a morning when the mountains around Soco Gap are looped with fog, is surely one of the most beautiful vistas in the state.

SIGHTS AND ENTERTAINMENT

In a state with countless attractions for automotive enthusiasts, Maggie Valley's **Wheels through Time Museum** (62 Vintage Lane, 828/926-6266, www.wheelsthroughtime.com, 9am-5pm Thurs.-Mon. Apr.-late Nov., adults $15, over age 65 $12, ages 6-14 $7, under age 4 free) stands out as one of the most fun. A dazzling collection of nearly 300 vintage motorcycles and a fair number of cars are on display, including rarities like a 1908 Indian, a 1914 Harley-Davidson, military motorcycles from both world wars, and some gorgeous postwar bikes. This collection, which dates mostly to before 1950, is maintained in working order—almost every one of the bikes is revved up from time to time, and the museum's founder has been known to take a spin on one of the treasures.

Elevated Mountain Distilling Co. (3732 Soco Rd., 828/944-0766, www. elevatedmountain.com, 10am-7pm Mon.-Sat., tastings and tours $5) is right on the main drag in Maggie Valley, but if you decide to go for more than a quick sample or two, bring a designated driver, because their moonshine, flavored or straight, is fiery. Tours and tastings (adults $5, under age 21 free) include a sample of five of their spirits. On the fourth Saturday of each month they have a bluegrass jam, and in September, they hold a miniature music festival; check for dates as they vary.

SHOPPING

As you might expect, Maggie Valley has its fair share of touristy T-shirt shops and places where you can pick up some fudge and a refrigerator magnet. **Maggie Mountaineer Crafts** (2394 Soco Rd., 828/926-3129, www. maggiemountaineercrafts.com, 9am-5pm daily) and their attached sister store, **A Day In The Valley,** has all that and more. They've

---

Previous: bridge over Tuckasegee River in Bryson City; fly-fishing on the Tuckasegee River; Joyce Kilmer Memorial Forest

Maggie Valley

got plenty of fudge (and they ship; seriously, it's that good) and shirts to choose from, but they also have a pretty large selection of quilts and home decor items; knives, moccasins, and toys; and a great section of local foodstuffs like apple butter, sorghum molasses, and some seasonal treats. Throw in the deck overlooking the creek and you have yourself a charming little souvenir store.

Antiques shopping at **Sutton and Son's Antiques** (3156 Dellwood Rd., Waynesville, 828/944-1212, www.suttonandsonsantiques.com, 10am-5pm Mon.-Sat., 1pm-5pm Sun.) is an experience best summed up by their tagline: "Treasure hunting in the Smokies." The store is large and loaded with a nicely curated selection of antiques such as mountain crafts, automotive memorabilia, kitchen goods, and records.

RECREATION
Hiking

Near Maggie Valley, the mountains become rough. Located on the valley floor, the town of Maggie Valley is surprisingly short on trails, and what trails there are can be quite strenuous. There's the 3.8-mile stroll around **Lake Junaluska,** but other than that, the majority

of the trails are at the crest of the mountains, along the Blue Ridge Parkway. To the east of Maggie Valley, the mountains are a little more forgiving, and there are many trails of various intensities and lengths, but in the immediate area, you'll have to take the Heintooga Spur Road, a connector road between the Parkway and Great Smoky Mountains National Park, to a mile-high campground, picnic area with unparalleled views, and the **Flat Creek Trail.** On Heintooga Spur Road, you'll pass into Great Smoky Mountains National Park and be treated to no fewer than five stunning overlooks, the best of which is the Mile High Overlook, offering a glimpse of Clingmans Dome, Mount LeConte, Mount Kephart, and Mount Guyot.

FLAT CREEK TRAIL

Distance: 5 miles round-trip

Duration: 3 hours

Elevation gain: 250 feet

Difficulty: moderate

Trailhead: Heintooga Ridge picnic area off Heintooga Spur Road, accessible at milepost 458.2

Though named the Flat Creek Trail, you will find a waterfall—the 200-foot Flat Creek Falls, a beautiful but difficult-to-see cascade—along the path. The main trail is easy, with little elevation gain or loss until you turn onto the short spur trail that leads to the falls. The falls trail is steep and slick, so be careful if you decide to explore in this area.

Heavy logging at the turn of the 20th century opened the forest up and allowed a thick swath of grass to grow here. Today, much of the grass remains, and the forest seems to rise from it like an island in a sea of green. It's a strange sight.

Winter Sports

Maggie Valley's **Cataloochee Ski Area** (1080 Ski Lodge Rd., off U.S. 19, 800/768-0285, snow conditions 800/768-3588, www.cataloochee. com, lift tickets $26-82, rentals $27-32) has slopes geared to every level of skier and snowboarder. Classes and private lessons are taught for all ages. At Cataloochee's sister snowsports area, **Tube World** (U.S. 19, next to Ski Area, 828/926-0285, www.cataloochee.com, late Nov.-mid-Mar., must be over 42 inches tall, $25), you can zip down the mountain on inner tubes, and there's a "Wee Bowl" area for children (call ahead, $5).

FOOD

★ **Joey's Pancake House** (4309 Soco Rd., 828/926-0212, www.joeyspancake.com, 7am-noon daily, about $2-9) has been flipping flapjacks for travelers and locals alike since 1966, and it's exactly the kind of place you picture: paper menu placemats; hot, weak, delicious coffee; a little kitschy; and packed with regulars. The pancakes, waffles, and country ham are so good that lines form on the weekends—get here early. And if you're as taken by the pancakes as I am, you'll pick up some of their mix to take home with you.

J. Arthurs Restaurant (2843 Soco Rd., 828/926-1817, www.jarthurs.com, 4:30pm-late Tues.-Sun., $11-32) serves the best steak around—no wonder considering steak is the house specialty and they've been perfecting their technique for nearly 30 years. The restaurant also has a variety of seafood and pasta dishes, but there are few vegetarian options.

The Italian food at **Frankie's Trattoria** (1037 Soco Rd., 828/926-6216, www. frankiestrattoria.com, 11:30am-9:30pm Mon.-Thurs., 11:30am-10pm Fri.-Sat., $9-23) is a bright spot in Maggie Valley. Pizzas are quite good, pasta dishes are shareably big and very tasty, and the wine list is great. All that makes Frankie's a good choice for a night out in Maggie Valley. You'll find that you're not the only out-of-towner in the dining room, and it seems no matter where the diners come from, they all leave raving and ready for more.

If you want barbecue, try ★ **Willie Brooks BBQ** (2550 Soco Rd., 828/944-1227, www.williebrooksbbq.com, 11am-8pm Mon. and Thurs.-Sat., 11:30am-6:30pm Sun., $7-24). A blend of Western North Carolina and Texas barbecue, it delivers on the menu variety and on flavor. Their pulled pork is smoky and moist, the brisket just right, and the smoked wings awesome. They have six sauces ranging from a spicy to a sweet North Carolina-style to an Alabama white sauce (perfect for those wings) to a mustard sauce. And if you're in the mood for a feast, they sell by the pound, or you can buy a whole pork butt, brisket, chicken, or turkey breast. Their pulled pork is smoky and moist, the brisket is excellent, and their sauces aren't too heavy-handed. All told, it's solid barbecue that's only going to get better.

ACCOMMODATIONS

Along Maggie Valley's main drag (Soco Rd./ U.S. 19) you'll see a lot of creek-side motels and mom-and-pop mountain inns. Among the pleasant independent motels are **The Valley Inn** (236 Soco Rd., 800/948-6880, www.thevalleyinn.com, from $79 in-season, $39 off-season) and **Jonathan Creek Inn and Villas** (4324 Soco Rd., 800/577-7812, www.jonathancreekinn.com, from $90), which has creek-side rooms with screened porches.

If you want to get a feel for the mountains, try one of the cabin rentals. **Bear Run Log Cabins** (1604 Moody Farm Rd., 828/926-7566, 888/926-7566, www.bearrunlogcabins. com, from $150 Apr.-Nov., from $120

Nov.-Mar.) has a quartet of cabins that sleep five and have Wi-Fi, a fireplace, and a small kitchen. Their decks overlook Jonathan Creek, one of the area trout streams. Cozy, comfy, and cabin-y, they're exactly what you picture when you think of a mountain cabin getaway.

The largest hotel in Maggie Valley is the **Maggie Valley Inn** (70 Soco Rd., 828/962-0201, www.maggievalleyhotel.com, from $100 Apr.-Nov., from $80 Nov.-Mar.). It's a basic hotel with excellent rates, a pool, a bar, and a pair of restaurants. **Rendezvous Restaurant** (3pm-9:30pm Mon.-Tues., 11:30am-9:30pm Wed., 11:30am-10pm Thurs., 11:30am-11pm Fri.-Sat., 11:30am-8:30pm Sun., $9-20) serves burgers, ribs, steaks, pasta, and plenty of dishes to fuel you up for a day on the trail. At **Maggie Valley Pizzeria** (3pm-9:30pm Mon.-Tues., 11:30am-9:30pm Wed., 11:30am-10pm Thurs., 11:30am-11pm Fri.-Sat., 11:30am-8:30pm Sun., $9-20) it's pizza and calzones, and while there aren't any specialty pies, what they have does the job.

There is one fantastic campground in the area: the ★ **Balsam Mountain Campground** (Heintooga Spur Rd., milepost 458.2, 828/497-9270, www.nps.gov/grsm, reservations www.recreation.gov, $18), the highest campground in Great Smoky Mountains National Park at 5,310 feet. This primitive campground has 43 sites for tents and RVs, with a dedicated tent-only section. It's a beautiful, isolated campground that's often overlooked, as it's slightly off the beaten path. Because it's also a primitive campground (pit toilets, no showers), most of the year you won't have many neighbors here. If you're driving a vehicle you feel comfortable taking on forest roads, Balsam Mountain Road, sometimes called Round Bottom Road, continues on from the campground, making a nice trip through the forest down to Cherokee. It's about two hours but worth the drive.

TRANSPORTATION

U.S. 19 is the main thoroughfare in these parts, leading from Asheville (45 minutes east) to the Great Smoky Mountains National Park (35 minutes west). If you're taking your time between Asheville, Boone, or parts north, the Blue Ridge Parkway is a beautiful but slow (three hours or more, depending on where you begin) drive to this part of the state. Maggie Valley is only 25 minutes off I-40 via exits 20, 24, or 27.

Cherokee and the Qualla Boundary

The town of Cherokee is a study in juxtapositions: the cultural traditions of the Cherokee people, the region's natural beauty, a 24-hour casino, and community-wide preparation for the future. Cherokee is the seat of government of the Eastern Band of the Cherokee, who have lived in these mountains for centuries. Today, their traditional arts and crafts, government, and cultural heritage are very much alive, although their language seems to be disappearing. The Qualla ("KWA-lah") Boundary is not a reservation but a large tract of land owned and governed by the Cherokee people. Institutions like the Museum of the Cherokee Indian and the Qualla Arts and Crafts Mutual provide a solid base for the Eastern Band's cultural life. As you drive around, take a look at the road signs: Below each English road name is that same name in Cherokee, a beautiful script created by Sequoyah, a 19th-century Cherokee silversmith. This language, once nearly extinct, is being taught to the community's youth now, and there is a Cherokee language immersion school on the Qualla Boundary. This doesn't mean the language is not in danger: Few Cherokee people speak it fluently.

The main street in Cherokee is a classic cheesy tourist district where you'll find "Indian" souvenirs—factory-made moccasins, plastic tomahawks, peace pipes, faux bear-skins, the works. In a retro way, this part of Cherokee, with its predictable trinket shops and fudgeries, is charming.

Aside from its proximity to the Great Smoky Mountains National Park and the Blue Ridge Parkway, the biggest draw in town is Harrah's Cherokee Casino, one of the largest casino hotels in the state and home to a world-class spa. The 24-hour entertainment opportunities attract visitors from far and wide, some of whom stay on the property the whole time, while others take a break from the slap of cards and the flash of slot machines to experience the natural and cultural wonders of Cherokee.

Take all of this that you see—the casino, the tacky tourist shops, and the stereotyping signs—with a grain of salt, as they don't represent the true nature of the Cherokee people and their long history.

★ CHEROKEE CULTURAL SIGHTS
Museum of the Cherokee Indian

The **Museum of the Cherokee Indian** (589 Tsali Blvd., 828/497-3481, www.cherokeemuseum.org, 9am-7pm Mon.-Sat., 9am-5pm Sun. late June-Aug., 9am-5pm daily Sept.-May, $12, ages 6-12 $7, under age 5 free) was founded in 1948 and was originally housed in a log cabin. Today, it is a well-regarded modern museum and locus of community culture. In the exhibits that trace the long history of the Cherokee people, you may notice the disconcertingly realistic mannequins. Local community members volunteered to be models for these mannequins, allowing casts to be made of their faces and bodies so that the figures would not reflect an outsider's notion of what Native Americans should look like. The Museum of the Cherokee Indian traces their history from the Paleo-Indian people of the Pleistocene, when the ancestral Cherokees were hunter-gatherers, through the ancient days of Cherokee civilization, and into contact with European settlers.

Cherokee

© MOON.COM

A great deal of this exhibit focuses on the 18th and 19th centuries, when a series of tragedies befell the Cherokee as a result of the invasion of their homeland. It was also a time of great cultural advancement, including Sequoyah's development of the script to write the Cherokee language. The forced relocation of Native Americans called the Trail of Tears began near here, along the North Carolina-Georgia border, in the early 19th century. A small contingent of Cherokees remained in the Smokies at the time of the Trail of Tears, successfully eluding, and then negotiating with, the U.S. military, who were trying to force most of the Native Americans in the Southeast to move to Oklahoma. Those who stayed out in the woods, along with a few others who were able to return from Oklahoma, are the ancestors of today's Eastern Band, and their history is truly remarkable.

A favorite part of the museum is the stories, legends, and myths described on placards throughout the building. There's the story of a boy who became a bear and convinced his entire clan to become bears also. There's one about Spearfinger, a frightening creature that some say still lives in these woods today. And there are tales about Selu, the corn mother, and Kanati, the lucky hunter. Cherokee member and contemporary writer Marilou Awiakta has written widely about Selu, tying the past and present together with taut lines of thought that challenge our views on culture and technology.

Qualla Arts and Crafts Mutual

Across the street from the museum is the **Qualla Arts and Crafts Mutual** (645 Tsali Blvd., 828/497-3103, http://quallaartsandcrafts.com, 8am-6pm Mon.-Sat., 9am-5pm Sun. Apr.-Nov., 8am-4:30pm Mon.-Sat. Nov.-Mar.), a community arts co-op where 250 local artists sell their work. The gallery's high standards and the community's thousands of years of artistry make for a collection of very special pottery, baskets, masks, and other traditional art. The Qualla co-op does a great service to this community by providing a year-round market for the work of traditional Cherokee artists, whose stewardship of and innovation in the arts are so important. The double-woven baskets are especially beautiful, as are the carvings of the masks representing each of the seven clans of the Cherokee people (the Bird, Deer, Longhair, Blue, Wolf, Paint, and Wild Potato).

Oconaluftee Indian Village

Oconaluftee Indian Village (778 Drama Rd., 828/497-2111, http://visitcherokeenc.com,

9:30am-4pm Mon.-Sat. Apr.-Nov., adults $20, children $12, under age 6 free) is a recreated Cherokee village tucked into the hills above the town. Here you'll see how the Cherokee people lived in the 18th century. Tour guides in period costumes lead groups on walking lectures with stops at stations where you can see Cherokee cultural, artistic, and daily-life activities performed as authentically as possible. From cooking demos to flint knapping (for arrowheads and spear points) to wood carving and clay work, you'll get a look at how the Cherokee lived centuries ago. The highlight of the tour is the ritual dance demonstration, showing a half-dozen dances and explaining their cultural significance.

RECREATION
Fishing

Cherokee has more than 30 miles of streams, rivers, and creeks ideal for fishing. The Eastern Band owns and operates a fish hatchery that releases around 250,000 trout into these waters every year, creating the perfect mix for fantastic fishing. Unlike in the rest of North Carolina, you don't need a North Carolina fishing license; you need a **Tribal Fishing Permit** (www.fishcherokee.com, 1 day $10, 2 days $17, 3 days $27, 5 days $47, full season permit $250), sold at a number of outlets in Cherokee. You'll find brook, brown, golden, and rainbow trout, and it's fly-rod only, so you have to have your cast down pat if you want to bring in a big one. There are both catch-and-release and catch-and-keep waters in the Qualla Boundary, but if you want to fish outside the boundary, you need a North Carolina or Tennessee fishing permit. Tennessee permits are only valid inside the Great Smoky Mountains National Park boundaries in North Carolina.

Mountain Biking

Mountain bikers, hikers, and trail runners take note: **Fire Mountain Trails** (trailhead 778 Drama Rd., near Oconaluftee Indian Village, www.visitcherokeenc.com, free) has 10.5 miles of paths, trails and single track

The Story of the Cherokee

Museum of the Cherokee Indian

The Cherokee people believe that the mountains of western North Carolina have been part of their homeland dating back to at least the last ice age, some 11,000 years ago. By the time Spanish soldiers encountered the Cherokee in the 1540s, the nation controlled around 140,000 square miles across what is now the southern United States, living in log cabins in towns and villages throughout their territory. They farmed corn, squash, and beans (known as "The Three Sisters"); hunted elk, deer, and bear; and prospered in peacetime and warred with other nations periodically.

During the first two centuries of earnest European contact, the Cherokee were peaceful and hospitable with the colonists they encountered. Through the course of those 200 years, strings of broken treaties and concessions by the Cherokee had shrunk their once-vast empire dramatically. When President Andrew Jackson insisted that all indigenous people in the Southeast be moved west of the Mississippi, the real trouble began.

As Jackson's forced march and relocation of the Cherokee and other nations, known as the **Trail of Tears,** pressed on, a small group of Cherokee avoided relocation by becoming North Carolina citizens. A band of resistance fighters stayed behind near modern-day Cherokee, hiding in the hills, hollows, and caves high in the mountains. These holdouts would become the core of the **Eastern Band of Cherokee Indians.** Unable to own any land, the Cherokee turned to an adopted member to purchase and hold land in his name. He did so, and in 1870, the Cherokee formed a corporation and took control of that land, which they called the **Qualla Boundary.**

Today, the Eastern Band of the Cherokee Indians has nearly 15,000 members (their counterparts in Oklahoma number 10 times as many), many of whom live within the 82-square-mile Qualla Boundary. Tribe members are fiercely proud of their heritage, traditions, stories, and language. An afternoon spent at the **Museum of the Cherokee Indian,** the **Qualla Arts and Crafts Mutual,** and the **Oconaluftee Indian Village,** followed by an evening showing of *Unto These Hills,* will give you a more complete understanding of their history.

waiting on you. There are plenty of terrain features, tabletops, and places to get air, but also trails perfect for beginners. If you didn't bring your own bike, head 15 minutes down the road to Bryson City, where **Tsali Cycles** (35 Slope St., Bryson City, 828/489-9020, www.tsalicycles.com, 10am-5pm Mon.-Sat., mountain-bike rentals adults half-day from $25, full-day $45, children half-day from $20, full-day $25) can get you set up with wheels.

Golf

The **Sequoyah National Golf Club** (79 Cahons Rd., Whittier, 828/497-3000, www.sequoyahnational.com, 18 holes, par 72, greens fees from $65), five miles south of Cherokee in Whittier, is a stunning mountain golf course. Making the most of the contours and elevation, the course offers tee boxes with breathtaking views of the fairway and the Smoky Mountains. The course record is 62, an impressive feat on a normal course, but here it's something else. Holes like number 12 and number 15 test a golfer's club knowledge and course IQ. This is a tough course for first-timers because so many of the holes have blind approaches, doglegs, or both, but it's enjoyable enough.

Water Sports

For fun on the water, try **Smoky Mountain Tube and Raft** (1847 Tsali Blvd., 828/497-4545, http://cherokeetubeandraft.com, 10am-6pm daily Memorial Day-Labor Day Weekend, weather permitting, $12). They do only one thing: rent tubes on which you'll drift down the river and splash your friends. Smoky Mountain Tubing has mountains of tubes, so rent one and float down the Oconaluftee River for two or three hours. They have a fleet of shuttle buses to pick you up a few miles downstream.

ENTERTAINMENT AND EVENTS

The Eastern Band of the Cherokee operates **Harrah's Cherokee Casino and Hotel** (777 Casino Dr., 828/497-7777, www.caesars.

com/harrahs-cherokee, 24 hours daily). This full-bore Vegas-style casino has more than 3,800 digital games and slot machines along with around 150 table games, such as baccarat, blackjack, roulette, and a poker-only room. Inside the casino complex is a 3,000-seat concert venue where acts like Alicia Keys and the Black Crows have performed, a huge buffet, and a grab-and-go food court next to the casino floor. Unlike in the rest of the state, smoking is allowed on the casino floor, though certain areas have been designated as nonsmoking. Inside the hotel portion of the casino are a restaurant, a Starbucks, and the **Mandara Spa,** which offers salon and spa services like massages and facials.

Of the several outdoor dramas for which North Carolina is known, among the longest running is Cherokee's **Unto These Hills** (Mountainside Theater, 688 Drama Rd., adjacent to Oconaluftee Indian Village, 866/554-4557, www.visitcherokeenc.com, 8pm Mon.-Sat. June-Aug. 15, adults $28-31, ages 6-12 $18-21, under age 6 free). For more than 60 summers, Cherokee actors have told the story of their nation's history, from ancient times through the Trail of Tears. Every seat in the house is a good seat at the Mountainside Theater, and the play is certainly enlightening. Be warned: If you're gun-shy or easily startled, there is some cannon fire and gunfire in the play.

Hear stories, learn dances, and interact with Cherokee storytellers at the **Cherokee Bonfire** (Oconaluftee Islands Park, Tsalagi Rd. and Tsali Blvd., where U.S. 19 and U.S. 441 intersect, 800/438-1601, www.visitcherokeenc. com, 5pm-7pm Mon., Wed., and Fri.-Sat. May-Oct., free, including marshmallows). Bring your bathing suit and some water shoes to the bonfire; afterward, you may want to go for a wade or a quick dip in the Oconaluftee River, which is wide, rocky, and fun.

FOOD

The arrival and expansion of Harrah's Cherokee Casino brought with it a bevy of restaurants, including **Ruth's Chris Steak**

House (777 Casino Dr., 828/497-7777, 828/497-8577, www.harrahscherokee.com, 5pm-10pm Mon.-Thurs., 5pm-11pm Fri., 4pm-11pm Sat., 4pm-9pm Sun., around $60), and like its other locations, it serves a variety of steaks and chops, a handful of seafood dishes, and more than 220 wines.

Brio Tuscan Grille (828/497-8233, www. brioitalian.com, 11:30am-10pm Sun.-Thurs., 11:30am-11pm Fri.-Sat., lunch $10-26, dinner $11-36) is a fine Italian restaurant specializing in dishes from northern Italy. This isn't a spaghetti-and-meatballs kind of place; it's more refined, with dishes like lasagna Bolognese al forno, lobster and shrimp ravioli with crab insalata, Tuscan grilled pork chops, and bistecca alla Fiorentina. The ambience is nice, the wine list is nicer, and the food is great.

What's a casino without a buffet? Anyone can find something that satisfies at **Chef's Stage Buffet** (4:30pm-10pm Mon. and Thurs., 4:30pm-11pm Fri.-Sat., 1pm-10pm Sun., from $29 Mon. and Thurs.-Fri., Sun. seafood buffet $37), where four chefs run four distinct micro-restaurants. There's everything here: Asian dishes, Latin, Italian, seafood, Southern, barbecue, a salad bar you could land an airplane on, and desserts for days. A second buffet option is the **Selu Garden Café** (7am-2:30pm daily, around $15), which offers up a hearty breakfast every day, a slightly more upscale brunch on weekends, and a bottomless soup and salad bar.

Downstairs in Harrah's is an airport-style food court that includes the **Earl of Sandwich** (11am-11pm daily, around $10), a deli serving hot and cold sandwiches and paninis; grab-and-go sandwiches are available 24 hours daily. There is also **Pizzeria Uno Express** (11am-11pm Sun.-Thurs., 11am-2am Fri.-Sat., around $10), serving thin-crust pizza, calzones, and pasta dishes; **Noodle Bar** (6pm-2am Mon.-Thurs., 5pm-3am Fri.-Sat., 5pm-2am Sun., around $18), serving Asian dishes like ramen and dim sum options;

Johnny Rockets (24 hours daily, around $10), serving burgers, sandwiches, fries, milk shakes, and breakfast; and a **Dunkin' Donuts Express** (24 hours daily, around $5) that has doughnuts and coffee. The food court also has a variety of snacks and drinks available 24 hours daily.

Just outside the town of Cherokee is **Granny's Kitchen** (1098 Painttown Rd., 828/497-5010, www.grannyskitchencherokee. com, breakfast 7am-11am Tues.-Sun. June-Aug., 7am-11am Fri.-Sun. Apr.-May, Sept., and Nov., lunch and dinner 11am-8pm Tues.-Sun. mid-Mar.-mid-Dec., $8-12), a country-buffet restaurant where you can get some of the best fried chicken in North Carolina. Granny is actually a man who likes to joke, "No one wants to eat at Grandpa's, so I became Granny."

ACCOMMODATIONS

Cherokee has many motels, including a **Holiday Inn** (376 Painttown Rd., 828/497-3113, www.ihg.com, from $113) and an **Econo Lodge** (20 River Rd./U.S. 19, 828/497-4575, www.choicehotels.com, from $85, pets allowed).

★ **Harrah's Cherokee Casino and Hotel** (777 Casino Dr., 828/497-7777, www. harrahscherokee.com, $100-510) is, without a doubt, the best place to stay in Cherokee. The rooms are spacious, comfortable, and well kept; there's the casino and a number of dining options an elevator ride away; and the spa provides an added layer of amenities you don't find at other hotels in town.

There's something about visiting a place and living where the residents live, and ★ **Panther Creek Cabins** (Wrights Creek Rd., 828/497-2461, www.panthercreekresort. com, cabins $100-150) gives you that chance with your choice of eight cabins, ranging from private two-person affairs to larger lodges that could easily sleep you and seven others in four beds. These quaint cabins are quiet, just outside downtown Cherokee, and comfortable.

TRANSPORTATION AND SERVICES

Cherokee is located on a particularly pretty winding section of U.S. 19 between Maggie Valley and Bryson City, 2.5 miles south of the southern terminus of the Blue Ridge Parkway. From the Blue Ridge Parkway, a six-minute drive south along U.S. 441 will take you right to the cultural center of Cherokee.

The **Cherokee Welcome Center** (498 Tsali Blvd., 800/438-1601, www.visitcherokeenc.com, 8am-5pm daily) can help you with tickets, directions, and things to do and see. There's one radio station in Cherokee, **WNCC** (101.3 FM), a country station, although you can pick up distant stations with a wider selection.

SYLVA

The small town of Sylva, southwest of Waynesville, is crowned by the pretty Jackson County Courthouse, an Italianate building with an ornate cupola, kept under wistful watch by the requisite courthouse-square Confederate monument. Visitors should stop by the **Jackson County Visitor Center** (773 W. Main St., 800/962-1911, www.mountainlovers.com) or visit them online to learn more about the communities here; tourist information is available through Discover Jackson County (www.discoverjacksonnc.com).

Sights

South of Sylva, the mysterious **Judaculla Rock** (off Caney Fork Rd., www.judacullarock.com) has puzzled folks for centuries. The soapstone boulder is covered in petroglyphs estimated to be at least 500 years old. The figures and symbols and squiggles are clearly significant but as of yet are not understood. I'm fascinated with petroglyphs, and these are some of the most mysterious I've encountered. The soft rock has eroded, and the pictures are not as clear as they were in generations past, but many of them can still be discerned. To reach the rock, drive south on Highway 107 eight miles past the intersection with Sylva's Business U.S. 23. Make a left on Caney Fork Road/County Road 1737 and drive 2.5 miles to a gravel road. Turn left, and after just under 0.5 miles you'll see the rock on the right and a parking area on the left.

Shopping

Sylva's City Lights Bookstore (3 E. Jackson St., 828/586-9499, www.citylightsnc.

Jackson County Courthouse in Sylva

com, 9am-9pm Mon.-Sat., 10am-3pm Sun.) is hardly a knockoff of the monumental Beat establishment in San Francisco with which it shares a name. Instead, it's a first-rate small-town bookstore with stock that has the novelty sought by vacationers and the depth to make regulars of the local patrons. In addition to the sections you'll find in any good bookstore, their selection of books of regional interest, including folklore, nature, recreation guides, history, and fiction and poetry by Appalachian and Southern authors, is excellent.

Founded by a pair of Appalachian Trail through-hikers, **Black Balsam Outdoors** (562 W. Main St., 828/631-2864, www.blackbalsamoutdoors.com, 10am-5:30pm Mon.-Thurs., 10am-6pm Fri.-Sat., noon-5pm Sun.) will get you geared up for a trip into the woods whether you're looking for hard-core trail gear to use on your own through-hike or if you're in the market for a day-hike kit that will serve you for this trip to the Smokies and many more. They know their gear, how to use it, and where to go to give it a good workout, so don't hesitate to inquire about their favorite hikes in the area and the national park.

Food

The North Carolina mountains are experiencing a booming organic foods movement, and you'll find eco-aware eateries throughout the area. ★ **Lulu's On Main** (678 W. Main St., 828/586-8989, www.lulusonmain.com, 11am-8pm Mon.-Thurs., 11am-9pm Fri.-Sat., $11-19) is one of the most acclaimed restaurants in the area. The menu is American gourmet at heart with splashes of Mediterranean and Nuevo Latino specialties. Try the cheese ravioli with tofu, the beef short ribs, or the paella. They have plenty of vegetarian options.

City Lights Café (3 E. Jackson St., 828/587-2233, www.citylightscafe.com, 8am-9pm Mon.-Sat., 9am-3pm Sun., breakfast $2-8, lunch and dinner $5-12), downstairs from the bookshop, has some excellent crepes, a mighty good biscuit, and fun tacos, and they serve wine and beer. It's a cool, casual spot to

dine and relax with your book and a bottle of wine, or to see a small local act play.

If you're in the mood for coffee and something light, try **White Moon** (545 Mill St., 828/331-0111, www.whitemoonsylva.com, 7am-6pm Tues.-Fri., 9am-5pm Sat., $3-11). White Moon is one street over from the main drag, it would be easy to overlook, but that would be a mistake. Friendly folks serve coffee, café drinks, and a small but tasty lunch and breakfast menu, so when you need your avocado toast fix, a savory breakfast bowl or a sandwich, this is the spot.

Soul Infusion (628 E. Main St., 828/586-1717, www.soulinfusion.com, 11am-10pm Mon.-Fri., noon-late Sat., $5-10) is a cozy hippie-gourmet teahouse in an old house on Main Street. You can get very good burritos, sandwiches, pizza, wraps, more than 60 kinds of tea, and even more selections of bottled beer. On weekends and some weeknights, local blues, folk, reggae, and experimental musicians put on a show. Seize the opportunity to hear some of the talent in this musical region.

Nightlife

It's a small town, so there's not a whole lot in the way of nightlife here, but **Innovation Brewing** (414 W. Main St., 828/586-9678, www.innovation-brewing.com, noon-midnight Mon.-Thurs., 11am-midnight Fri.-Sun.) has 22 beers in their regular rotation with 10 on tap at any time. The Nitro Irish Stout, Nut Brown, and Midnight Rye-der Black IPA are mainstays, but they also make a few sours. Keep an ear out for live music in the taproom, as bands drop by often. If you're hungry, you're in luck: **Cosmic Carry-Out** (828/506-2830, www.cosmiccarryout.com, noon-9pm Mon.-Thurs., 11am-10:30pm Fri.-Sat., 11am-9pm Sun., $3-9) has burgers, tacos, grilled-cheese sandwiches, and fries for your dining enjoyment.

Balsam Falls Brewing (506 W. Main St., 828/631-1987, www.balsamfallsbrewing.com, noon-10pm Sun.-Wed., noon-midnight Thurs.-Sat.) comet to Sylva by way of the

Tampa, Florida, homebrew scene, where owners Corey and Laure Bryson got their start. But Balsam Falls is far from homebrew. The pair went on to get their Cicerone certification (think sommelier for beer), and Corey's a certified beer judge, so the brews they put on draft are top notch. Every beer has a fun name—Ole Granny Smathers Decrepitude Tonic, Grass Ripper 2000 Summer Kolsch—and the variety runs the gamut from IPAs to barley wine to Russian imperials to lightly hopped American pale ales. They have plans to expand, opening a restaurant next door, so keep your eyes open for what's next.

For cocktails, head to **The Cut Cocktail Lounge** (610 W. Main St., 828/631-4795, 5pm-2am Mon.-Fri., noon-2am Sat.-Sun.) in a former barber shop downtown. The drinks are excellent, the atmosphere on the right side of dive-y, and they serve food until 2am every night—sometimes chili, sometimes gourmet popcorn, sometimes barbecue (it's a sort of potluck thing).

Accommodations

The **Blue Ridge Inn** (756 W. Main St., Sylva, 828/586-2123, from $110) is a great place to stay in Sylva. Located at the far end of downtown, it's an eight-minute walk to the breweries at the other end of town and a three-minute walk to dining spots like Lulu's and City Lights. The rooms are comfortable and priced right, and the staff is exceptionally polite.

DILLSBORO

Next door to Sylva is Dillsboro, a river town of rafters and crafters. **Dogwood Crafters** (90 Webster St., 828/586-2248, www. dogwoodcrafters.com, 10am-6pm Mon.-Sat. and 11am-4pm Sun. Mar.-Dec., 11am-4pm Fri.-Sun. Feb., closed Jan.), in operation for more than 30 years, is a gallery and co-op that represents around 100 local artists and artisans. While the shop carries some of the ubiquitous country-whimsical stuff, mixed in is the work of some very traditional Blue Ridge

weavers, potters, carvers, and other expert artisans, making the shop well worth a visit.

In November, Dillsboro's population grows significantly when potters and pottery lovers descend on the town for the annual **Western North Carolina Pottery Festival** (828/586-3601, www.wncpotteryfestival.com). This juried pottery show features more than 40 potters, a street fair, and the Clay Olympics. The Clay Olympics are timed competitions to make the tallest cylinder or widest bowl, as well as blindfolded pot-making. It's odd, but the crowd and the artists get into it, making the one-day festival worth seeing.

Recreation

Dillsboro River Company (18 Macktown Rd., 828/507-2428, www.northcarolinarafting.com, 10am-6pm daily June-Sept., tubing $20, guided trips $27-37), across the river from downtown Dillsboro, will set you afloat on the Tuckasegee River, a comparatively warm river with areas of Class II rapids. It's pronounced "tuck-a-SEE-jee" but is often referred to simply as "the Tuck." Dillsboro River Company rents rafts, "ducks," and inflatable and sit-on-top kayaks. If you'd like to hire a river rat, guides will be happy to lead you on tours twice daily, and for an extra fee you can share a boat with the guide. There are minimum weight restrictions for these watercraft, so if you are traveling with children, call ahead to ask if the guides think your young ones are ready for the Tuckasegee.

Nightlife

Sylva's Innovation Brewing has an outpost in Dillsboro, **Innovation Station** (40 Depot St., Dillsboro, 828/226-0262, www.innovation-brewing.com, noon-midnight Mon.-Thurs., 11am-midnight Fri.-Sun.). Housed in an former train depot, it's got the right feel for this railroad town, and their generous taps—there are nearly three dozen—mean plenty of brews to choose from. Innovation also has a barrel-aging program here, and it's home to their pilot brew house, so you'll likely find a few experimental brews to sample.

The Fly-Fishing Trail

Jackson County is the home of the first Fly-Fishing Trail in the country; it includes 15 spots on some of the best trout waters in the Smokies where you can catch rainbow, brook, and brown trout, and even the occasional golden trout. Because of its proximity to many mountain communities, the Fly-Fishing Trail has become the epicenter of fly-fishing in the region. Easy access to these waters, convenient complimentary maps (www.flyfishingtrail.com and http://mountainloversnc. com), and the excellent support the trail receives make it a choice spot for trout fishing no matter which community you're visiting.

Top spots include Panthertown Creek, where a two-mile walk from the end of Breedlove Road (Hwy. 1121) leads you to what some have called the "Yosemite of the East" because of its picturesque rocky bluffs. You'll catch more brook trout than you may have thought possible on this three-mile stream, which is catch-and-release only.

For an "urban" fishing experience, try the Tuckasegee River as it passes through Dillsboro. You can park and fish at a number of places between Dillsboro Park and the Best Western River Escape Inn, and you run a good chance of catching a large rainbow or brown trout.

The Lower Tuckasegee River, running from Bakers Creek Bridge to Whittier along U.S. 19/74, is around 10 miles of excellent fishing for rainbow and brown trout as well as smallmouth bass.

Fly-Fishing Trail cofounder Alex Bell, who knows the waters of western North Carolina intimately, operates AB's Fly Fishing Guide Service (828/226-3833, www.abfish.org, half-day wading trips 1 person $200, 2 people $275, 3 people $350, full-day with lunch 1 person $300, 2 people $375, 3 people $450; full-day float trips with lunch 1-2 people $450). AB's supplies tackle and waders if you need them, as well as extensive lessons in proper casting, water reading, and fly selection, but you're responsible for securing your own North Carolina fishing license and trout stamp.

In Bryson City the Fly Fishing Museum of the Southern Appalachians (210 Main St., Bryson City, 828/867-9246, 9am-5pm Mon.-Fri., 11am-5pm Sat. Apr.-Aug. and Oct., 8am-4pm Mon.-Fri. Sept. and Nov.-Mar., free) has displays of commonly used flies, historic rods and reels, and a Fly Fishing Hall of Fame.

Food

★ Haywood Smokehouse (403 Haywood St., 828/631-9797, www.haywoodsmokehouse. com, 11am-8pm Tues.-Sat., $8-26) is a funky little barbecue shack serving some fine western North Carolina 'cue, craft beers, and house-made smoked barbecue sauces. The menu is small, but if it's pork or chicken and it's barbecuable, it's here. The Haywood Smokehouse is biker-friendly, so don't be surprised if you see a line of Harleys outside.

It's not surprising to find a restaurant bragging about their farm-to-fork philosophy these days, even in a town as small as Dillsboro, but it is surprising to find one living up to that boast and delivering great food. ★ Foragers Canteen (42 Depot St., 828/631-4114, www.foragerscanteen.com, 7am-8:30pm Mon.-Thurs., 7am-9:30pm

Fri.-Sat., 10am-8pm Sun., breakfast $6-14, lunch and dinner $8-30) serves three meals a day. Whether you want breakfast tacos or a big stack of pancakes to start the day, a veggie-friendly mushroom taco, a fish taco, or a loaded burger for lunch, or something substantial like a pair of huge pork chops for dinner, they've got it covered. Rest assured that what you're eating was raised as responsibly as possible.

The Jarrett House (100 Haywood St., 828/477-4948, www.jarretthouse.com, 11:30am-2:30pm and 4:30pm-7:30pm Fri.-Sun. Mar.-Nov., 4:30pm-9pm Tues.-Sun. Dec.-Feb., $12-18) is famous for its dining room, an extravaganza of country cooking. You can order many other mountain specialties, including fried catfish, fried chicken, sweet tea, biscuits, and for dessert the daily cobbler or vinegar pie (a strange but tasty pie that's similar to a pecan pie without the pecans). There are few options for vegetarians, but if you like heavy Southern fare, you'll think you're in heaven.

If you're sweet tooth is calling, give it a little satisfaction with a stop at **Dillsboro Chocolate Factory** (28 Church St., 828/631-0156, www.dillsborochocolate.com, 10am-7pm Mon.-Thurs., 10am-8:30pm Fri., 10am-9pm Sat., noon-5pm Sun. summer-fall, 10am-5pm Wed.-Sat., noon-5pm Sun. winter). They have truffles, chocolate, fudge, candy, and other assorted sweets, many of which they make in house.

Accommodations

Of the many historic inns in this region, one of the oldest is Dillsboro's **Jarrett House** (100 Haywood St., 828/477-4958, www.jarretthouse.com, from $129, includes full country breakfast). The three-story 1880s lodge was built to serve passengers on the railroad, and today it's once again a busy rail stop, now for the Great Smoky Mountains Railroad's excursion trains. The guest rooms have old-fashioned furniture, air-conditioning, and private baths, but the only TV is in the lobby.

The **Best Western Plus River Escape Inn & Suites** (248 WBI Dr., 828/586-6060, www.bwiriverescape.com, from $130 Mar.-Aug., from $180 Sept.-Oct., from $110 Nov.-Feb.) isn't what you think of when you think chain hotel; it's much more. The rooms are more attractive and comfortable (and more frequently updated) than you'd expect, the big patio overlooking the river includes a fire-pit area, and it's close to Dillsboro, the road to Cherokee, and the national park.

CULLOWHEE

The unincorporated village of Cullowhee (CULL-uh-wee), on Highway 107 between Sylva and Cashiers, is the home of Western Carolina University (WCU). The university's **Mountain Heritage Center** (Hunter Library, WCU campus, 828/227-7129, www.

wcu.edu, 10am-4pm Fri.-Mon., 10am-7pm Thurs., free) is a small museum with a great collection that will fascinate anyone interested in Appalachian history. The permanent exhibit *Migration of the Scotch-Irish People* is full of artifacts like a 19th-century covered wagon, wonderful photographs, and homemade quilts, linens, and musical instruments. The Mountain Heritage Center also hosts two traveling exhibits in addition to the permanent installation as well as the annual festival **Mountain Heritage Day** (www.mountainheritageday.com, late Sept.), which brings together many of western North Carolina's best and most authentic traditional musicians and artisans in a free festival that draws up to 25,000 visitors.

CASHIERS

Cashiers is about as quaint a mountain town as you'll find. The full-time population is small, but there are plenty of vacation and second homes here, so this little town gets busy in fall when the leaves are at their best. Fall also brings an unusual play of light and shadow on the nearby mountains. The **Shadow of the Bear,** a bear-shaped shadow that appears for only 30 minutes a day mid-October to early-November when the sun hits a certain ridge just right, brings carloads of visitors to the Rhodes Big View Overlook on Highway 64 just west of Cashiers. To go "bear hunting," as the locals call it, the window is small, typically from 5:30pm to 6pm, maybe 6:15pm, but you'll want to arrive earlier to get a prime viewing spot.

While you're in Cashiers, stay at **High Hampton Inn** (1525 Hwy. 107 S., 828/743-2411, www.highhamptonresort.com, inn from $170, homes $400-800), a gorgeous and historic inn as well as cabins and vacation homes. On the 1,400-acre campus you'll find hiking (easy to moderate, and all with excellent views and well-marked trails), swimming and boating in the lake, and a concierge who can help you find the right mix of things to do nearby. In 2018 the resort closed for a massive renovation, including work to the golf course, inn, dining, and activities areas; construction is expected to be finished by mid-2020.

There are a number of good places to dine in Cashiers, and my favorite coffee shop, **Buck's Coffee Café** (6 Hwy. 107 N., 828/743-9997, 7am-6pm daily, $2-10), serves up a great latte and has a cool little upcycled antiques shop attached. **On the Side Barbecue** (78 Hwy. 64 E., 828/743-4334, www.cashiersfarmersmarket.com, 11am-6pm daily, $10-20) has pulled pork sandwiches, brisket, and ribs in a blend of barbecue styles, plus it's in a great little farmers market loaded with produce and locally made foods. Finally, **The Orchard** (905 Hwy. 107 S., 828/743-7614, www.theorchardcashiers.com, 5:30pm-late Mon.-Sat., $15-40) is one of the best restaurants around; their menu of seasonally driven dishes—trout and grits, wild mushroom ravioli, bourbon-sorghum rib-eye—and an outstanding wine list makes this a must-dine if you're in Cashiers.

GETTING THERE AND AROUND

The towns of Sylva and Dillsboro are easily reached from Asheville by heading west on I-40, then following U.S. 23/U.S. 74 to U.S. 441 south, a drive of about an hour. Sylva and Dillsboro are five minutes apart via Haywood Road/West Main Street. Cullowhee is an easy 15-minute drive south along U.S. 441 and Highways 116 and 107. Cashiers is 22 miles farther south along Highway 107.

Bryson City and the Nantahala Forest

To look at the mountains here, you'd think that the defining feature in this part of North Carolina would be the surrounding peaks, but you're only partly right. This is a land dominated by water: Smoke-thick fog crowds valleys in the predawn hours. The peaks stand ringed in clouds. Moss, ferns, and dense forests crowd the edge of rivers and streams. When you're in the Nantahala Gorge, it feels like you've stepped into a fairy tale. According to Cherokee legends, a formidable witch called Spearfinger lived here, as did a monstrous snake and even an inchworm so large it could span the gorge. Spearfinger and her cohorts haven't been seen in years, and the Nantahala River, which runs through the narrow gorge, attracts white-water enthusiasts.

Nearby Bryson City is a river town whose proximity to white water makes it a favorite haunt for rafters, kayakers, and other thrill seekers. If you approach Bryson City from the north on U.S. 19, you're in for a strange sight: The banks of the Tuckasegee River are shored up with crushed cars.

SIGHTS
★ Great Smoky Mountain Railroad

The **Great Smoky Mountains Railroad** (GSMR, depots in Bryson City and Dillsboro, 800/872-4681, www.gsmr.com, adults from $50, children $29) is one of the best and most fun ways to see the Smokies. On historic trains, the GSMR carries sightseers on excursions from two to several hours long, through some of the most beautiful scenery in the region. Trips between Dillsboro and Bryson City, with a layover at each end for shopping and dining, follow the banks of the Tuckasegee River, while round-trips from Bryson City follow the Little Tennessee and Nantahala Rivers deep into the Nantahala Gorge. Many other excursions are offered, including gourmet dining, wine-, beer-, and moonshine-tasting trips, rides on a steam locomotive, autumn leaf-peeping trips, and more. There are Thomas the Tank Engine and the Little Engine That Could trips for kids, and runs to and from river-rafting outfitters.

Museums

Inside Great Smoky Mountains Railroad gift shop is the **Smoky Mountain Trains Museum** (100 Greenlee St., 800/872-4681, www.gsmr.com, hours vary, generally 9am-4pm daily late May-Dec., 9:30am-4:30pm daily Jan.-late May, call ahead, adults $10, children $5, free with train ticket) The **Fly Fishing Museum of the Southern Appalachians** (210 Main St., Bryson City, 828/867-9246, 8am-4pm Mon.-Fri. Sept. and Nov.-Mar., 9am-5pm Mon.-Fri. and 11am-5pm Sat. Apr.-Aug. and Oct., free) tells the story of fly fishing on the 14,000 miles of trout waters in North Carolina and across the southern Appalachians. Displays of hand-tied flies, antique rods and reels, drift boats, and even live fly-tying demos round out this free museum. Across the street is the **Swain County Heritage Museum** (12 Everett St., 828/488-7857, www.swainheritagemuseum.com, 9am-6pm daily Apr.-Dec., 10am-5pm daily Jan.-Mar., free); downstairs is a Great Smoky Mountain Association Book Store, and upstairs is a small but thorough museum telling the history of Bryson City and Swain County.

SPORTS AND RECREATION

★ Nantahala River Gorge

The stunningly beautiful **Nantahala River Gorge,** just outside Bryson City in the Nantahala National Forest, supports scores of river guide companies, many clustered along U.S. 19 west. Nantahala is said to mean "land of the noonday sun," and there are indeed parts of this gorge where the sheer rock walls above the river are so steep that sunlight only hits the water at the noon hour. Eight miles of the Nantahala River flow through the gorge over Class II-III rapids. The nearby Ocoee River is also a favorite of rafters, and the Cheoah River, when there are controlled

water releases, has some of the South's most famous and difficult Class III-IV runs.

Outfitters and Tours

There's a lot to do in and around Bryson City beyond the borders of Greats Smoky Mountains National Park. White-water rafting, kayaking, and tubing are popular ways to spend a day, but so are zip-lining, hiking, and mountain biking. Fortunately several outfitters can help you arrange for guided tours, rentals, and just about anything else you need to make your time here memorable.

Carolina Bound Adventures (35 Slope St., 828/569-6699, www.carolinaboundadventures.com) offers guide and concierge services, taking visitors on hikes, mountain bike rides, overnight camping trips, waterfall tours, and brewery and winery tours, and they'll assist in planning just about any aspect of your getaway, even pet-sitting if you plan on a long day in the park; rates vary but start at $29.

Endless River Adventures (14157 U.S. 19 W., near Bryson City, 828/488-6199, www.endlessriveradventures.com, $24-45) gives white-water and flat-water kayaking instruction, rentals, and guided trips on the Nantahala, Ocoee, and Cheoah Rivers. They'll be able to suggest a run suited to your skill level.

In addition to river guide services, **Wildwater Rafting** (10345 U.S. 19 W., 12 miles west of Bryson City, 866/319-8870, www.wildwaterrafting.com) leads **Wildwater Jeep Tours** ($50-110), half- and full-day Jeep excursions through back roads and wilderness to waterfalls and old mountain settlements.

You can explore the mountains around Bryson City with the **Nantahala Outdoor Center** (13077 U.S. 19 W., Bryson City, 828/785-4845 or 828/366-7502, www.noc.com, 9am-5pm daily, from $30), which offers a variety of adventure options that include white-water rafting, stand-up paddleboarding on the flat-water sections of the river, hiking, mountain biking, and zip-lining. Half-day, full-day, and overnight trips are possible, and

1: Great Smoky Mountain Railroad in Bryson City
2: Nantahala River Gorge

excursions like the Rapid Transit combine a relaxing morning train ride with an afternoon rafting trip.

★ Fly-Fishing the Tuckasegee River

The mountain streams around Bryson City are teeming with fish; a few outfitters can help you catch them. **Fly Fishing the Smokies** (Bryson City, 828/488-7665, www.flyfishingthesmokies.net) has a number of guides and options for a day or more of fishing. Wade the streams with them for a half-day (1 person $200, 2 people $250) or full-day (1 person $275, 2 people $325) outing, try a float trip (half-day $225 per boat, full-day $325 per boat), or go backcountry camping and fly-fishing in the Great Smoky Mountains National Park ($500-850 pp). They also go bass fishing on nearby Fontana Lake (half-day $275).

Another top fishing guide in the Bryson City area is **Steve Claxton's Smoky Mountain Adventures** (Bryson City, 828/736-7501, http://steveclaxton.com), who specializes in leaving civilization behind in favor of camping, catching wild mountain trout, and getting a true taste of the wilderness. Three-day, two-night camping trips for five to seven people run around $400 pp, and four-day, three-night trips are $575-700 pp. They also offer half-day (1 person $150, 2 people $200, 3 people $250) and full-day fishing trips (1 person $225, 2 people $275, 3 people $325) on nearby streams and lakes.

Nantahala Fly Fishing Co. (Robbinsville, 828/479-8850 or 866/910-1013, www.flyfishnorthcarolina.com, guided trips and private lessons half-day 1 angler $150, $75 per additional person, full-day 1-2 anglers $300, $75 per additional person) provides guided trips for fly-rod fishing, but if you've never held one of these odd fishing rods in your hand, they also provide a fly-fishing school ($300 for 2 days) and private instruction. Best of all, they have a "No Fish, No Pay" guarantee.

For fly fishers who don't need a guide, a number of streams around are packed with fish, but be sure to inquire about regulations for individual streams; some are catch-and-release, while a neighboring stream is catch-and-keep, and some have regulations about the types of hooks you can use. Once you're ready to put your line in the water, try **Hazel Creek** on the north shore of Fontana Lake, where you'll find pristine waters and a good number of fish. Other nearby creeks, like **Eagle Creek** and any of the feeder creeks that empty into the lake, are prime spots as well.

Hiking

The Great Smoky Mountains National Park has more than 800 miles of wilderness trails, and with around 40 percent of the park located in Swain County, more trails than you could hike in a week are within striking distance from Bryson City. **Deep Creek Loop** is a 4.9-mile loop that passes two waterfalls on its easy, mostly flat, track. You can also take the strenuous **Deep Creek Trail** to Newfound Gap Road, a 14.2-mile one-way hike that will require a return ride. The **Noland Creek Trail** is a fairly easy 6-mile trail near the end of the Road to Nowhere (a failed road-building project from the 1930s and 1940s). At the end of the Road to Nowhere, just past the tunnel, is the **Goldmine Loop Trail,** a 3.1-mile track that's beautiful and enjoyable, and the nature and lake views are especially welcome after trekking through the dark 0.5-mile tunnel on the way in (bring a flashlight; you won't regret it).

SHOPPING

Bryson City Outdoors (169 Main St., 828/342-6444, www.brysoncityoutdoors.com, 10am-7pm Mon.-Sat., 10am-6pm Sun.) carries just about all the gear you need to head into the Smokies for a few days, plus recommendations on everything from where to hike or bike or raft to where you should get lunch. They also run a hiker shuttle ($17-210), kayak and stand-up paddleboard rentals on Fontana Lake (1 hour $25, $10 per additional hour up to $55 for 4 hours), sunrise and sunset tours (from $155), and stand-up paddleboard yoga classes ($15 if you have a board, $35 with board rental). And if you want to give backpacking or camping a try but you're not ready to throw down a few hundred bucks for gear, they rent equipment. I love their adjacent **taproom** (10am-9pm Mon.-Wed., 10am-10pm Thurs.-Sat., 10am-8pm Sun.), where they keep a dozen brews from North Carolina and the region on tap and another 200 beers in bottles and cans. It's an awesome collection of beer, and they know their stuff, so if you're stuck, want to try something new, or have a favorite that you don't see, strike up a conversation and find a new draft to enjoy.

There are a number of T-shirt and souvenir shops in Bryson City, but **Appalachian Mercantile** (158 Everett St., 828/488-2531, www.appalachianmercantile.net, 10am-7pm Mon.-Wed. and Sat., 10am-9pm Thurs.-Fri., 10am-6pm Sun., call for hours from Nov.-Mar.) is top on the list. Their selection doesn't overwhelm you, and there's not as much souvenir flotsam as you'll find elsewhere; instead the foodstuffs, playing cards, games, and toys have been winnowed down to the best in each category. The owner, Lance, was a backcountry guide in the area and then a location scout for the film industry; now he's an author of local histories and a shopkeeper, and he's ready with a story if you've got a minute to listen.

FOOD

The Bistro at The Everett Boutique Hotel (24 Everett St., 828/488-1934, www.theeveretthotel.com, dinner from 4:30pm daily, brunch 8:30am-3pm Sat.-Sun., dinner $14-35, brunch $6.50-16) serves an excellent dinner that's contemporary Appalachian in nature but that includes one or two vegetarian-friendly dishes, typically noodle bowls. Regardless of what you order, the flavor will be on point and you'll find a cocktail, wine, or North Carolina beer to pair with it.

You can't beat breakfast at **Everett Street Diner** (126 Everett St., 828/488-0123, www.brysoncityrestaurant.com, 7am-2pm daily,

breakfast $4.50-14, lunch $6-11), where the biscuits and gravy are filling without weighing you down on the trail, and the pancakes are fluffy. At lunch the burgers are great and the light lunch—salad and half a sandwich—is a bargain. If you want a real treat—Bryson City gossip and local news—sit at the counter in back.

For coffee and a quick breakfast, lunch, or snack, visit **Mountain Perks Espresso Bar & Café** (9 Depot St., 8282/488-9561, 7am-4pm Sun.-Mon. and Thurs., 7am-5pm Fri.-Sat., closed Tues.-Wed., $2-16). They make a good cappuccino, and the quiche, wraps, and bagel sandwiches hit the spot whether you eat them in-house or take them on your park adventure.

The Appalachian Trail passes only a few feet from **River's End Restaurant** (13077 Hwy. 19 W., 828/488-7172, www.noc.com, 8am-8pm daily, $6-22) at the Nantahala Outdoor Center. Given its proximity to the trail (really a footbridge over the river, but on the trail nonetheless) and to the center's rafting, paddling, and hiking nexus, it's a popular spot for outdoorsy sorts. The menu reflects this with dishes like the Sherpa bowls (rice, veggies, and optional meat) that are packed with protein, calories, and carbs to fuel you through a day on the trail.

Nantahala Brewing Brewpub (116 Ramseur St., 828/585-5885, www.nantahalabrewing.com, 4pm-10pm daily, $7-25) carries a full slate of Nantahala Brewing beer, but also a menu of elevated pub grub. The salads are sizable and fresh, the pot roast and brown ale chicken are pleasant surprises, and the tacos and sharable plates exceed your bar food expectations.

Speaking of bars and bar food, **Mountain Layers Brewing Company** (90 Everett St., 828/538-0115, 2pm-10pm Mon.-Thurs., noon-11pm Fri.-Sat., 1pm-9pm Sun.) has an excellent rooftop deck overlooking the Tuckasegee River and a board of tasty beers to go with it. Their Russian Imperial Stout, Dragon Tamer New England IPA, and The Helles You Say Helles are top notch. Food trucks like The Rice Wagon (828/593-9931, $6-14), serving Hawaiian barbecue, South of Philly Cheesesteaks (828/586-0550, www. southofphillync.com, $6-10), and The Chili Chomper 2 (828/508-1957, $4-12), a taco truck, are at the brewery most every night.

ACCOMMODATIONS

Bryson City has a surprising number of high-quality inns and bed-and-breakfasts. On Schoolhouse Hill overlooking Bryson City is the ★ **McKinley Edwards Inn** (208 Arlington Ave., 828/488-9626, www. mckinleyedwardsinn.com, from $149), a lovely 12-room house and inn built in 1922. The grounds are magnificent, and breakfast, a drink, or just quiet time on the deck looking at the mountains will sell you on coming back again and again. The **Folkestone Inn** (101 Folkestone Rd., 828/488-2730 or 888/812-3385, www.folkestoneinn.com, $132-176) is one of the region's outstanding bed-and-breakfasts, a roomy 1920s farmhouse expanded and renovated into a charming and tranquil inn. Each room has a balcony or porch. Baked treats at breakfast include shortcake, kuchen, cobblers, and other delicacies.

An 85-year-old hotel on the National Register of Historic Places, the **Fryemont Inn** (245 Fryemont St., Bryson City, 828/488-4879, www.fryemontinn.com, mid-Apr.-late Nov. $125-310, includes meals, late Nov.-mid-Apr. $115-215, no meals) has a lodge with a cozy, rustic feel with chestnut-paneled guest rooms and an inviting lobby with an enormous stone fireplace, balcony suites, a log cabin that sleeps six, and suites.

★ **The Everett Boutique Hotel & Bistro** (24 Everett St., 828/488-1934, www. theeveretthotel.com, $199-349) has 10 suites, a rooftop hangout area, and an excellent restaurant attached. The rooms are spacious, comfortable, and mountain chic, but best of all, the beds are so comfortable you might want to move in. The hotel opened in 2015 but was built in 1908 and served as the Bryson City Bank (you can still see the vault door in the restaurant) until 1960. It's as lovely a place

to stay as you can imagine, and it's within a 10-minute walk to everything Bryson City has to offer.

Way back in the forest by Fontana Lake, the **Fontana Village Resort** (300 Woods Rd., Fontana Dam, 828/498-2211 or 800/849-2258, www.fontanavillage.com) was originally built as housing for the workers building the dam, a massive wartime undertaking that created a whole town out in the woods. Renovated into a comfortable resort, Fontana Village features a lodge ($113-173), cabins ($113-353), camping ($15-40), and a variety of boat rentals, including pontoon boats and fishing charters.

Some river outfitters offer lodging, which can be a cheap way to pass the night if you don't mind roughing it. The **Rolling Thunder River Company** (10160 U.S. 19 W., near Bryson City, 800/408-7238, www. rollingthunderriverco.com, no alcohol permitted) operates a large bunkhouse with beds ($10-12 pp) for its rafting customers. **Carolina Outfitters** (715 U.S. 19, Topton, 828/488-9819, www.carolinaoutfitters.com) has a number of accommodations ($80-100), including two-room cabins, two-bedroom apartments, and three-bedroom cabins suitable for a large group. Many of the outfitters also offer camping on their properties.

Camping

Among the nicest camping options available in the Nantahala Forest is **Standing Indian Campground** (90 Sloan Rd., Franklin, 877/444-6777, www.recreation.gov, Apr.-Oct., $20-75). Standing Indian has a nice diversity of campsites, from flat grassy areas to cozy mountainside nooks. Drinking water, hot showers, flush toilets, and a phone are all available on-site, and leashed pets are permitted. At 3,400 feet elevation, the campground is close to the Appalachian Trail.

Another nice campground is the **Deep Creek Tube Center and Campground** (1090 W. Deep Creek Rd., Bryson City, 828/488-6055, www.deepcreekcamping. com, Apr.-late Oct., camping $27-50, cabins

$80-195), with more than 50 campsites, 18 cabins, and access to Deep Creek, which runs right by many campsites, where you can go tubing ($6 per day). You can also go gem "mining" here, a great mountain tradition; they sell bags and buckets of gem-enriched dirt in the camp store. The best part is that the campground is within walking distance of the Great Smoky Mountains National Park.

TRANSPORTATION

Bryson City can be reached via U.S. 19 and U.S. 74, if you're coming south from Maggie Valley and Cherokee; it's only 15 minutes from Cherokee and 45 minutes from Maggie Valley. It's 20 minutes to the Great Smoky Mountains National Park's Oconaluftee Visitors Center, just north of Cherokee. Asheville is 1 hour, 20 minutes east along U.S. 74 and I-40.

Robbinsville and the Valley Towns

Between Robbinsville and the Georgia state line is another region at the heart of Cherokee life. Snowbird, not far from Robbinsville, is one of the most traditional Cherokee communities, where it's common to hear the Cherokee language, and Cherokee arts, crafts, and folkways are flourishing. The burial site of Junaluska, one of the Eastern Band's most prominent leaders, is here.

As moving as it is to see the memorial to one of the Cherokee heroes, the town of Murphy is forever linked with tragedy for the Cherokee people and a dark incident in American history—the Trail of Tears. Around 16,000 Cherokee people, including warriors and clan leaders, men, women, children, the elderly, and the infirm, were forced to leave their homes in North Carolina, Tennessee, and Georgia; they were arrested and marched under guard to Fort Butler, here in Murphy, and from Fort Butler they were forced to walk to Oklahoma. You'll find the names of these people, many of whom died along the way, inscribed in Cherokee on a memorial at the L&N Depot in Murphy.

In addition to places of historic significance in Cherokee culture, this farthest southwestern corner of North Carolina has other compelling sights. Brasstown, a tiny village on the Georgia state line, is the home of the John C. Campbell Folk School, an artists' colony nearly a century old, where visitors can stroll among studios and along trails and stop in to a gallery shop with some of the

most beautiful crafts you'll find in the region. Back up toward Robbinsville, the relentlessly scenic **Cherohala Skyway** (www.cherohala. org) crosses 43 miles of the Cherokee and Nantahala Forests. This road is a major destination for motorcyclists and sports-car drivers as well as day-trippers and vacationers.

ROBBINSVILLE

The whole southwestern corner of North Carolina is rich with Cherokee history and culture, and the Robbinsville area has some of the deepest roots of great significance to the Cherokee people. In little towns and crossroads a few miles outside Robbinsville, several hundred people known as the Snowbird community keep alive some of the oldest Cherokee ways. The Cherokee language is spoken here, and it's a place where some of the Eastern Band's most admired basket makers, potters, and other artists continue to make and teach their ancient arts. If you're visiting and want to enjoy an adult beverage, you'd better bring your own, as Graham County is North Carolina's one and only dry county.

Sights

Outside Robbinsville, in the ancient Stecoah Valley, is an imposing old rock schoolhouse built in 1930 and used as a school until the mid-1990s. It has been reborn as the **Stecoah Valley Center** (121 Schoolhouse Rd., Stecoah, 828/479-3364, www.stecoahvalleycenter.com), home of a weavers' guild, a native plants

Junaluska

One of the most important figures in the history of the Eastern Band of the Cherokee is Junaluska, who was born near Dillard, Georgia, in 1776. During the wars against the Creek Indians from 1812 to 1814, the Cherokee people fought beside U.S. forces, and it's said that the fierce young Junaluska saved the life of Andrew Jackson at the battle of Horse Shoe Bend in Alabama.

Twenty years later, Jackson, by then president, repaid Junaluska's bravery and the loyalty of the Cherokee people by signing the Indian Removal Act, which ordered that they, along with four other major Southern nations, be forced from their homelands and marched to the new Indian Territory of Oklahoma. Junaluska traveled to Washington and met with Jackson to plead for mercy for the Cherokee nation; his pleas were ignored, and in 1838, Junaluska joined 16,000 members of the Cherokee nation who were force-marched close to 1,000 miles to Oklahoma. Midway across Tennessee, he led a failed escape attempt and was captured and chained; he completed the march in leg irons and manacles. It was during this time that Junaluska supposedly said, "If I had known what Andrew Jackson would do to the Cherokees, I would have killed him myself that day at Horse Shoe Bend." In 1841 he was finally able to leave Oklahoma and made the 17-day trip to North Carolina on horseback.

He spent his final years in Cherokee County, on land granted to him by the state of North Carolina. He and his third wife, Nicie, are buried at Robbinsville, at what is now the Junaluska Memorial and Museum. His grave was originally marked according to Cherokee tradition—with a pile of stones—but in 1910 the Daughters of the American Revolution commissioned a marker for his gravesite. During the dedication ceremony, Reverend Armstrong Cornsilk delivered a eulogy in the Cherokee language:

He was a good man. He was a good friend. He was a good friend in his home and everywhere. He would ask the hungry man to eat. He would ask the cold one to warm by his fire. He would ask the tired one to rest, and he would give a good place to sleep. Juno's home was a good home for others. He was a smart man. He made his mind think well. He was very brave. He was not afraid. Juno at this time has been dead about 50 years. I am glad he is up above [pointing up-ward]. I am glad we have this beautiful monument. It shows Junaluska did good, and it shows we all appreciate him together—having a pleasant time together. I hope we shall all meet Junaluska in heaven [pointing upward] and all be happy there together.

preservation group, a concert series, several festivals, and a great **Gallery Shop** (828/497-3098, 10am-5pm Mon.-Sat. Apr.-Nov., 10am-5pm Mon.-Fri. Mar. and Dec.) of local artisans' work. Concerts in the Appalachian Evening summer series, featuring area musicians, are preceded by community suppers of traditional mountain cuisine.

On Robbinsville's Main Street is the **Junaluska Memorial** (Main St., 0.5 miles north of the Graham County Courthouse, 828/479-4727, 9am-5pm Mon.-Sat. Apr.-Oct., call for hours Nov.-Mar.), where Junaluska, a 19th-century leader of the Eastern Band of the Cherokee, and his third wife, Nicie, are buried.

Down a winding country road 14 miles outside Robbinsville, **Yellow Branch Pottery and Cheese** (136 Yellow Branch Circle, Robbinsville, 828/479-6710, www. yellowbranch.com, noon-5pm Tues.-Sat. Apr.-Nov. or by appointment) is a beautifully rustic spot for an afternoon's excursion. Bruce DeGroot, Karen Mickler, and their herd of Jersey cows produce prizewinning artisanal cheeses and graceful, functional pottery. Visitors are welcome at their farm and shop.

Entertainment and Events

Every year on the Saturday of Memorial Day weekend in late May, the Snowbird Cherokee host the **Fading Voices Festival** (www. grahamcountytravel.com) in Robbinsville. The festival features a mound-building ceremony along with typical festival attractions—music, dancing, storytelling, crafts, and lots of food—but in the deeply traditional forms carried on by the Snowbird community.

★ Joyce Kilmer Memorial Forest

The **Joyce Kilmer Memorial Forest** (Joyce Kilmer Rd., off Hwy. 143 west of Robbinsville, www.grahamcountytravel.com) is one of the largest remaining tracts of virgin forest in the eastern United States, with more than 3,800 acres of old-growth forest. Some of the tulip poplar trees are 450 years old and have grown to more than 100 feet tall and 20 feet around. The forest is named in honor of Joyce Kilmer, a soldier killed in action in France during World War I. His poem "Trees" inspired this living memorial. The only way to see the forest is on foot, and a two-mile loop or two one-mile loops make for an easy hike through a remarkable woodland. A pair of loop trails winds for two miles through the forest, and these easy well-maintained paths allow visitors to experience the woods that so inspired Kilmer and his poem.

The Joyce Kilmer Memorial Forest abuts the 17,410-acre Slickrock Wilderness Area that stretches into Tennessee; **Slickrock Creek Trail** is one of its longest trails. This 13.5-mile (one-way) trail starts out easy, but the final 5.5 miles are fairly strenuous. *Backpacker* magazine named this one of the toughest trails in the country several years ago, in part because the hike can be a 21.7-mile loop by connecting with the **Haoe Lead, Hangover Lead,** and **Ike Branch Trails.** Be forewarned that this is a big trip, but it's rewarding, with views of waterfalls (the first is only a few miles in, on the easy part) and rhododendron thickets. Its name is apt: The rocks here can be incredibly slick.

On the **Hangover Lead South Trail,** the trailhead is adjacent to the parking area at Big Fat Gap (off Slick Rock Rd., about 7 miles from U.S. 129). The trail is only 2.8 miles long, but it's strenuous. The payoff is the view from the Haoe summit at 5,249 feet. There are backcountry campsites here, and the rule is to keep campsites 100 yards from streams and practice Leave No Trace guidelines.

A handy collection of **trail maps** for Joyce Kilmer Memorial Forest, Slickrock Creek, Snowbird Back Country, and Tsali Recreation Area is available from the Graham Chamber (http://grahamchamber.com). The maps provide a rough idea of the locations and routes of these trails, but they are not a replacement for topographic maps, which you should have with you while on any of these rugged or isolated trails. A slightly better map is available through the Partners of the Joyce Kilmer Slickrock Wilderness (www.joycekilmerslickrock.org).

Food and Accommodations

The **Snowbird Mountain Lodge** (4633 Santeetlah Rd., 11 miles west of Robbinsville, 828/479-3433, http://snowbirdlodge.com, $290-475) was built in the early 1940s, a rustic chestnut-and-stone inn atop a 3,000-foot mountain. The view is exquisite, and the lodge is perfectly situated among the Cherohala Skyway, Lake Santeetlah, and the Joyce Kilmer Forest. Guests enjoy a full breakfast, picnic lunch, and four course supper created from seasonal local specialties.

Another pleasant place to stay near Robbinsville is the **Tapoco Lodge Resort** (14981 Tapoco Rd., 15 miles north of Robbinsville, 828/498-2800, www.tapocolodge.com, Thurs.-Sat. Nov.-Sept., daily Oct., rooms and suites $179-329, cabins $149-249). Built in 1930, the lodge is on the National Register of Historic Places, and it has the feel of an old-time hotel. Guest rooms in the main lodge and surrounding cabins are simple but comfortable, and the resort overlooks the Cheoah River, a legendary run for rafters several times each year when controlled releases of water form crazy-fast rapids. Dine here at **Tapoco Tavern** (828/498-2800, 7:30am-10am and 11am-9pm Sun.-Thurs., 11am-10pm Fri.-Sat., $9-25) on pizzas, steaks, trout, fried chicken, sandwiches, and salads.

Mountain Ivy Rentals (56 Airport Rd.,

2.5 miles east of Robbinsville, 828/735-9180, www.mountainivy.com, 2-night minimum, $125) has one log-sided cabin that sleeps six and is steps away from great trout fishing in the stream that runs alongside the cabin. An indoor fireplace and a space outside for a campfire help make it cozy in any season. The garage is handy for motorcycle travelers, as it gives them a place to secure trailers, bikes, and other gear. At the **Simple Life Campground** (88 Lower Mountain Creek Rd., 828/788-1099, www.thesimplelifecampground.com, Mar.-Nov., cabins $32-144, RVs $48-58, tents $18, pop-up campers $28) the cabins, RV sites, and tent sites have access to hot showers and Wi-Fi. This campground is near the Cherohala Skyway, Joyce Kilmer National Forest, and Lake Santeetlah.

If you're RVing your way through the Smokies, the six-acre **Teaberry Hill RV Campground** (77 Upper Sawyers Creek Rd., 828/479-3953, http://teaberryhill.com, May-Oct., $55, $600 weekly, $900 monthly) is one of the nicest campgrounds you'll find, with large pull-through sites to accommodate any size RV. Amenities include 30- and 50-amp electrical hookups, water and sewer, and Wi-Fi access.

HAYESVILLE, BRASSTOWN, AND MURPHY

Between Hayesville and Brasstown, you can get a really good sense of the art that has come out of this region over the years. These three small towns are along the Georgia border on U.S. 64.

Murphy River Walk

The **Murphy River Walk** is a three-mile trail along the Hiwassee River and Valley River, winding from Konehete Park to the Old L&N Depot through this charming tiny town. It gives you the chance to see Murphy up close and personal, and it's a great way to stretch your legs after a long ride.

After a walk along the river, take a look in some of the many antiques stores in Murphy.

Marketplace Antiques (41 Peachtree St., 828/837-1060, 10am-5pm Mon.-Fri., 10am-4pm Sat., noon-4pm Sun.), **Black & White Market** (40 Valley River Ave., 828/516-1634, www.black-and-white-market.com, 10am-5pm Mon.-Fri., 10am-4pm Sat.), and **In With the Old** (980 W. U.S. 64, 828/557-0030, noon-5pm Mon. and Wed.-Fri., 10am-2pm Sun.) will have you covered in the antiques department, and **Serenity Mountain Gift Shop** (35 Tennessee St., 828/361-7543, 10:30am-5:30pm Tues.-Fri., 10am-5pm Sat.) has all the shirts, souvenirs, and gifts you'll want. If you're looking for beer, wine, or cigars, swing by **The Murphy Co.** (50 W. U.S. 64, 828/516-1630, www.themurphycompany.net, 10am-7pm Mon.-Thurs., 10am-9pm Fri.-Sat.).

★ John C. Campbell Folk School

One of North Carolina's most remarkable cultural institutions, the **John C. Campbell Folk School** (1 Folk School Rd., Brasstown, 800/365-5724, www.folkschool.org) was created by a pair of Northern honeymooners who traveled through Appalachia 100 years ago to educate themselves about Southern highland culture. John C. and Olive Dame Campbell, like other high-profile Northern liberals of their day, directed their humanitarian impulses toward the education and economic betterment of Southern mountain dwellers. John Campbell died a decade later, but Olive, joining forces with her friend Marguerite Butler, set out to establish a "folk school" in the Southern mountains that she and John had visited. She was inspired by the model of the Danish *folkehøjskole,* workshops that preserved and taught traditional arts as a means of fostering economic self-determination and personal pride in rural communities. Brasstown was chosen as the site for this grand experiment, and in 1925, the John C. Campbell Folk School opened its doors.

Today, thousands of artists travel every year to this uncommonly lovely remote valley, the site of an ancient Cherokee village. In weeklong and weekend classes, students of all ages and skill levels learn about the traditional arts of this region, such as pottery, weaving, dyeing, storytelling, and chair caning, as well as contemporary and exotic crafts such as photography, kaleidoscope making, bookmaking, and paper marbling. The website outlines the hundreds of courses offered every year, but even if you're passing through the area on a shorter visit, you can explore the school's campus. Visitors are asked to preserve the quiet atmosphere of learning and concentration when viewing the artist studios, but you can have an up-close look at some of their marvelous wares in the school's **Craft Shop** (bottom floor of Olive Dame Campbell Dining Hall, 8am-5pm Mon.-Wed. and Fri.-Sat., 8am-6pm Thurs., 1pm-5pm Sun.), one of the nicest craft shops in western North Carolina; you'll be wowed by what you find here. Exhibits about the school's history and historic examples of the work of local artists of past generations are on display at the **History Center** (8am-5pm Mon.-Sat., 1pm-5pm Sun.), next to Keith House.

There are several nature trails on campus that thread through this lovely valley. Be sure to visit the 0.25-mile **Rivercane Walk,** which features outdoor sculpture by some of the greatest living artists of the Eastern Band of the Cherokee. In the evenings you'll often find concerts by traditional musicians, or community square, contra, and English country dances. A visit to the John C. Campbell Folk School, whether as a student or a traveler, is an exceptional opportunity to immerse yourself in a great creative tradition.

Food and Accommodations

The western terminus of the North Carolina Barbecue Trail is **Herb's Pit Bar-B-Que** (15725 W. U.S. 64, Murphy, 828/494-5367, 11am-8pm Wed.-Sun., $2-30) and should be your first or last stop on it. Here you can sample more than the 'cue that pit masters in the deep mountains make—you can also order plates of tasty fried trout and chicken and thick steaks off the grill.

The Parson's Pub (19 Tennessee St.,

828/837-4151, www.theparsonspub.com, 11am-9pm Mon.-Thurs., 11am-10pm Fri.-Sat., $6-12) is an Irish-style pub, with the shepherd's pie, corned beef and cabbage, and Irish pasty you'd expect to find on the food side of the menu, and more than 80 beers on draft, in bottles, and in cans.

At **The Daily Grind & Wine** (46 Valley River Ave., 828/835-7322, www.thedailygrindandwine.com, 8am-6pm Mon.-Tues., 9am-8pm Wed.-Fri., 9am-4pm Sat., breakfast $2-7, lunch $4-11) you'll find plenty of coffee and a great cheap breakfast menu as well as a more filling lunch and snack menu loaded with sandwiches and salads, a very tasty spicy black bean burger, and a Guinness beer brat that's top-notch. They also have a wine shop and bar serving wine and regional craft beer.

In nearby Hayesville, 15 miles east along U.S. 64, there are two spots to keep on your radar. **The Copper Door** (2 Sullivan St., Hayesville, 828/389-8460, http://thecopperdoor.com, 5pm-10pm Tues.-Sat., $16-48) is an upscale joint serving a nice selection of seafood, steaks, and other meat-centric dishes, but they can accommodate vegetarians and vegans. This elegant restaurant is run by a chef from New Orleans, and his influence is all over the menu, from crawfish to mussels to other French- and creole-inspired creations. Over at **Nocturnal Brewing Company** (893 U.S. 64 Business, Hayesville, 828/305-7337, www.nocturnalbrewing.com, 4pm-9pm Wed.-Thurs., 4pm-10pm Fri.-Sat., 11am-3pm Sun., dinner $5-25, brunch $5-18) they have a solid burger, a really good lentil sloppy joe, and tempeh tacos if you're hungry, and their beer—saisons, goses, pale ales, and bier de gardes—is proof positive that in North Carolina, there's a great brewery anywhere you go.

Angels Landing Inn Bed & Breakfast (94 Campbell St., Murphy, 828/360-7700, $88-105) is one of the only B&Bs in town. Fortunately, the price is right, and the breakfast is a good one. As with most B&Bs, and as with most North Carolinians, the folks here are friendly and ready with a recommendation if you're ready to explore like a local (or just get a little local gossip).

Harrah's Casino in Cherokee opened a sister location here in Murphy in 2015: **Harrah's Cherokee Valley River Casino & Hotel** (777 Casino Pkwy., Murphy, 828/422-7777, www.caesars.com, $99-499) has 300 rooms and a huge 50,000-square-feet gaming floor with 70 table games and more than 1,000 slot machines. The dining options are **Nathan's Famous Hot Dogs** (11am-11pm Sun.-Thurs., 11am-3am Fri.-Sat., around $6), **Panda Express** (11am-11pm Sun.-Thurs., 11am-3am Fri.-Sat., about $14), **Earl of Sandwich** (24 hours daily, breakfast 6am-11am daily, around $12), **The Landing Cafe** (8am-10pm daily, around $12), **Starbucks** (6am-11pm Sun.-Thurs., 6am-1am Fri.-Sat.), and **Moe's Southwest Grill** (11am-11pm Sun.-Thurs., 11am-3am Fri.-Sat., around $12). Still, who comes to a casino to eat?

TRANSPORTATION

This is the southwesternmost corner of North Carolina, in some places as close to Atlanta as to Asheville. From Murphy to Asheville is 2.5 hours along U.S. 74 and I-40, and to Atlanta the drive is closer to 3 hours. Robbinsville and Murphy are about 45 minutes apart along U.S. 129 and U.S. 74. It's 1 hour from Murphy to Bryson City, and to get to the Oconaluftee Visitors Center in Cherokee from Murphy is a 1.5-hour drive.

Asheville

There's an energy in the mountain town of Asheville that you don't find in many other places in North Carolina. For more than a century Asheville has been a hive of progressive thinking and has a surprisingly cosmopolitan level of living.

With all the writers, artists, musicians, dancers, wealthy industrialists, and eclectic personalities that have inhabited this town, it's easy to understand how it earned the nickname "Paris of the South." Built on a series of hills around the confluence of the Swannanoa ("swan-uh-NO-uh") and French Broad Rivers, commerce found its way here in the 18th and 19th centuries via water routes and a mountain stagecoach road. In the late 1800s the town experienced a boom as railroad lines began to bring vacationers by the tens of thousands. It was around that time that George Vanderbilt, scion of the massively wealthy Vanderbilt dynasty, began building his mountain home, the Biltmore, just south of downtown. From the 1880s to the 1930s the mountain town underwent a long and rapid expansion, eventually becoming a small city in its own right.

Asheville's proximity to Great Smoky Mountains National Park (it's a little more than an hour to the south and west) makes it a convenient travel hub. Use Asheville as a starting or ending point, or as a base of operations. The city also offers diverse dining and lodging options.

SIGHTS
Downtown Architecture

As beautiful as Asheville's natural environment may be, the striking architecture is just as attractive. The Montford neighborhood, a contemporary of the Biltmore, is a mixture of ornate Queen Anne houses and Craftsman-style bungalows. The Grove Park Inn, a huge luxury hotel, was built in 1913 and is decked out with rustic architectural devices intended to make vacationing New Yorkers and wealthy people feel like they were roughing it. In downtown Asheville is a large concentration of art deco buildings on the scale of Miami Beach. Significant structures dating to the boom before the Great Depression include the **Buncombe County Courthouse** (60 Court Plaza, built in 1927-1929), the **First**

Greater Asheville

© MOON.COM

Baptist Church (Oak St. and Woodfin St., 1925), the **S&W Cafeteria** (56 Patton Ave., 1929), the **Public Service Building** (89-93 Patton Ave., 1929), and the **Grove Arcade** (1 Page Ave., 1926-1929).

The **Jackson Building** (22 S. Pack Square, built in 1923-1924) is a fine example of neo-Gothic architecture with a disturbing back-story. According to legend, on the day of the stock market crash in 1929 that started the Great Depression, one of the wealthiest men in Asheville lost it all and leaped to his death from the building. Three or four (depending on who's telling the story) more of Asheville's wealthiest followed suit. What is known to be true is that there's a bull's-eye built into the sidewalk in front of the building as a morbid monument to the story.

★ Biltmore Estate

Much of downtown Asheville dates to the 1920s, but the architectural crown jewel, the **Biltmore Estate** (1 Lodge St., 800/411-3812, www.biltmore.com, house 9am-5pm daily, gardens 9am-8pm daily, ticket office 8:30am-6:30pm daily, adults $59-89, ages 10-16 $30-45, under age 10 free, additional fees for activities), predates that by decades. It was built in the late 1800s for owner George Vanderbilt, grandson of Gilded Age robber baron Cornelius Vanderbilt. He found himself so awestruck by the land that he amassed a 125,000-acre tract south of Asheville where he would build his "country home." He engaged celebrity architect Richard Morris Hunt to build the home in the style of a 16th-century French château. Vanderbilt also hired the esteemed Frederick Law Olmsted, creator of New York City's Central Park, to design the landscape for the grounds, gardens, and surrounding forest.

A three-mile-long approach road leads through manicured forests, revealing bits of the landscape and hiding the house until you are upon it, creating a sense of drama and wonder for arriving visitors. While the Biltmore Estate's original 125,000 acres are now greatly diminished—the estate comprises a little more than 8,000 acres today—it's easy to see just how big it was.

The Biltmore Estate was once the largest privately owned home in the country, and most of the house is open to visitors on self-guided tours. Other parts—like the roof and some servants' areas—are accessible on behind-the-scenes tours. As astounding as this may be, it's nothing compared to the art collected here. There are paintings by Renoir, James Abbott Whistler, and John Singer Sargent; a collection of European antiques including Napoleon's chess set; and room upon room of masterwork in tiling, woodworking and carving, masonry, and stone carving.

Visitors can eat, shop, tour, explore, relax, and unwind without leaving the grounds, and there's easily enough here to fill a weekend. Other sights include the **Biltmore Winery** and **Cedric's** brewery in Antler Hill Village, **River Bend Farm,** which features traditional crafts, and the **Equestrian Center.**

Admission cost for the Biltmore Estate varies by season and includes the house, gardens, and winery; activities such as horseback riding, rafting, and behind-the-scenes tours cost extra. Special events, like the Christmas Candlelight Tour (Nov.-Dec.) also have additional fees. Parking is free, and a complimentary shuttle runs to the house.

Asheville Art Museum

In mid-2019 the **Asheville Art Museum** (2 S. Pack Square, 828/253-3227, www.ashevilleart. org, 10am-5pm Tues.-Sat., 1pm-5pm Sun., adults $8, students $7, over age 60 $7, under age 6 free) reopened after nearly two years of renovations to the exterior and galleries. There are new galleries, a rooftop sculpture garden and café, and the redesign has allowed them to expand the permanent collection space by 70 percent and to double rotating exhibit spaces. The wing facing Pack Square has been sheathed in glass and conveys from the exterior what the gallery space does inside: blend the old and the new, and invite you in for some artistic discoveries. The museum has been around since 1948, so this update was

Downtown Asheville

© MOON.COM

needed. The permanent collection includes a wide array of media and styles, ranging from photo portraits to ceramics to statuary to beautiful modern pieces. A large collection from the nearby experimental school, Black Mountain College, shows the highlights of works created by faculty and students.

North Carolina Arboretum

The enormous **North Carolina Arboretum** (100 Frederick Law Olmsted Way, 828/665-2492, www.ncarboretum.org, 8am-9pm daily Apr.-Oct., 8am-7pm daily Nov.-Mar., bonsai exhibition garden 9am-5pm daily, parking $14 cars, $50 RVs) is considered by many to be one of the most beautiful in the country. The 434 natural and landscaped acres back into the Pisgah National Forest, just off the Blue Ridge Parkway. Major collections include the National Native Azalea Repository, where you can see almost every species of azalea native to the United States as well as several hybrids, and the very special Bonsai Collection, where staff horticulturists care

for more than 200 bonsai plants, many of their own creation.

Bicycles and leashed dogs are permitted on many of the trails. Walking areas range from easy to fairly rugged, but with 10 miles of hiking and biking trails, you will find one that suits your skill level. To learn more about the history of the Arboretum, the plants themselves, and the natural history of the region, join one of the guided tours (1pm Tues. and Sat.). These two-mile walk-and-talk tours happen rain or shine, so dress for the weather. The Arboretum also has a very nice café, the **Bent Creek Bistro** (11am-4pm Tues.-Sun. Mar.-Nov., $4-9), and a gift shop, the **Connections Gallery** (9am-4pm daily Apr.-Oct., 11am-4pm daily Nov.-Mar.).

Botanical Gardens

The **Botanical Gardens at Asheville** (151 W. T. Weaver Blvd., adjacent to UNC-Asheville campus, 828/252-5190, www.ashevillebotanicalgardens.org, dawn-dusk daily year-round, donation) is a 10-acre preserve for the region's increasingly threatened native plant species. Laid out in 1960 by landscape architect Doan Ogden, the gardens are an ecological haven. The many "rooms" are planted to reflect different environments of the mountains, including the Wildflower Trail, the Heath Cove, and the Fern and Moss Trail. Spring blooms peak in mid-April, but the gardens are an absolutely lovely and visually rich place to visit any time of year. Because of its serious mission of plant preservation, neither pets nor bicycles are allowed. Admission is free, but as the gardens are entirely supported by donations, your contribution will have a real impact. On the first Saturday in May, the **Day in the Gardens** brings food and music to this normally placid park, and garden and nature enthusiasts from all around come to tour and to buy native plants for their home gardens. There is also a visitors center and gift shop (11am-3pm daily Mar., 10am-4pm Mon.-Sat., noon-4pm

Sun. Apr.-Oct., noon-4pm daily Nov.-Dec. 6, closed Dec.-late Feb.).

Western North Carolina Nature Center

Asheville, and western North Carolina generally, tend to be very ecologically conscious, as reflected in the **Western North Carolina Nature Center** (75 Gashes Creek Rd., 828/259-8080, www.wildwnc.org, 10am-5pm daily, closed Thanksgiving Day, Dec. 24-25, and Jan. 1, adults $11, over age 64 $10, ages 3-15 $7, under age 3 free). On the grounds of an old zoo—don't worry, it's not depressing—wild animals that are unable to survive in the wild due to injury or having been raised as pets live in wooded habitats on public display. This is the place to see some of the mountains' rarest species—those that even most lifelong mountain residents have never seen: cougars, wolves, coyotes, bobcats, and even the elusive hellbender. What's a hellbender, you ask? Come to the Nature Center to find out.

Folk Art Center

Anyone with an interest in Appalachian handicrafts and folk or fine art should stop by the **Folk Art Center** (Blue Ridge Parkway, milepost 382, 828/298-7928, 9am-5pm daily Jan.-Mar., 9am-6pm daily Apr.-Dec., free). Home to the Southern Highland Craft Guild, the Folk Art Center has around 30,000 square feet of space that includes three galleries, an auditorium, a research library, a tiny Blue Ridge Parkway info booth, and the Allanstand Craft Shop. Allanstand is the oldest continuously operated craft shop in the United States. It was started in 1897 by a Presbyterian missionary and carries out the same vision it had the year it was born: to help preserve traditional art forms and raise the visibility of the arts and crafts of the Appalachian Mountains. Although the folk arts are well represented in beautiful pottery, baskets, weaving, and quilts, you'll also find the work of contemporary studio artists in an array of media, including gorgeous handcrafted furniture, clothing,

1: Biltmore Estate 2: North Carolina Arboretum

jewelry, and toys. Bring your holiday shopping list even if it's April.

Every day, one or more members of the Southern Highlands Craft Guild are on hand to demonstrate their craft at the entrance to the Folk Art Center. They may be whittling away at a chunk of wood with a pocket knife, spinning wool into yarn or weaving, or tying brooms. No matter what they're doing, they're happy to talk to you and explain their process and the history of their craft.

SPORTS AND RECREATION

Asheville is a "go out and do it" kind of town. It's not unusual to see mountain bikers, road riders, runners, hikers, flat-water kayakers, and their daredevil white water-loving cousins all on the streets in town. A number of gear shops call Asheville home, and trails, rivers, and mountain roads are all accessed right here.

Zip-Lining

For a different perspective on the Asheville area, head north for 30 minutes along I-26 west and spend the day at **Navitat** (242 Poverty Branch Rd., Barnardsville, 855/628-4828 or 828/626-3700, www.navitat.com, 8am-5pm daily). You can streak through the forest canopy on a pair of zip-line courses like an overgrown flying squirrel. The Mountaintop Tour (from $99) has the tallest zip line here; it's an incredible 350 feet high—they say "Don't look down," but do; it's amazing. The longest is more than 3,600 feet, and you can reach speeds of 65 miles an hour. Two rappels, a pair of sky bridges, and three short hikes provide interludes from all the zipping and flying, and there are plenty of opportunities for photos and action-camera videos. The smaller course, the Treetop Tour ($99), has 10 zip lines up to 2,000 feet long, a pair of bridges, and two rappels. You can combine the two courses ($179) into one giant day of adventure. If you're not into zip-lining, they have an RTV Shadow Tour ($50) that takes you on a tour of the surrounding mountains

while the rest of your party plays at being flying squirrels for the afternoon.

If you're tempted to zip-line but want something a little less heart-pounding, think about **The Adventure Center of Asheville** (85 Expo Dr., 877/247-5539, www.ashevilletreetopsadventurepark.com, 9am-5pm daily). The Adventure Center has a number of high-flying adventures to try. Their **Treetops Adventure Park** ($49) has 60 challenges (read: rope swings, sky bridges, cargo nets, short zip lines, leaps from tall platforms) spread over five different adventure trails, allowing you to face the trail that presents you with the best challenges. If you want more climbing, you can scale a few trees with their **Tree Quest** ($15), which gets you geared up for a 1.5-hour tree climbing extravaganza, but don't think you're just going limb to limb; you'll be using climbing ropes, ascenders, and other pieces of specialized gear. The **Zip Line Canopy Tours** ($59-79) has 11 zips, three sky bridges, and so many great views you'll forget about the zip lines. **Kid Zip** ($49) is a zip-line course designed for kids ages 4-10. They also have the **KOLO Mountain Bike Park** (full-day access adults $21, youths $16, with rental bikes 2-hour pass adults $49-64, children $44) where you can challenge yourself or build up your skills before you head out onto some of the single-track trails south of town.

Bicycling

In town, take a tour by bicycle. I know what you're thinking; "It's too hilly, I'll never be able to climb that." **The Flying Bike Electric Bike Tours** (meeting point 225 Coxe Ave., 828/393-0326, www.flyingbiketours.com. 9am, 1pm, 4pm daily Feb.15-Dec.15, $62 per rider, ages 12 and under free) provide you with pedal-assisted bikes that make the hills easier and the flats seem like nothing at all. To show off how well the pedal-assist system works, you start with the hill to the Grove Park Inn, the first stop on a two-hour tour

1: floating down the French Broad River with Zen Tubing 2: zip-lining at Navitat

around Asheville's historic and cultural sites. The bikes really are ingenious; rather than rely on a throttle like a moped or electric scooter, they use their power to make pedaling easier, meaning you still have to work, just not as hard, to get where you're going. If you're ready to create your own bicycle tour of Asheville, Flying Bike **rents** their pedal-assisted machines (2 hours $29, 4 hours $49, 8 hours $79).

There are countless miles of **bicycle trails** on the Biltmore Estate, and you can bring your bike or rent one in Antler Hill Village from the **Bike Barn** (828/225-1331, beach cruiser $15 per hour, half-day mountain and hybrid bikes adults $25, children $20, tandem bikes $50, estate admission not included). Riding on paved roads is not allowed (they're too narrow to share with cars), so stick to the marked paths, which will take you past prime photo spots and some of the most beautiful land on the estate.

In a town with as much beer as Asheville, I'd be remiss if I didn't mention the **Amazing Pubcycle** (828/214-5010, www. amazingpubcycle.com, $25, pickup at Aloft Hotel, 51 Biltmore Ave., and Renaissance Hotel, 33 Woodfin St.). Yes, it's a strange pedal-powered pub on wheels that you see loaded down with bachelorette parties, guys getaways, and assorted rascals out to drink a heroic number of brews while working off a few of those calories as they pedal around town. On the tour you'll make two quick stops for beer; the rest is BYOB (beer and wine, no hard liquor), so pay a visit to one of the excellent bottle shops in town before you saddle up.

Water Sports

Wai Mauna Asheville SUP Tours

(159 Riverside Dr., 828/808-9038, www. waimaunaashevillesuptours.com, rentals $40, tours $80-95) is a natural fit for Asheville given that "wai mauna" is Hawaiian for "mountain waters." Where most SUP outfitters ignore the two most beautiful parts of the day, dawn and dusk, these guys embrace it: Wai Mauna offers two tours, one of the River Arts District (5 tours daily: dawn, sunset,

mid-morning, mid-afternoon, late afternoon) and the Biltmore Estate (3 tours daily: early morning, mid-morning, mid-afternoon). And as much as people rave about sunsets, there's something to the Dawn Patrol tour. At that time, the river's often shrouded in fog, the birds are waking up, and the river is as still as it will ever be; it's a perfect time to paddle. If you want to do something wild, try their six-person paddleboard ($300 guided tour, $175 self-guided). Wai Mauna also rents boards if you want to explore on your own ($44-69).

Tubing isn't a sport, inasmuch as you simply recline in an inner tube and float from point A to point B, but it's a lot of fun. If you want to go tubing in Asheville, do it with **Zen Tubing** (855/936-8823, www.zentubing.com, trips 10am-3pm daily, $20, cooler carrier $5). The French Broad is a calm river, especially on the sections where Zen sends their tubers (what else would you call one who rides a tube?). If you pick up a six-pack of your favorite canned beverage, you'll want the cooler carrier tube so you can keep any snacks and beverages close at hand. Tube trips take a while, but you'll have plenty of company, as the river is mobbed by tube enthusiasts. They have two locations, one in midtown Asheville (608 Riverside Dr.) and one in south Asheville (1648 Brevard Rd.).

French Broad Outfitters (704 Riverside Dr., 828/505-7371, www. frenchbroadoutfitters.com, 10am-6pm daily, rentals $15-75 per day) specializes in sports that get you wet, namely stand-up paddleboards, kayaks, and white-water kayaks, if you're that adventurous. If you've come to Asheville equipped with your own paddleboard or kayak, Adventure Rentals rents helmets, dry suits, PFDs, kayak skirts, and more. Guided tours of the River Arts District ($45) and the Biltmore ($45) are available, as are tubing trips (adults $20, children $10) and there are options for a self-guided multiple-day camping and paddling trips along the French Broad (2.5-day kayak or canoe rentals from $135, additional cost to rent camping gear).

Asheville and the Southern Blue Ridge

© MOON.COM

The French Broad and Swannanoa Rivers offer a lot of opportunities to try your hand a stand-up paddleboarding. It's much different than on a lake, marsh creek, or even the ocean, and you have to know how to read the river for underwater hazards and how to fall off correctly. **Asheville Outdoor Center** (521 Amboy Rd., 828/232-1970, www.ashevilleoutdoorcenter.com, tours $30-65) provides rentals and lessons to make sure you're safe on the river. They offer tours ranging from a few to many miles, but it's all scenic and mostly downstream.

Hiking

Ready for mountain air? Join **Blue Ridge Hiking Co.** (36 Montford Ave., 828/713-5451, http://blueridgehikingco.com) on private hikes (half-day 1-3 people $175, $35 per additional person, full-day 1-3 people $275, $50 per additional person) in the Pisgah National Forest, as well as group hikes (Fri.-Sun. Apr.-Oct., $80); they even do private overnight trips (from $380). Founder Jennifer Pharr Davis has hiked more than 11,000 miles of long-distance trails and became the first woman to be the overall record holder for fastest through-hike of the Appalachian Trail: She hiked its 2,181 miles in 46.5 days. Don't worry, she and her guides don't go that fast on the trail; they like to slow down, enjoy the moment, and make sure everyone gets a look and feel for what they love about hiking.

Asheville Hiking Tours (828/476-8687, www.ashevillehikingtours.com) leads day hikes (from $45), waterfall and Blue Ridge Parkway tours (from $75), photo tours into the Smoky Mountains (from $75), and private hikes (good for groups, from $99/pp). Backpacking trips are also available (starting around $350) and are built around themes like fall color and destination-specific hikes. Their guides are experts in a number of fields—zoology, forest ecology, primitive skills—and are naturalists, storytellers and experienced backpackers.

Hiking on the **Biltmore Estate** can mean anything from walking the 2.5 miles of mulched paths in the manicured gardens to exploring the hills, meadows, streams, and riverbank on more than 22 miles of trails. None are rugged, so you don't need any special equipment, just water, your camera, and maybe a walking stick. The Outdoor Adventure Center in Antler Hill Village has maps and can help you identify the right hike.

SHOPPING

Asheville is full of boutiques and one-off shops, and standing near the center of it all is the 1929 **Grove Arcade** (1 Page Ave., 828/252-7799, www.grovearcade.com), a beautiful and storied piece of architecture that is now a chic shopping and dining destination in the heart of downtown. The expansive Tudor Revival building, ornately filigreed inside and out in ivory-glazed terra-cotta, was initially planned as the base of a 14-story building, a skyscraper by that day's standard. Inside there are jewelry shops and home decor stores, fossils and crystals, and clothing stores. **Mountain Made** (Suite 123, 828/350-0307, www.mtnmade.com, 10am-6pm Mon.-Sat., noon-5pm Sun.) carries arts and crafts from more than 80 regional artisans, and you'll be surprised by the handiwork, fine art, and jewelry you find here. At **Battery Park Book Exchange & Champagne Bar** (Suite 101, 828/252-0020, www.batteryparkbookexchange.com, 11am-9pm Sun.-Thurs., 11am-10pm Fri.-Sat.) you'll find a menu of sharable plates and snacks ($9-23), a long list of champagne, beer and other bubbly beverages, and a whole lot of books to browse.

There are a number of art galleries in Asheville, and two stand out as especially notable. First, **Woolworth Walk** (25 Haywood St., 828/254-9234, www.woolworthwalk.com, 11am-6pm Mon.-Thurs., 11am-7pm Fri., 10am-7pm Sat., 11am-5pm Sun.) has works from more than 140 artists working in a range of mediums all in a renovated Woolworth department store; **The Soda Fountain** (11am-5pm Mon.-Thurs., 11am-6pm Fri., 10am-6pm Sat., 11am-4pm Sun., $4-8) serves milk shakes and malts, sandwiches and salads à la the

Woolworth lunch counter. On the South Slope, **ZaPow** (150 Coxe Ave., Suite 101, 828/575-9112, www.zapow.com, noon-8pm Sun.-Thurs., noon-10pm Fri.-Sat.) has made a name for itself as a gallery devoted to illustration, narrative, and pop-culture art, so when you want something colorful, singular, and very attuned to the zeitgeist, this is your spot.

One of my favorite shops is **Mast General Store** (15 Biltmore Ave., 828/232-1883, www.mastgeneralstore.com, 10am-6pm Mon.-Wed., 10am-9pm Thurs.-Sat., noon-6pm Sun.). There are several locations around Western North Carolina and a few in East Tennessee, but the Asheville spot is a must-visit for me. There's an area packed with bins and barrels of candy; clothes and jackets for men, women, and kids; cast-iron cookware and Appalachian foodstuffs; and a basement full of hiking and outdoor gear and clothes.

There are a trio of bottle shops that every beer lover should visit while in Asheville: **Appalachian Vintner** (745 Biltmore Ave., 828/505-7500, www.appalachianvintner.com, 10:15am-8pm Mon.-Wed., 10:15am-9:30pm Thurs.-Sat., noon-6pm Sun.), **Bruisin' Ales** (66 Broadway St., 828/252-8999, www.bruisin-ales.com, noon-6pm Sun.-Mon., noon-8pm Tues.-Thurs., noon-9pm Fri.-Sat.), and **Tasty Beverage Co.** (162 Coxe Ave., 828/232-7120, www.tastybeverageco.com, 11am-9pm Mon.-Thurs., 11am-10pm Fri.-Sat., noon-6pm Sun.). Which one should you go to? Do what I do and drop by all three. Their selection of Asheville and North Carolina brews has a lot of overlap (naturally), but their international and specialty selections vary, making a hunt for a particular brew, brewery, or style half the fun. In each of these you'll find staff and patrons ready with opinions, guidance and recommendations, so don't be afraid to ask.

Antiques

For lovers of vintage, retro, and aged things, the **Antique Tobacco Barn** (75 Swannanoa River Rd., 828/252-7291, www.atbarn.com, 10am-6pm Mon.-Thurs., 9am 6pm Fri. Sat., 1pm-6pm Sun. Mar.-Oct., 10am-5pm Mon.-Sat., 1pm-5pm Sun. Nov.-Feb.) has more than 77,000 square feet of goodies to plunder through. This perpetual winner of the *Mountain XPress* "Best Antiques Store in Western North Carolina" category has toys, art, tools, furniture, radios, sporting equipment, folk art, farm relics, oddball bric-a-brac, mid-century furniture, and all those great weird things you can only find in a collection this massive. It takes a while to explore this humongous shop, so carve out some time.

Asheville's Grove Arcade

NORTH CAROLINA GATEWAYS

ASHEVILLE

Along Swannanoa River Rd., you'll find yourself in the **Biltmore Antiques District** (120 Swannanoa Rd.), a small shopping district that's packed with an intriguing group of antiques shops like **Nostalgique Antiques** (126 Swannanoa River Rd., 828/505-3556, 11am-5pm Mon.-Sat., noon-5pm Sun.). Some specialize in imports; others in lamps, European furniture, or fine jewelry. Exploring here is always a good time because you never know what you'll find or where you'll find it. **Sweeten Creek Antiques and Collectables** (115 Sweeten Creek Rd., 828/277-6100, 10am-5pm Mon.-Sat., noon-5pm Sun.) and **Screen Door** (115 Fairview Rd., 828/277-3667, www.screendoorasheville. com, 10am-6pm Mon.-Sat., 1pm-6pm Sun. Mar.-Nov., 10am-5pm Mon.-Sat. and noon-5pm Sun. Nov.-Mar.) offer antiques, collectibles, and mid-century pieces from hundreds of vendors and pickers.

Along the Swannanoa River, many of Asheville's old warehouses and industrial buildings have been transformed into studio spaces, galleries, restaurants, and breweries in an area known as the **River Arts District** (www.riverartsdistrict.com). More than 160 artists have working studios here, and twice a year, during the first weekend of June and November, nearly every artist in the district opens their studios to the public for a two-day **Studio Stroll.** On the second Saturday of each month, some of the studios (they rotate based on medium, so one month may be photography, the next clay, and so on) are open for **A Closer Look,** a day of artist demonstrations, classes, workshops, and creative activities.

NIGHTLIFE AND ENTERTAINMENT

My favorite spot for live music is the **Orange Peel Social Aid and Pleasure Club** (101 Biltmore Ave., 828/398-1837, www. theorangepeel.net, noon-midnight or later daily). They're billed as "the nation's premier live music hall and concert venue," and they can back that up with some powerful acts

taking the stage. The Orange Peel is a cool concert hall with a great big dance floor, great sound, and great history.

There's live music all over Asheville, and of late there are exceptional spots for cocktails too. **Sovereign Remedies** (29 N. Market St., 828/919-9518, www.soverignremedies. com, light bites 2pm-4pm, late-night menu 4pm-2am Mon., light bites 2pm-4pm, dinner 4pm-10pm, late-night 10pm-2am Tues.-Fri., brunch 10am-3pm, dinner 4pm-10pm, late-night 10pm-2am Sat.-Sun., $4-24) rose to the top of Asheville's cocktail scene and has stayed there. They stay stocked with wild herbs, berries, fruits, and roots to make cocktails, infuse or macerate various liquors, craft bitters, and create shrubs (drinking vinegars; don't make that face, they're delicious). As we've gotten to know the bartenders, we like to sit and chat (when it's not busy) and challenge them to create something new from strange spirits.

Aux Bar (68 N. Lexington Ave., 828/575-2723, www.auxbarasheville.com, 11am-2am nightly, lunch $8-14, dinner $7-24, brunch $8-12, late-night menu $3-15) has that highbrow-lowbrow thing down pat thanks to a menu where you can get Cheerwine Sangria and King Cobra bottle service to go with your fried chicken and crumpets, Buffalo-style duck wings, pickled eggs, and beef heart tartare. It's a fun spot that gets weirder as the night grows longer, but it's also a place where you'll spot a number of Asheville chefs and personalities on the right night.

The Waterbird Asheville (197 Charlotte St., 828/552-3662, www.thewaterbirdasheville. com, 8am-11pm daily, breakfast $2-12, lunch and dinner $4-19, late-night snacks $5-19) opens early with coffee and a solid breakfast menu, transitions to a lunch-dinner-snacks situation, and wraps it up with an outstanding array of drinks. Yeah there's coffee and hand-squeezed juice, but the cocktails are where it's at. Apricot liqueur tempers pisco in the delicate Pisco Flower. An odd array of ingredients—falernum, amaro flora, yellow chartreuse—go into an Appalachian Negroni.

And simple drinks like the old fashioned and the sidecar get quirky updates here.

North Carolina's first board game café is in Asheville, and an afternoon or evening at **Well Played** (58 Wall St., 828/232-7375, www. wellplayedasheville.com, noon-10pm Sun.-Thurs., noon-1am Fri.-Sat., $5 Sun.-Thurs., $7 Fri.-Sat.) is one well spent. They have the largest board game library in the state with more than 600 on the shelves and more coming in every week (hence the cover charge), so whether you want a kid-friendly game of Sorry, a rousing game of cards, or want to try to figure out the latest iteration of Settlers of Catan, this is your spot. In addition to their huge selection of games, they serve food ($4-12) like pizzas, snacks, dips, and sandwiches as well as wine, beer and café drinks. It's easy to spend some time there whether you're a family looking for a new game to try out or if you're a hard-core Ticket to Ride player looking to enjoy some adult libations while you attempt a new winning strategy.

EVENTS

Asheville's home to **Chow Chow** (www.chow-chowasheville.com, tickets $15-150), a food festival celebrating the flavors of Southern Appalachia. The city's biggest chefs and culinary personalities were joined by noted guests Chefs Jose Andreas, Vivian Howard, Ashley Christensen and others for demos, tastings, charity dinners and swank soirees. It's a great opportunity to taste outstanding dishes and meet some culinary legends, and the mid-September event takes place in a perfect time to visit Asheville.

FOOD

Asheville is a town that clearly loves its food, with 17 active farmers markets, nearly 300 independent restaurants, and more breweries per capita than any other city in the country. They set out to prove it at every meal.

One of the most amazing restaurants in Asheville—and that's quite the qualification given the food scene here—is ★ **Rhubarb** (7 N. Pack Square, 828/785-1503, http://

rhubarbasheville.com, 3pm-9:30pm Mon., 11:30am-9:30pm Wed.-Thurs., 11:30am-10:30pm Fri., 10:30am-10:30pm Sat., 10:30am-9:30pm Sun., $11-48). Chef John Fleer is a culinary magician with a kitchen full of talented cooks helping create masterful dishes. Using the best of farmed, foraged, and pasture-raised ingredients, dishes like the pork belly with daylily-walnut slaw, the peanut-braised collard greens, the wood-roasted whole trout, or the seared duck breast with seasonal berries are dishes you'll have dreams about. On Sunday they do a three-course communal meal (adults $34, children $13) that's inventive (braised chicken-of-the-woods mushrooms doubling as coq au vin) and delicious.

Nearby is another of chef Fleer's projects, **Benne on Eagle** (35 Eagle St., 828/552-8833, www.benneoneagle.com, breakfast 7am-10:30am daily, dinner 5pm-9:30pm Mon.-Sat., brunch 10:30am-3pm Sun., breakfast $6.50-12.50, dinner $7-31, brunch $7-21). In the heart of Asheville's historically African-American neighborhood, The Block, Benne on Eagle seeks to revitalize the foodways and energy of this community. The menu is rootsy and grounded in the soul-food world, but with that impeccable twist Fleer and his crew deliver every time. Think black-eyed pea hummus, buttermilk-cornbread soup, cabbage pancakes, catfish and waffles, oxtail with creamed peas, and braised rabbit; you're going to make yourself so hungry you need to make a reservation.

Somehow ★ **Cúrate** (13 Biltmore Ave., 828/239-2946, www.katiebuttonrestaurants. com, 11:20am-10:30pm Tues.-Thurs., 11:30am-11pm Fri., 10am-11pm Sat., 10am-10:30pm Sun., lunch and dinner $8-60, brunch $6-12), one of Asheville's best restaurants, keeps getting better. This Spanish tapas restaurant is headed up by chef Katie Button, who cut her culinary teeth at the legendary El Bulli in Spain, cooked at Jean Georges and several of José Andrés's restaurants, and is a perpetual James Beard Award nominee and semifinalist. The menu here is all hers,

though. Favorites include the rossejat negro (paella-style thin noodles in squid ink sauce), pincho moruno (lamb skewers with Moorish spices), honey-topped bacalao fritters, and the spectacular cochinillo (a roasted quarter of a suckling pig). Do yourself a favor and make a reservation.

In West Asheville, **Biscuit Head** (733 Haywood Rd., 828/333-5145, www.biscuitheads.com, 7am-2pm Mon.-Fri., 8am-3pm Sat.-Sun., around $8) serves up Appalachian specialty cat-head biscuits, so named because they're huge—the size of a cat's head. These biscuits are dynamite. Try The Asheville Benedict—an open-faced biscuit with charred scallion cream cheese, fresh tomatoes, poached eggs, roasted red peppers, and a kale salad. Or just get the "Biscuit And," which comes with a biscuit and your choice of crazy butters, jams, hot sauces, infused honeys, and toppings from the biscuit bar, featuring all house-made spreadables. There's a second location (417 Biltmore Ave., Suite 4F, 828/505-3449, 7am-2pm Mon.-Fri., 9am-3pm Sat.-Sun.) in town too.

BimBeriBon (697 Haywood Rd., 828/505-0328, www.bimberibon.com, 8am-8:30pm Mon.-Thurs., 8am-9pm Fri.-Sat., 8am-2pm Sun., breakfast $8-13, lunch and dinner $11-15) serves an eclectic menu of international flavors for breakfast, lunch, and dinner. There's bibimbap from Korea, India's tandoori chicken and pakora, bing from China, and Latin-inspired omelets. Toss in a cool location and delicious coffee and you can see why they stay busy. Nearby is **Hole Doughnuts** (168 Haywood Rd., 828/774-5667, www.holedoughnuts.com, 7:30am-2pm Wed.-Sat., $2-3) one of my worldwide top-three doughnuts (I eat a lot of doughnuts; don't judge). Yeasted dough cooked to order, they're always hot, always fresh, and always interesting. My favorite from here had a sugared sumac glaze, making that yeasty little doughnut that much more tart.

1: Orange Peel Social Aid and Pleasure Club
2: Buxton Hall Barbeque

★ **The Admiral** (400 Haywood Rd., 828/252-2541, www.theadmiralasheville.com, 5pm-10pm daily, $16-45) has been West Asheville's prime food destination since it opened in a humble cinderblock building in what they call "the wage-earning side of town." Blue-collar roots aside, the kitchen here is driven by talent and culinary curiosity. The menu is an ever-evolving collection of New American dishes and simple plates. Their rib-eye is served with roasted potato and cabbage, the half chicken comes with Carolina Gold rice and pole beans, and the pork chop is the picture of perfection. It's a small, cozy, chic-but-divey spot with a great cocktail program.

With West Asheville becoming a dining center in its own right, one more restaurant to check out is **Jargon** (715 Haywood Rd., 828/785-1761, www.jargonrestaurant.com, 5pm-9pm Sun.-Thurs., 5pm-10pm Fri.-Sat., $9-32). This menu holds true to Asheville's "eat local" philosophy but casts a wider net for inspiration. You'll find some Southern classics like shrimp and grits, shrimp and crawfish étouffée, pickled watermelon rind salad, and deviled eggs on the menu, but you'll also find Spanish octopus, spaetzle, and beef tartare served with bone marrow. Unexpected twists to elements of otherwise familiar dishes orange absinthe butter, smoked marinara, pumpkin seed brittle—make each menu iteration a new dining experience.

Over Easy Cafe (32 Broadway St., 828/236-3533, www.overeasyasheville.com, 8am-2pm daily, $6-14) is adorable. It's a bright, colorful, feel-good place that serves a breakfast that will make you smile. They're not reinventing the breakfast wheel here, just doing it better and with a little local flair. Breakfast sandwiches on buttery brioche, English Pea toasts, strawberry buckwheat hotcakes, daily eggs benedict specials, and packed-to-the-ceiling veggie omelets are solid choices, but you won't be mad at the seared octopus with poached egg or the huevos rancheros.

What's a trip to North Carolina without barbecue? ★ **Buxton Hall Barbeque** (32

Banks Ave., 828/232-7216, www.buxtonhall. com, 11:30am-3pm and 5:30pm-9:30 Sun.-Thurs., 11:30am-3pm and 5:30pm-10pm Fri.-Sat., $5-16) is a blend of old-school barbecue at its best with new-school spins and sides courtesy of chef Elliot Moss. Moss and company crisscrossed the Carolinas, dining in dozens of barbecue joints to create his menu. Chicken Bog (rice, chicken, and sausage) from the low country of South Carolina is right there beside Eastern North Carolina whole-hog barbecue; South Carolina Barbecue Hash; and smoked sausages, fried catfish, and smoked chicken, all accompanied by an excellent selection of classic barbecue sides. A personal favorite here isn't barbecue (I know that's crazy); it's a fried chicken sandwich that's an homage to one you'll find at a popular Southern chain restaurant known for being closed on Sundays, and it's way better.

One of two restaurants that are on my "Every Time I'm in Asheville I Eat Here" list is ★ **Cucina 24** (24 Wall St., 828/254-6170, www.cucina24restaurant.com, 5:30pm-9:30pm Sun.-Thurs., 5pm-10:30pm Fri.-Sat., $10-35, prix fixe $48). A decidedly Italian restaurant where the chef is dedicated to using as much as possible from local farms, ranches, and fishing is a challenge, but chef Brian Canipelli does it with style. The three-course prix-fixe menu will take some of the question out of what to get, but the menu is tight and enticing, and everything is the right thing to order, so go wild. Pizza and veggies are roasted in a wood-fired oven, pasta is made in house, the sauce is to die for, and whether you want to go old-school with rigatoni, meatballs, and pecorino or new-school with troccoli, sea urchin, and parsley, you'll leave ready to make a reservation for next time.

If you're in the mood for a killer hot dog, burger like no other, or a Cuban sandwich that will make you think about proposing marriage to the guy or gal operating the grill, or even a bologna sandwich (seriously), head to **Foothills Food Truck** (2 Huntsman Place, at Hi-Wire's Big Top, 828/606-9372, www.

foothillslocalmeats.com, 4pm-9pm Mon.-Thurs., 4pm-10pm Fri., noon-10pm Sat., 1pm-8pm Sun., $8-14). I love this place and it has become one of my go-tos in Asheville. We meet friends at Hi-Wire's Big Top, grab a couple of orders of poutine and a sandwich (I go back and forth between the Cuban, the bologna melt, and the classic li'l cheeseburger), then enjoy the beer and food and company.

In a town with so many great restaurants, it's difficult to stand out, but **En La Calle** (15 Eagle St., 828/232-7012, www.enlacalleasheville.com, 5pm-11pm Mon.-Thurs., 5pm-midnight Fri.-Sat., 5pm-10pm Sun., $6-25) does. And for the right reasons. The name translates to "in the street," and this Latin street food-inspired restaurant is like the perfect upscale food truck: great energy, a quick kitchen and even faster service, delicious small plates that you'll want to order 25 of, and exceptional cocktails. The carnitas taco, spicy fried cauliflower, selection of ceviche, roasted duck pancake, and cotija-coated street corn are addictive.

When you've been at the Grey Eagle or the Orange Peel, the show has just let out, it's the middle of the night, and you need to refuel with some good food, the lights are on at **Rosetta's Kitchen** (116 N. Lexington Ave., 828/232-0738, www.rosettaskitchen.com, 11am-11pm Mon.-Sat., $6-12). There's so much to recommend about this place: The food is very good, it's all vegetarian and mostly vegan, and it's made with local produce in season. They compost everything that makes its way back to the kitchen, recycle all their trash, and make sure their used vegetable oil goes to power biodiesel cars—it's Asheville's signature countercultural reinterpretation of the South, and it's one of the best vegetarian places in town. Downstairs is **The Buchi Bar,** where they serve Buchi kombucha and kombucha-based cocktails, as well as beer, wine, cocktails and all-natural sodas.

Driven by the dual nature of food—it's both

1: BimBeriBon 2: Sourwood Inn

a way to explore and get out of your comfort zone, and a thing that offers comfort and peace—**Gan Shan Station** (143 Charlotte St., 828/774-5280, www.ganshanstation.com, 5pm-9:30pm Sun.-Thurs., 5pm-10:30pm Fri.-Sat., $7-19) digs deep into pan-Asian cuisine for inspiration and serves up dishes like Thit Bo, Pork Ramen, Mapo Doufu, dry fried green beans, and okonomiyaki that are on point when it comes to flavor and authenticity. If the regular menu isn't enough (with the complexity they coax out of these dishes, you could eat the menu four times through and not be tired of it, so "if their regular menu isn't enough" may be a stretch), try the Chef's Table (reserve at least 48 hours in advance, $55 pp) where the kitchen gets to play with their food and will send out more food than you know what to do with.

White Duck Taco Shop (12 Biltmore Ave., 828/232-9191; 388 Riverside Dr., 828/254-1398, www.whiteducktacoshop. com, 11:30am-9pm daily, $4-6) serves tacos that intrigue and delight. I know that sounds trite in a world where it seems every other restaurant serves tacos, but White Duck lives up to the hype. You can get jerk chicken, fried chicken, Korean beef bulgogi with kimchi, duck confit with mole and cranberry salsa, even a banh mi tofu taco that tastes like the awesome Vietnamese sandwich. Priced so you can scarf down two or three without breaking the bank, they're just about perfect, but if you're a taco fan and someone who likes to try things that are a little left of center, this is your place.

Local favorite **Chai Pani** (22 Battery Park Ave., 828/254-4003, www.chaipaniasheville. com, lunch 11:30am-3:30pm Mon.-Sat., noon-3:30pm Sun., dinner 5pm-9:30pm Sun.-Thurs., 5:30pm-10pm Fri.-Sat., under $14) continues to win fans because of its cool atmosphere and great food. The restaurant's name means "tea and water," a phrase that refers to a snack or a small gift. This restaurant is inspired by Indian street food vendors and serves casual and affordable specialties from all over India.

ACCOMMODATIONS

The **Asheville Bed & Breakfast Association** (www.ashevillebba.com) has a constantly growing membership of inns and B&Bs in the area that band together to promote getaways, tours, and seasonal packages. Check with them for any current specials.

In the heart of downtown overlooking Pack Square, **Kimpton's Hotel Arras** (7 Patton Ave., 833/221-9044 or 828/255-0303, www. hotelarras.com, from $150) transformed an otherwise dull former bank building into a swank 128-room boutique hotel with some serious eats. It's hard to miss as it's in the tallest building in Western North Carolina and the hotel's restaurants, Bargello and District 42, stay busy. **Bargello** (breakfast 7am-3pm Mon.-Fri., lunch 11am-3pm Mon.-Fri., dinner 5pm-3pm daily, brunch 7am-3pm Sat.-Sun., $8-28) serves Mediterranean and Mediterranean-inspired dishes. **District 42** (3pm-midnight daily) serves cocktails and shared plates with a side of outstanding Blue Ridge Mountain views; the menu is globally inspired, so expect everything from Chinese pork buns to gussied up frankfurters and other delicious surprises.

Just off the Blue Ridge Parkway north of Asheville, a true retreat is the ★ **Sourwood Inn** (810 Elk Mountain Scenic Hwy., Asheville, 828/255-0690, www.sourwoodinn.com, $155-195, from $190 cabin). It charmed me so much the first time I saw it, I made reservations for an anniversary weekend. Situated on the end of a ridgeline, the inn offers a view of nearly 270 degrees from every bedroom window and balcony. Your cell phone won't work here, and there's no Wi-Fi (by design), so you can truly unplug. There are a couple of miles of easy hiking trails, a pond, a bamboo grove, and some sculptures tucked in the woods nearby, but if you're feeling adventurous, they have a couple of options. The innkeeper's son-in-law happens to be a fly-fishing guide and an active hawker—that means he hunts with a hawk named Rocket Girl; packages are available that will put you on the fish or put Rocket Girl on your arm. Other specials include a

Craft Brews in Beer City

Asheville is regarded as the epicenter of North Carolina's beer and culinary scenes, and it's well deserved. Asheville itself is packed with award-winning restaurants and breweries, and every time a new one opens, it makes the news. Winner of the title "Beer City USA" and perpetually at the top of any beer geek's list of cities to visit, Asheville's brewery scene is exemplary in terms of variety, innovation, and sheer volume. When you're in town you'll have no problem finding a brewery to visit, but this list will give you a head start on your search for the perfect brew.

- **Hi-Wire Brewing** (www.hiwirebrewing.com) has a pair of locations, on the South Slope (197 Hilliard Ave., 828/738-2448) and the Big Top (2 Huntsman Place, 828/575-9675). At the Big Top you'll find their flagship brews and a great food truck, and on the South Slope you'll find experimental quaffs to try.

- **Zillicoah Beer Company** (870 Riverside Dr., Woodfin, 828/424-7929, www.zillicoahbeer. com) is new to the scene but strong with beer aged in French oak, collaboration brews with local breweries, and an exceptional kölsch.

- **Burial Beer Co.** (40 Collier Ave., 828/475-2739, www.burialbeer.com) makes intriguing brews with intriguing names. Their taproom, with its indoor and outdoor spaces, excellent food truck, and funky mural, make it a great place to stop and enjoy one of the double IPAs.

- **Bhramari Brewing Co.** (101 S. Lexington Ave., 828/214-7981, www.bhramaribrewing. com) delivers the unexpected: black gose with orange blossom, sour pale ales, dry hopped berliner weisse, a sour beer that tastes like fruit punch, even a foeder-aged honey-infused beer.

- **Highland Brewing Company** (12 Old Charlotte Hwy., Suite H, 828/299-3370, www. highlandbrewing.com) has the honor of being the first microbrewery in Asheville, and it's a fine one. They continue to keep their flagship brews relevant by tweaking the recipes, but they also continue to innovate, releasing an impressive set of single-hop brews.

- **Archetype Brewing** (www.archetypebrewing.com) has locations downtown (174 Broadway St., 828/505-8305) and in West Asheville (265 Haywood Rd., 828/505-4177) where you'll find their interpretations of Belgian beers like a saison, witbier, strong ale, and more.

- **Green Man Brewery** (27 Buxton Ave., 828/252-5502, www.greenmanbrewery.com) has lagers, fruity IPAs, even tart berliner weisses, but their monster Rainmaker Double IPA is a hit, as are their barrel-aged and sour beers like Bootsy and Snozzberry.

- **Catawba Brewing Co.** (32 Banks Ave., 828/552-3934, www.catawbabrewing.com) has a relaxing tap room with a bevy of crushable beers on tap. Their White Zombie white ale, Drum Circle Haze double IPA, and Festbier lager are favorites.

- **New Belgium Brewing Company** (21 Craven St., 828/333-6900, www.newbelgium. com) is one of the biggest in the area, and their tour is exceptional. Most craft beer fans know Fat Tire and their other brews, but the taproom here carries specialties and barrel-aged beers not available elsewhere.

- **Sierra Nevada Brewery** (100 Sierra Nevada Way, Fletcher, 828/708-6242, www. sierranevada.com) was described to me as "the Taj Mahal of Beer" and "like Willy Wonka's factory, but with beer," and it's mighty impressive. There's a good restaurant on-site, a great tour, an impressive facility, and a *long* tap list that goes beyond what you expect from Sierra Nevada.

- **Oskar Blues Brewery** (342 Mountain Industrial Dr., Brevard, 828/883-2337, www. oskarblues.com) is the East Coast outpost for this Colorado staple. Old Chub Scotch Ale, Mama's Little Yella Pils, and their Pinner IPA are made fresh here.

Blue Ridge Parkway package that includes fly-fishing, a massage, horseback riding, Biltmore Estate passes, and wild food foraging. Call for directions—it's tricky to find.

★ **Zen Asheville Inn & Spa Retreat** (128 Hillside St., 828/255-0051, www.ashevillespa.com, $189-419) is one of my favorite places in town to stay. Every room has a big, comfortable bed and a two-person hot tub; there's a sauna and a cold shower for guests to use as well as a European steam shower. Breakfast is a healthy, filling affair, and most importantly, the rooms are private and quiet. Massage therapists and estheticians are kept on call, so you can arrange for treatments of almost any kind on-site. Throughout the house, comfortable seating areas make it easy to find a spot for breakfast or tea or just to read or talk; my favorite spot is the tatami porch overlooking the Japanese garden at the front of the house.

A truly lovely bed-and-breakfast is **Sweet Biscuit Inn** (77 Kenilworth Rd., 828/250-0170, www.sweetbiscuitinn.com, $160-250). I have to admit, I was drawn here by the name, but the place, the host, the breakfast, all of it conspired to make me like it even more. The seven bedrooms and carriage house are accented by tiger oak wood floors and high ceilings. Queen or king beds are comfy, and breakfast is excellent, especially the biscuits.

In the days of yore, before budget hotels became the norm, the motor court or cottage court was the stay-over of choice for middle-class travelers. Today, these motor courts and cottage courts are relics of the past, and few remain, but the mountains of North Carolina still contain a handful of fine examples; in the Asheville area, at least two are still operating today, providing travelers with retro accommodations. **Asheville Log Cabin Motor Court** (330 Weaverville Rd., 828/645-6546, www.theashevillecabins.com, 2-night minimum weekends, $94-305, 1 pet $15 per night, 2 pets $25 per night) was constructed around 1930 and appears in the 1958 Robert Mitchum movie *Thunder Road*. The cabins have cable TV and wireless internet access but no phones. Some are air-conditioned, but that's not usually a necessity at this elevation. Another great cabin court is the **Pines Cottages** (346 Weaverville Rd., 828/645-9661, http://ashevillepines.com, $103-204, $15 per pet, up to 2). Billed as "A nice place for nice people," how could you resist staying here?

Downtown, several new hotels will be completed in 2020 and beyond. **AC Hotel by Marriott Downtown Asheville** (10 Broadway St., 828/258-2522, www.marriott.com, $120-535) is one of my favorites for the spacious rooms, generally excellent views, and a great rooftop bar, **Capella on 9** (828/771-5156, 6:30am-10am Mon.-Fri., 7am-11am Sat.-Sun., 4pm-11pm Mon., 4pm-midnight Tues.-Thurs., 2pm-1am Fri.-Sat., 2pm-11pm Sun. $6-16) On the roof you can get cocktails, wine, and beer, and order from a tasty tapas menu—olives, charcuterie and cheese boards, patatas bravas, even pan-fried trout—while you take in the views.

Aloft Asheville Downtown (51 Biltmore Ave., 828/232-2838, www.aloftashevilledowntown.com, $126-602) has a great location that's walkable to most everything downtown or on the South Slope. There is a trendy bar serving rock-star cocktails, plush modern guest rooms, and fantastic city and mountain views from most rooms; others are poolside. Excellent dining, great drinks, and all the live music you could ever want (courtesy of The Orange Peel) are only a short walk away.

Want to stay in a tree house? How about a retro camper with a hot tub? Or a dome with skylight windows so you can watch the stars? Or a yurt? If this sounds good, you need **Asheville Glamping** (www.ashevilleglamping.com, 828/450-9745, $110-400). They have a trio of properties with a host of quirky but refined places and ways to stay, from safari-style tents to tree houses to yurts and more. When you book they'll send you the address of your particular property. It's a slight inconvenience but it's their way to keep their immensely Instagrammable campgrounds and properties free of lookers and lurkers and a haven to their guests.

If you've spent the day touring Biltmore House, viewing the incredible splendor in which a robber baron of the Gilded Age basked, it may be jarring to return to real life. You can soften the transition with a stay at the luxurious **Inn on Biltmore Estate** (866/336-1245, www.biltmore.com, from $629 peak season, from $269 off-season, suites up to $2,000). It's everything you'd wish for from a hotel in this location. The suites are beautifully furnished and luxurious, the views are magnificent, and the lobby, dining room, and library have the deluxe coziness of a turn-of-the-20th-century lodge. **Village Hotel on Biltmore Estate** (rooms from $400, packages from $550) in Antler Hill Village has 209 rooms and is a testament to the ongoing and growing popularity of the Biltmore.

Resorts

The **Grove Park Inn Resort & Spa** (290 Macon Ave., 828/252-2711 or 800/438-5800, www.groveparkinn.com, $270-1,900, spa and golf packages available) is the sort of place Asheville residents bring their out-of-town houseguests when giving them a grand tour of the city, simply to walk into the lobby to ooh and aah. The massive stone building constructed by a crew of 400 who had only mule teams and a single steam shovel to aid them—was erected in 1912 and 1913, the project of St. Louis millionaire E. W. Grove, the name behind Grove's Tasteless Chill Tonic, a medicinal syrup that outsold Coca-Cola in the 1890s.

The opening of the Grove Park Inn was cause for such fanfare that William Jennings Bryan addressed the celebratory dinner party. In the coming years, at least eight U.S. presidents would stay here, as would a glittering parade of early-20th-century big shots, among them Henry Ford, Thomas Edison, Eleanor Roosevelt, Harry Houdini, F. Scott Fitzgerald, Will Rogers, and George Gershwin. Even if you don't stay at the Grove Park while you

are visiting Asheville, swing by just to see it. You can drive right up to the front door, and if you tell the valets that you just want to go in and see the lobby, they'll probably be willing to watch your car for five minutes (a tip helps). The lobby is amazing, a cross between a Gilded Age hunting lodge and the great hall of a medieval castle. There are 14-foot fireplaces at each end, and the elevators, believe it or not, are inside the chimneys. It's easy to imagine flappers, foreign dignitaries, mobsters, and literati milling about the lobby with their martinis when this hotel was young.

You can also park your car and head inside for a cocktail or dinner at one of their many on-site establishments. Each of their venues has phenomenal views: **Vue 1913** (5:30pm-9pm daily, $32-169) has French and American dishes that are well done but not particularly creative; **Edison Craft Ales + Kitchen** (4pm-11pm Mon.-Thurs., 4pm-midnight Fri., 11am-midnight Sat., 11am-11pm Sun., $8-28) serves some high-quality bar food and craft beer; **Blue Ridge** (6:30am-10:30am daily, breakfast $15-26, brunch $42, dinner $45) is a farm-to-table artisanal buffet (yes, I too am confused as to how artisanal and buffet work together); and the **Sunset Terrace** (11am-9pm daily, $15-30 lunch, $26-60 dinner) and **Sunset Cocktail Terrace** (11am-9pm daily).

Being a guest at the Grove Park is quite an experience. In addition to the spectacle of the lodge and its multiple restaurants, cafés, bars, and shops, for an additional charge guests have access to its world-famous **spa** ($90 daily). The pass gives access to the lounges, pools, waterfall, steam room, inhalation room, and outdoor whirlpool tub. The indoor pool is a fantastic place, a subterranean stone room with vaulted skylights and tropical plants. For extra fees ($120-540, most $200-300), guests can choose from a long menu of spa treatments: massages, facials, manicures, aromatherapy, and body wraps. For $70 you can have your aura photographed before and after the treatment to gauge the depth of your relaxation.

TRANSPORTATION

Car

From Asheville it's easy to get to Great Smoky Mountains National Park. In just over an hour you can be in Cataloochee, at the north end of the park, to camp, hike, and watch for elk in a serene mountain cove; to get there, take I-40 west to exit 20 and follow the signs. You can also take I-40 west into Tennessee, follow the Foothills Parkway to U.S. 321, and skirt the edge of the national park to Gatlinburg, Tennessee, and the entrance to the national park (a trip of about 90 minutes). From Gatlinburg, you can make a loop back to Asheville by taking Newfound Gap Road across the national park to Cherokee, North Carolina (about 2.5 hours), and then back to Asheville via U.S. 441 to U.S. 19 to I-40, a total loop of about 3.5 hours and some 175 miles.

You can also head straight to Cherokee from Asheville and enter the national park via Newfound Gap Road there. It's an hour's drive following I-40 west to exit 27, then taking U.S. 19 south to U.S. 441, which takes you right to Cherokee. Alternately you can take the more scenic, but much longer, route and get to Cherokee via the Blue Ridge Parkway. This route is only 83 miles, but it takes 2-2.5 hours. If you want to go this way, head south out of Asheville along U.S. 25 and pick up the Blue Ridge Parkway about 5.5 miles out of town; turn south on the Parkway and drive until you reach Cherokee and the national park. And, of course, you can reverse the course if you're making that grand loop and return to Asheville via the Blue Ridge Parkway by picking it up in Cherokee and driving north.

Air

Asheville Regional Airport (AVL, 61 Terminal Dr., 828/684-2226, www.flyavl.com) is a 20-minute drive on I-26 south of the city in Fletcher. American Airlines, Delta, United, Spirit, and Allegiant offer nonstop flights to Charlotte, Atlanta, Chicago, Washington DC, New York City's Newark and LaGuardia, Denver, and more. A taxi from the airport will run around $45.

Bus

There is a **Greyhound station** (2 Tunnel Rd., 828/253-8451, www.greyhound.com) in Asheville. Asheville has an extensive public bus system called **ART** (www.ashevillenc.gov, 6am-11:30pm Mon.-Sat., $1, seniors $0.50), connecting most major points in the metropolitan area, including the airport, with downtown. See the website for routes and schedules.

BREVARD

Brevard is the pleasant seat of the improbably named Transylvania County (unlike in vampire stories, it's not creepy, but beautiful in a Gothic forest way) only 48 minutes southwest of Asheville. Brevard has a population of rather startling and odd-looking white squirrels. The local legend about their origins is that their ancestors escaped from an overturned circus truck in Florida in 1940 and made their way to Brevard as pets. More likely, say researchers, they came from an exotic pet breeder in Florida and were acquired by a Brevard-area family. In any case, the white squirrels escaped into the wild of Transylvania County, and you'll probably see their descendants in the area when you visit.

Sports and Recreation
DUPONT STATE RECREATIONAL FOREST

About 10 miles south of Brevard, **DuPont State Recreational Forest** (U.S. 276, 828/877-6527, www.dupontstaterecreational forest.com) has more than 90 miles of hiking trails on 10,000 acres. Some of Transylvania County's beautiful waterfalls are located within the forest and accessible on foot via moderate or strenuous forest trails, or, for people with disabilities only, with special permits and advance reservation, by vehicle. Visitors should use caution, wear brightly colored clothing, and leave that bearskin cape at home September-December, when hikers share the woods with hunters. The Aleen Steinberg Visitor Center (89 Buck Forest Rd., Cedar Mountain, 9am-5pm daily mid-Mar.-Dec., 10am-4pm Sat.-Sun. Jan.-Mar. 14) has restrooms and trash cans and is staffed by volunteers who are happy to help with trail recommendations. The visitors center is near the trailhead to Hooker Falls.

Many of the hiking and mountain biking trails are true rugged forest paths; others, like those that lead to a trio of waterfalls—Hooker, Triple, and High Falls—are wide maintained avenues through the woods. The hike, or hikes, as you'll follow several trails, to Triple and High Falls can be hot, sweaty affairs in spring and summer, so bring water. But the views are more than worth it, and in fall it's a phenomenal hike. After you make this longer hike, make the shorter one to the lower Hooker Falls and go for a swim in the crisp mountain water. Already cool, it will feel downright cold—and quite refreshing on a hot day. If you hike the three falls, you're looking at a 2-mile loop for High Falls, a 0.4-mile trail to Triple Falls, and another 0.4-mile trail to Hooker, for a total of 2.8 miles. Downloadable maps and more information are available through **Friends of DuPont Forest** (www.dupontforest.com).

Entertainment and Events

The **Brevard Music Center** (349 Andante Lane, 828/862-2100, www.brevardmusic.org) has attracted the highest-caliber young musicians for more than 70 years for intensive summer-long classical music instruction. Throughout the summer, Brevard Music Center students, as well as visiting soloists of international fame, put on world-class concerts, performing works that have included Tchaikovsky as well as Gilbert and Sullivan.

There's a lot more live music to be had in and around Brevard. The **DFR Room** (36 E. Main St., 828/877-9906, www.dfrroom.net, from 5pm Mon. and Wed.-Sat.) is home to the B-Town live radio show and jam session, evenings of karaoke and dance, and bands; check their calendar for the month's schedule. There's blues every Wednesday night at **The Tavern** (14 S. Gaston St., 828/884-5556, www.the-tavern-night-club.business.site,

4:30pm-11pm Wed.-Sat., 11am-8pm Sun., $9-21), and bluegrass, rock-and-roll, jam bands, and more every night they're open. There's a full bar and grill, so wear your dancing shoes and come hungry and thirsty. **Ecusta Brewing Company** (49 Pisgah Hwy., Pisgah Forest, 828/966-2337, www.ecustabrewing.com, 1pm-8pm Mon.-Thurs., 1pm-10pm Fri., noon-10pm Sat., noon-9pm Sun.) has live music and in-brewery events like yoga as well as a dozen or so beers on draft. The other breweries in town also have live music on weekends and occasionally throughout the week.

Shopping

A great outdoor shop, T-shirt spot, and place for a beer is **DD Bullwinkel's Outdoors** (60 E. Main St., 828/862-4700, www.ddbullwinkels.com, 10am-6pm Mon., 10am-8pm Tues.-Sat., noon-6pm Sun.). This is your spot for serious trail and climbing gear, outerwear and yoga duds, and some excellent T-shirts. I stop here every time I'm in town for a new shirt or sticker, or to replace some worn bit of equipment. Now that The Map Room, their tap room, is open, it's a good spot to have a pint and listen to the local gossip too.

Named for the town's namesake tree-dwelling oddity, **The White Squirrel Shoppe** (2 W. Main St., 828/877-3530, www.whitesquirrelshoppe.com, 10:30am-5:30pm Mon.-Thurs., 10am-6pm Fri.-Sat., 11:30am-5pm Sun.) is one of those quaint souvenir emporiums that has a bit of everything. Need a candle that smells like cookies? They got it. Want some hand towels embroidered with Brevard's legendary white squirrel? Got those too. The shop is charming, and the owners are nice; it's the kind of place where I buy a little something for my mom or mother-in-law when I'm in town.

Where the Brevard Music Center hosts concerts, **Southern Comfort Records** (16 W. Main St., 828/884-3575, www.celestialmtnmusic.com, 10am-5:30pm Mon.-Fri., 10am-4pm Sat.) is a music center of a different sort, and many bluegrass musicians come here for their instruments. Among more usual musical items, this nice little shop carries two lines of locally made instruments. Cedar Mountain Banjos, of the open-backed, old-time variety, are beautifully crafted and ring clear and pretty. The work of local fiddle builder Lyle Reedy is also sold at Celestial Mountain Music. His fiddles are handmade of a variety of fine woods and have a deep, biting sound. Musicians and woodworkers alike will enjoy a stop at this Main Street shop.

At **O.P. Taylor's** (16 S. Broad St., 828/883-2309, www.optaylors.com, 10am-6pm Mon.-Thurs., 10am-8pm Fri.-Sat., noon-5pm Sun.) you'll find a toy shop loaded with Lego and Playmobil toys, board and card games for the family, gags and gifts, and playthings old fashioned and newfangled. This is a fun shop, especially if you're traveling with or bringing back a gift for kids.

Brevard is also home to a number of artists. If you're here for a quick bite and then it's back to the Parkway, take the time to stick your head in **Number 7 Fine Arts and Crafts Cooperative** (2 W. Main St., 828/883-2294, www.number7arts.org, 10am-5pm Mon.-Sat., noon-4pm Sun.). This gallery has featured works by a diverse group of around 25 Transylvania County artists for more than 15 years. Many of the works are inspired by and created in the midst of the phenomenal nature here.

Food

One of the top restaurants in Brevard is ★ **The Square Root** (33 Times Arcade Alley, 828/884-6171, www.squarerootrestaurant. com, 11am-9pm Sun.-Mon. and Wed.-Thurs., 11am-10pm Fri.-Sat., lunch $7-18, dinner $7-25, brunch $6-12). Inside, the exposed brick walls create a warm room where the food is more like delicious art. Something as simple as a burger and onion rings comes out as a tower of food, and fine dinner entrées, like peach glazed pork and coffee and peppercorn-crusted steak, are almost too pretty to eat. Almost.

In the South, there are a few food traditions that have caught a cultural wave. One is barbecue; the other is the meat and three. Meat-and-three restaurants are just what they sound like: a serving of meat and three sides. ★ **Magpie Meat & Three** (170 King St., Unit C, 828/877-3773, www.magpiemeatandthree. com, 11am-9pm Tues.-Sat., $8-15) is doing it right, sticking to the traditions but using a chef for every part of the meal, which means a prettier presentation, higher quality ingredients, and a tastier preparation. You'll find pulled pork barbecue here on weekends, ribs at dinner, and fried chicken any time. For sides you'll want an order of okra, grits, collard greens, slaw, red rice, and all the rest, which really makes it a meat and eight if you're counting. Oh, and they carry a small but sensational selection of craft beer and cider.

The Falls Landing Eatery (18 E. Main St., 828/884-2835, www.thefallslanding.com, 11:30am-3pm Mon.-Sat., 5pm-9pm Tues.-Sat., lunch $7-14, dinner $10-25) is a spot popular among locals. They specialize in seafood (foreshadowed by the rainbow trout on their sign), and their North Carolina trout sautéed in lemon butter and bourbon is particularly good. Don't discount their burgers, steaks, or lamb chops, which deliver on flavor and value.

When the weather's right, dining on the patio at **Jordan Street Café** (48 W. Jordan St., 828/883-2558, www.thejordanstreetcafe. com, 4pm-10pm Thurs.-Sat., 11am-3pm and 4pm-10pm Sun., $9-12) is the way to go. They serve a little bit of everything—fish-and-chips, blackened chicken sandwiches, burgers, salads, daily flatbread pizza and quesadilla specials—but the menu is simple enough to keep it focused.

There's something soothing about getting a burger at a spot like **Cardinal Drive-In** (344 S. Broad St., 828/884-7085, 10am-11pm daily, $3-10). Maybe it's the quaintness of the drive-in, from ordering through the little speakers to someone bringing a tray of food to your car, but it's special. As are the burgers, and the onion rings. It looks a little rough, but that's part of the charm—along with the milk shakes.

For a quick bite or a shake, malt, or ice cream soda, check out **Rocky's Grill & Soda Shop** (50 S. Broad St., 828/877-5375, 10am-7pm Mon.-Thurs., 10am-9pm Fri.-Sat. 11am-6pm Sun.). This place has been around since 1942, and the nostalgic counter with its line of chrome stools takes you back to the heyday of this soda fountain. You can grab lunch for around $8, and for $5 or less you can get a malt, a milk shake, an ice cream soda, a root beer float, or even an egg cream (try one if you've never had one). It's a must-stop, especially as a reward after a morning hike or bike ride.

There are four breweries in Brevard as of the writing of this book. One of the most popular is **Oskar Blues Brewery** (342 Mountain Industrial Dr., 828/883-2337, www.oskarblues.com, noon-9pm Mon.-Thurs., noon-10pm Fri.-Sat., noon-8pm Sun.), a brewery born in Colorado that chose Brevard as the home of its East Coast brewery because of the small-town vibe, proximity to awesome mountain biking, and ease of distribution from here. Tour the brewery any day of the week (4pm Mon.-Thurs., hourly 2pm-5pm Fri.-Sun.) and grab a taste of one of their brews; my friends are partial to the Pinner Throwback IPA and Mama's Little Yella Pils (a pilsner), but I prefer the Old Chub Scotch Ale. Speaking of Old Chub, you can grab a bite to eat here at the **Oskar Blues Chubwagon** (noon-8pm Mon.-Thurs., noon-9pm Fri.-Sat., noon-7pm Sun., $3-12), which serves grilled cheese sandwiches, hot dogs, burgers, and fries.

Brevard Brewing Company (63 E. Main St., 828/885-2101, www.brevard-brewing.com, 2pm-11pm Mon.-Thurs., noon-midnight Fri.-Sat., 2pm-10-pm Sun.) specializes in German-style lagers and pilsners, though they also brew IPAs, dunkels, and some seasonal specialties. The tap room is wide open and friendly; they don't serve food, but you're welcome to bring some in from elsewhere.

PISGAH RANGER DISTRICT

Just north of Brevard in the town of Pisgah Forest is the main entrance to the **Pisgah**

Ranger District (U.S. 276, Pisgah Forest, 828/877-3265, www.fs.usda.gov, 9am-5pm Mon.-Sat. mid-Apr.-Oct., 9am-4:30pm Mon.-Fri. Nov.-mid-Apr.) of the Pisgah National Forest. The forest covers 500,000 acres, which is a large swath of western North Carolina, but this 157,000-acre ranger district has many of the forest's favorite attractions. A good topographic map is available from National Geographic (www.natgeomaps.com). In the ranger district are more than 275 miles of hiking trails and several campgrounds; the most easily accessible, and one of the most popular in the area, is **Davidson River Campground** (828/862-5960, reservations at 877/444-6777 or www.recreation.gov, year-round, $22-44), which is 1.5 miles from the Brevard entrance. It has showers and toilets.

The **Shining Rock Wilderness** and the **Middle Prong Wilderness,** which adjoins Shining Rock to the southwest, are a rugged terrain that rises from 3,200 feet at its lowest point, along the West Pigeon River, to a towering 6,400 feet at Richmond Balsam. **Cold Mountain,** made famous by the book and movie of the same name, is a real peak located within the Shining Rock Wilderness, and seeing it helps make the struggles of the fictional characters more real. These mountains are steep, and the forests dense, and what trails there are have no signage. This is a popular area among experienced backwoods trekkers, but it is not recommended for casual visitors because it is exceedingly easy to get lost. At a minimum, hikers should be adept at using both a compass and a topographic map before venturing into these wilderness areas.

Not to be confused with Shining Rock, **Sliding Rock** is an easily accessible waterfall and swimming spot with a parking lot ($2), bathhouse, and lifeguards (10am-6pm daily late May-early Sept.). You can actually ride down the 60-foot waterfall, a smooth rock face (not so smooth that you shouldn't wear sturdy britches), over which 11,000 gallons of water rush every minute into the chilly swimming hole below.

If you have kids with you, make sure

you stop at the **Cradle of Forestry** (U.S. 276, Pisgah Forest, 828/877-3130, www.cradleofforestry.com, 9am-5pm daily mid-Apr.-early Nov., adults $6, ages 4-12 $3). This museum and activity complex commemorate the rise of the forestry profession in the United States, which originated here at a turn-of-the-20th-century training school in the forests once owned by George Washington Vanderbilt, master of Biltmore. Plow days and living history days throughout the year give an interesting glimpse into this region's old-time methods of farming and frontier living. Self-guided trails lead through the woods to many interesting locations of this campus of America's first school of forestry. Most of what's here is geared toward little ones.

Accommodations

Slip back in time at the ★ **Sunset Motel** (523 S. Broad St., 828/884-9106, www.thesunsetmotel.com, $89-129). This kitschy motel is a throwback to the days of the classic roadside motel experience: It's cheap, comfortable, and has chairs right outside your door so you can visit with your neighbors. It also has the best modern convenience—free Wi-Fi. The staff is super friendly and ready to help with suggestions for places to eat and things to do. You can add on tickets to the Brevard Music Center, waterfall tours, and more when you book your room. For film buffs, Robert Mitchum stayed here when he was filming *Thunder Road*.

The modernized **Campbell House Bed and Breakfast** (243 W. Main St., 800/553-2853, www.campbellhousebrevard.com, from $159) has five rooms that feature queen beds and private baths—none are suites, but all are spacious. Though other accommodations in town are bicycle-friendly, Campbell House is the home of bicycle enthusiasts. **The Inn at Brevard** (315 E. Main St., 828/884-2105, www.theinnatbrevard.

com, $165-235) is spacious, beautiful, and kid-friendly. The stately 14-room B&B was built in 1885 and makes a good picture; the rooms are well appointed, and there's a full breakfast every day.

CAMPING

Davidson River Campground (Davidson River Circle, reservations 800/444-6777, local information 828/862-5960, www.recreation.gov, open year-round, sites $22-44) is just outside Brevard in the Shining Rock Wilderness Area. There are around 160 sites here, some with river access, but all have access to hot showers and flush toilets; each site comes equipped with a picnic table, a fire ring, and a grill. It's the most convenient campground for exploring the hiking and fishing in the area as well as checking out the waterfalls here.

Just 10 minutes outside Brevard, on 14 mountaintop acres, is **Ash Grove Mountain Cabins and Camping** (749 East Fork Rd., Brevard, 828/885-7216, www.ash-grove.com, tents and RVs $28-46, cabins $118-138). This retreat is open year-round, unlike others in the area, so you can experience all four seasons in this lovely spot. The cabins are quaint and cozy, and the tent and RV sites are well maintained. Common areas include a bonfire pit, a few lawn games, and a tiny waterfall.

Just 12.5 miles south of downtown Brevard, **Black Forest Family Camping Resort** (280 Summer Rd., Cedar Mountain, 828/884-2267, www.blackforestcampground.com, Mar. 15-Oct., limited facilities in winter, tent sites $32, RV sites $32, full hookups $39-44, cabin $57, travel trailer rentals $94) has 100 campsites that are level and, more importantly, shaded. Nearby you'll find hiking, fishing, rock climbing, and mountain biking; on-site, you'll find a playground complete with horseshoe pits, a large heated swimming pool, and a video arcade. There's also Wi-Fi (a must these days, even if you're car camping).

Background

The Landscape

GEOGRAPHY

The Mountain Region forms the western border of North Carolina. The ridges of the Blue Ridge and Great Smoky Mountains, both subranges of the Appalachian Mountain chain, undulate like the folds of a great quilt, running northeast to southwest from Virginia along the border with Tennessee and into the southwestern corner, where the inland tip of North Carolina meets Georgia. This is a land of waterfalls, rivers, and fast-flowing creeks, and rugged beautiful peaks of smaller mountain configurations. Hemmed in among the peaks and

Geographical Vocabulary

This region has some unusual landscapes and environments, and some unusual vocabulary to describe them. As you explore, you may encounter the following terms.

HOLLER

Here's a term that's really more of a regional pronunciation than a unique word. A holler is what is on paper termed a "hollow"—a mountain cove. It's just that in the South we aren't much for rounding words that end in "ow." If you don't believe me, just beller out the winda to that feller wallering in yonder meada.

BALD

An ecological mystery, the Appalachian bald is a mountaintop area on which there are no trees, even though surrounding mountaintops of the same elevation may be forested. Typically, a bald is either grassy or a heath. Heaths are more easily explained, as they are caused by soil conditions that don't support forest. Grassy balds, though, occur on land where logically trees should be found. Some theories hold that grassy balds were caused by generations of livestock grazing, but soil studies show that they were grassy meadows before the first cattle or sheep arrived. Grazing may still be the answer, though: The balds may originally have been chomped and trampled down by prehistoric megafauna—ancient bison, mastodons, and mammoths. Today, in the absence of mammoths or free-ranging cattle, some balds are gradually becoming woodland, except where deliberately maintained.

hollows of the Blue Ridge and the Smokies are the Black Mountains, the Pisgah Range, and the Unka Range. The Black Mountains are only about 15 miles wide and are confined mostly to Yancey County, but they're the highest in the state, and 6 of the 10 highest peaks in the eastern United States are here, including Mount Mitchell, the highest at 6,684 feet.

This is a region rich in resources, with coal seams, limestone and marble quarries, natural gas deposits, and, surprisingly, pockets and veins of precious and semiprecious gems. The rivers here are old, with the ironically named New River, one of the oldest in the world, flowing northward from North Carolina's Blue Ridge through Virginia and into West Virginia.

CLIMATE

The mountains are much cooler than either the Piedmont or the coast, and winter lasts longer. North Carolina towns like Asheville

and Boone can be blanketed in snow while less than 100 miles away the trees in Piedmont towns aren't even showing their fall colors. The coldest temperature ever recorded in North Carolina, −34°F, was recorded in 1985 on Mount Mitchell. Spring and fall can bring cool to temperate days and chilly nights, while summer days can hit the 80s, and the evenings bring a welcome relief. The Piedmont, on the other hand, can be brutally hot during the summer and quite warm on spring and fall days, though winter is milder. The coast sees long hot summers and cool—not cold—winters with rare snowfall.

The Smoky Mountains experience four distinct seasons, with temperatures and microclimates that can vary wildly depending on elevation and sun exposure. Temperatures can swing drastically with those elevation shifts, changing as much as 15 or 20 degrees as you go from the lowest elevations to the highest. That means on warm summer days, when cities like Asheville might see temperatures in the 80s, Mount Mitchell, 6,000 feet above sea level, will be in the low 50s and possibly cooler, depending on the wind.

During spring, temperatures in this region range from the low 40s to the mid- or upper 60s, and rain or even an early-spring snowfall is common. Summer sees higher temperatures, reaching 80 degrees with some regularity, higher on rare occasions; summer lows can dip down into the 60s and may be even lower at high elevations along the Blue Ridge Parkway. In fall, temperatures are similar to spring, with daytime temperatures in the 40s to 60s, and nights plunging to 30 degrees on occasion. Winter is cold, with ranges from the low 30s to the high 40s; nighttime temperatures, and temperatures in the deepest hollows, can fall into the teens and single digits. Temperatures that low are possible across the region during the coldest periods of winter, even lower at elevations where it's not uncommon to experience a few freezing days.

This is a wet place, with regular snowfall from late fall through early spring, and rains common any time of year. Winter storms can dump a few inches of wet snow on the mountains here, or they can dust it with some fine, powdery snow. Thunderstorms in spring, summer, and fall can be heavy, although the worst of the weather is only occasional; regular rain showers contribute to the 50-80 inches of precipitation falling annually.

Tornadoes, most common in the spring, can cause trouble any time of year. A rare November twister touched down in 2006, smashing the Columbus County community of Riegelwood, killing eight people and leaving a seven-mile swath of destruction. Even plain old **thunderstorms** can be dangerous, bringing lightning, flash flooding, difficult driving conditions, and even hail. **Snowstorms** are rare, and usually occur in the mountains. The Piedmont sees more snow than the coast, which sees flurries once or twice each winter and the occasional dusting of snow. Outside the mountains, most

North Carolinians are woefully inexperienced snow drivers, and the state Department of Transportation doesn't have the equipment in coastal counties to handle much more than a little snow.

ENVIRONMENTAL ISSUES

The parklands and forests along the routes through the Smoky Mountains are preserved so future generations can enjoy nature in as pristine a state as possible. That's why there's no gas available on the Blue Ridge Parkway. It also explains the constant reminders to adhere to **Leave No Trace** (www.lnt.org) principles. Leave No Trace principles are similar to the Boy Scouts of America teachings: Plan ahead and prepare, travel and camp on durable surfaces, dispose of waste properly, leave what you find, minimize campfire impacts, respect wildlife, be considerate of other visitors. These easy rules can improve the outdoor experience for everyone.

If you pack something in, pack it out, and consider carrying a **trash bag** on trails to pick up after less responsible hikers. If each of us would make this a habit, we could clean up a lot of litter that clutters up our view and is detrimental to the environment.

Dogs are allowed on some trails throughout this route, though they must be on leash or under physical control at all times. Please check with rangers for pet-friendly trails. If you have Fido out on the trail or let him use the grassy facilities at an overlook or wayside, be sure to pick up what he's putting down.

You'll pass several ponds and lakes as you travel this region, but unless there's a designated **swimming** area, going for a dip isn't cool. There are exceptions, but those exceptions are noted near the potential swimming hole. When in doubt, ask before you dive in.

You'll spot lots of **wildlife** on your trip. Common animals include white-tailed deer, raccoons, opossums, turtles, bobcats, and even black bears. Coyotes are becoming a more frequent sight along the way, and in certain areas of the Smoky Mountains, you can even see the occasional elk. Many times, a herd of deer will be in a pasture off the parkway. If you see deer (or any other animal), and you want to get a photograph, keep a safe distance from the animal and don't offer them any food; this makes them grow accustomed to people and can have negative impacts on their health.

Plants

In the early 1700s, John Lawson, an English explorer who would soon be one of the first victims of the Tuscarora War, wrote of a magnificent tree house somewhere in the very young colony of North Carolina.

I have been informed of a Tulip-Tree that was ten Foot Diameter; and another, wherein a lusty Man had his Bed and Household Furniture, and liv'd in it, till his Labour got him a more fashionable Mansion. He afterwards became a noted Man, in his Country, for Wealth and Conduct.

Whether or not there was ever a tulip poplar large enough to serve as a furnished bachelor pad, colonial forests must have seemed miraculous to the first Europeans to see them.

FORESTS

Today, after generations of logging and farming across the state, few old-growth forests exist. In the Smoky Mountains, stands of old-growth timber, like the Joyce Kilmer Memorial Forest, are a sight to behold, and some of the trees almost validate Lawson's anecdote. Across the state, scores of specialized ecosystems support a marvelous diversity of plant and animal life. In the east, cypress swamps and a few patches of maritime forest still stand; across the Sandhills are longleaf pine forests; in the mountains are fragrant balsam forests and stands of hardwoods.

Both North Carolina and Tennessee are geographically and climatically varied, so there's a greater diversity in tree species. But in Great Smoky Mountains National Park, the biodiversity is incredible. More than 1,600 species of flowering plants and shrubs grow here; 450 mosses, liverworts, and hornworts; and 50 types of fern. In short, there's a lot that grows here.

The science and profession of forestry were born here: In the 1880s and 1890s, George W. Vanderbilt, lord of the manor at Biltmore, engaged Fredrick Law Olmsted, who designed New York City's Central Park, to plan a managed forest of the finest, healthiest, and hardiest trees. Vanderbilt hired Gifford Pinchot and later Carl Schenck to be the stewards of the thousands of wooded acres he owned in the Pisgah Forest south of Asheville. The contributions these men made to the nascent field are still felt today and are commemorated at the Cradle of Forestry Museum near Brevard.

FLOWERS

In the park there are more than 1,500 species of flowering plants (the most of any North American national park), and much of the region's flora puts on great annual shows, drawing flocks of admirers—the gaudy **azaleas** of springtime, the **wildflowers** of the first warm weather in the hills, the **rhododendrons** and **mountain laurel** of the Appalachian summer. The Ericaceae family, a race of great woody bushes with star-shaped blossoms that includes azaleas, rhododendrons, and laurel, is the headliner in the floral fashion show.

The **flame azalea** makes a late-spring appearance on the mountainsides of the Blue Ridge and Great Smokies, joined by its cousins the mountain laurel and Catawba rhododendron in May and June. The ways of the rhododendron are a little mysterious; not every plant blooms every year, and there's no sure fire way of predicting when they'll put on big shows. The area's widely varying elevation also figures into bloom times. If you're interested in timing your trip to coincide with some of these flowering seasons, your best bet is to call ahead and speak with a ranger from Great Smoky Mountains National Park to find out how the season is coming along.

Around the end of April and into May, when spring finally arrives in the mountains but the forest floor is not yet sequestered in leafy shade, a profusion of delicate flowers emerges. **Violets** and **chickweed** emerge early on, as do the white **trillium** and the wake-robin, a trillium that looks something like a small poinsettia. Every year since 1950, around the end of April, Great Smoky Mountains National Park has hosted the **Spring Wildflower Pilgrimage** (www. springwildflowerpilgrimage.org), a weeklong festival featuring scores of nature walks that also reveal salamanders, birds, and wild hogs, along with workshops and art exhibits. See the website for a schedule of events.

Surprisingly, one of the best places to view displays of wildflowers is along the major highways. For more than 20 years the state Department of Transportation has carried out a highway beautification project that involves planting large banks of wildflowers along highways and in wide medians. The displays are not landscaped but are allowed to grow up in unkempt profusion, often planted in inspired combinations of wildly contrasting colors that make the flowerbeds a genuinely beautiful addition to the environment. The website of the state's **Department of Transportation** (www.ncdot.org) offers a guide to the locations and seasons of the wildflower beds.

FALL FOLIAGE

Arriving as early as mid-September at the highest elevations and gradually sliding down the mountains through late October, autumn colors bring a late-season wave of visitors. Dropping temperatures change trees' sugar production, resulting in a palette of colors, while simple fatigue causes the green to fade in others, exposing underlying hues. Countless climatic factors can alter the onset and progress of leaf season, so the mountains blush at slightly different times every year. The latter weeks of October tend to be the peak; during those weeks it can be difficult to find lodging in the mountains, so be sure to plan ahead. Some of the best places for leaf peeping are along the Blue Ridge Parkway and in Great Smoky Mountains National Park.

Animals

Continuing the theme of the astounding biodiversity in Great Smoky Mountains National Park, there are 65 species of mammal, more than 200 varieties of birds, 67 native fish species, and more than 80 types of reptiles and amphibians in the park. And researchers are finding more every year. Among the familiar wildlife most commonly seen in the state, **white-tailed deer** are out in force in the countryside and in the woods; they populate suburban areas in large numbers as well. **Raccoons** and **opossums** prowl at night, happy to scavenge from trash cans and the forest floor. **Skunks** are common, particularly in the mountains, and are often smelled rather than seen. They leave an odor something like a cross between grape soda and Sharpie markers. There are also a fair number of **black bears,** not only in the mountains but in swamps and deep woods across the state.

In woods and yards alike, **gray squirrels** and a host of familiar **songbirds** are a daily presence. Different species of **tree frogs** produce beautiful choruses on spring and summer nights, while **fireflies** mount sparkly shows in the trees and grass in the upper Piedmont and mountains.

The Carolina woods harbor colonies of

Southern flying squirrels. It's very unlikely that you'll see one unless it's at a nature center or wildlife rehabilitation clinic because flying squirrels are both nocturnal and shy. They're also almost unspeakably cute. Fully extended, they're about nine inches long snout to tail, weigh about four ounces, and have super-silky fur and pink noses, and like many nocturnal animals have comically long whiskers and huge, wide-set eyes that suggest amphetamine use. When they're flying—gliding, really—they spread their limbs to extend the patagium, a membrane that stretches between their front and hind legs, and glide along like little magic carpets.

Also deep in the Smokies are some herds of **wild hogs,** game boars brought to the area about 100 years ago and allowed to go feral. The official line among wildlife officials is that **mountain lions**—in this region called panthers—have been extinct in North Carolina for some time. But mountain dwellers claim there are still panthers in the Blue Ridge and Smokies, and most people here have seen or heard one—their cry sounds like a terror-filled scream. There are even tales of a panther in the inland woods of Brunswick and Columbus Counties on the southeast coast.

REINTRODUCED SPECIES

The Smokies proved a hospitable place for the reintroduction of **elk.** Now the largest animals in Great Smoky Mountains National Park, elk, which can grow up to 700 pounds, are most often observed in the Cataloochee section of the park, grazing happily and lounging in the mist in the early morning and at twilight.

AMPHIBIANS

Dozens of species of **salamanders** and their close kin, including **mudpuppies, sirens,** and *Amphiuma,* call this region home, and Great Smoky Mountains National Park harbors so many of them that it's known as the Salamander Capital of the World. Throughout the state, **frogs** and **toads** are numerous and

vociferous, especially the many species of dainty **tree frogs.** Two species, the gray tree frog and the spring peeper, are found almost everywhere, and beginning in late winter they create the impression that the trees are filled with ringing cell phones.

Hellbenders are quite possibly the strangest animal. They are enormous salamanders—not the slick little pencil-thin five-inch salamanders easily spotted along creeks, but hulking brutes that grow to more than two feet long and can weigh five pounds. Rare and hermetic, they live in rocky mountain streams, venturing out from under rocks at night to gobble up crayfish and minnows. They're hard to see even if they do emerge in the daytime because they're lumpy and mud-colored, camouflaged against streambeds. Aggressive with each other, the males often sport battle scars on their stumpy legs. They've been known to bite humans, but as rare as it is to spot a hellbender, it's an exponentially rarer occurrence to be bitten by one.

REPTILES

Turtles and **snakes** are the state's most common reptiles. **Box turtles,** found everywhere, and **bog turtles,** found in the Smokies, are the only land terrapins. A great many freshwater turtles inhabit the swamps and ponds, and on a sunny day every log or branch sticking out of fresh water will become a sunbathing terrace for as many turtles as it can hold. Common water turtles include **cooters, sliders,** and **painted turtles. Snapping turtles** can be found in fresh water throughout the state, so mind your toes. They grow up to a couple of feet long and can weigh more than 50 pounds. Not only will they bite—hard!—if provoked, they will actually initiate hostilities, lunging for you if they so much as disapprove of the fashion of your shoes. Even the tiny hatchlings are vicious, so give them a wide berth.

The vast majority of snakes are shy, gentle, and totally harmless to anything larger than a rat. There are a few species of venomous snakes that are very dangerous. These include three kinds of **rattlesnake:** the huge diamondback, whose diet of rabbits testifies to its size and strength; the pigmy; and the timber or canebrake rattler. Other venomous species are the beautiful mottled **copperhead** and the **cottonmouth or water moccasin,** famous for flinging its mouth open in hostility and flashing its brilliant white palate, although you'll rarely see a cottonmouth or moccasin in the Smokies.

Most snakes are entirely benign to humans, including old familiars such as **black racers** and **king snakes** as well as **milk, corn,** and **rat snakes.** One particularly endearing character is the **hognose snake,** which can be found throughout North Carolina but is most common in the east. Colloquially known as a spreading adder, the hognose snake compensates for its total harmlessness with amazing displays of histrionics. If you startle one, it will first flatten and greatly widen its head and neck and hiss most passionately. If it sees that you're not frightened by plan A, it will panic and go straight to plan B: playing dead. The hognose snake won't simply lie inert until you go away, though; it goes to the dramatic lengths of flipping onto its back, exposing its pitiably vulnerable belly, opening its mouth, throwing its head back limply, and sticking out its tongue as if it had just been poisoned. It is such a devoted method actor that should you call its bluff and poke it back onto its belly, it will fling itself energetically back into the mortuary pose and resume being deceased.

Local Culture

TOURISM

In the mountains, the main industries have been mining and logging, agriculture, and tourism. As the way we care for our environment has evolved, mining and logging have largely fallen by the wayside and been replaced by small pockets of manufacturing from national and international companies or larger local companies. Through this, the importance of tourism has increased. The region has always drawn visitors to its mountains, waters, and cities, and as the economy evolves, the tourism sector has become vital to the state's well-being. In the mountains, **Great Smoky Mountain National Park** is a recognizable, even marquee, name for visitors, and **Asheville,** with its superb dining and much-lauded craft beer scene, is atop many visitors' lists. Heritage tourism is helping small towns as visitors follow quilt and craft trails across rural counties. This is helping grow interest in lesser-known cities and small towns throughout the mountains.

INDIGENOUS CULTURES

In the Great Smoky Mountains, the town of Cherokee on the Qualla Boundary, which is Cherokee-administered land, is the governmental seat of the Eastern Band of the Cherokee. The Eastern Band are largely descended from those Cherokee people who escaped arrest during the deportation of the Southeast's Native Americans on the Trail of Tears in the 19th century, or who made the forced march to Oklahoma but survived and walked home to the mountains.

The early 19th century in North Carolina was a good deal more peaceful than the previous hundred years had been. Yet despite the relative peace, there was also conflict. Andrew Jackson's administration presided over the passage of the Indian Removal Act in 1830, which assigned reservations in the Indian Territory of present-day Oklahoma to the "Five Civilized Tribes" of the southeastern United States—the Cherokee, Choctaw, Creek, Chickasaw, and Seminole. Thousands of Cherokee people were forced out of western North Carolina, northern Georgia, eastern Tennessee, and Alabama and marched west on the Trail of Tears. About 4,000 died along the way. Another 1,000 or so Cherokee people, through hiding, fighting, and

Understanding Local Lingo

Regional speech features delightful and sometimes perplexing regional vocabulary and grammar. Following are some of the common phrases most likely to stump travelers.

- **Bless your/his/her heart:** A complex declaration with infinitely varied intentions, interpreted depending on context or tone. In its most basic use, "Bless your heart" is a sincere thank-you for a favor or a kindness paid. It's also an exclamation of affection, usually applied to children and the elderly, as in, "You're *not* 92 years old! You are? Well, bless your heart." Frequently, though, hearts are blessed to frame criticism in a charitable light, as in, "Bless his heart; that man from New York don't know not to shout."

- **buggy:** a shopping cart, as at a grocery store.

- **carry:** convey, escort, give a ride to. "I carried my mother up to the mountains for her birthday."

- **cattywampus:** topsy-turvy, mixed up. Used especially in the Piedmont and farther west.

- **Coke:** any soft drink; may be called "pop" in the mountains.

- **come back:** often uttered by shopkeepers as a customer leaves, not to ask them to return immediately, but simply an invitation to patronize the establishment again someday.

- **dinner:** the midday meal.

- **evening:** not just the twilight hours, but all the hours between about 3pm and nightfall.

- **ever-how:** however; similarly, "ever-when," "ever-what," and "ever-who."

- **fair to middling:** so-so, in response to "How you?"; a holdover term from North Carolina's moonshining days, the term originally applied to grading 'shine by examining bubbles in a shaken mason jar.

- **fixing:** about to or preparing to do something. "She's fixing to have a baby any day now."

- **holler:** hollow, a mountain cove.

- **mash:** press, as a button. "I keep mashing the button, but the elevator won't come."

negotiation, managed to win the right to stay in North Carolina—an act of resistance that was the birth of the modern Eastern Band of the Cherokee, still centered on the town of Cherokee on the Qualla Boundary in North Carolina's Great Smoky Mountains.

The Cherokee people depict emblematic episodes in their history in the outdoor drama *Unto These Hills,* in production since 1950. It's especially important to note that among the characteristics of outdoor drama in North Carolina is the fact that the cast, crew, and often the producers and playwrights are members of the communities whose stories the plays tell.

Throughout the town of Cherokee, North Carolina, you'll see many street and commercial signs written in English and a set of pretty, twisty symbols that look like a cross between Khmer or Sanskrit and Cyrillic. This is Cherokee, written in the alphabet famously devised by Sequoyah in the early 19th century. Cherokee also survives as a spoken language, though typically among the elders in traditional communities. To combat the slow death of the language, Eastern Band of Cherokee leadership has started a program to teach tribal youth to speak and write the language, though the pool of fluent speakers is very small.

ARTS AND CRAFTS

Several communities are known worldwide for their local traditions, and countless

- **mess:** Discombobulated, in a rut, not living right. "I was a mess until I joined the church."

- **might could/should/would:** could/should/would perhaps. "Looks like it's fixing to rain. You might should go roll up your car windows."

- **piece:** a vague measure of distance, as in, "down the road a piece" (a little ways down the road) or "a fair piece" (a long way).

- **poke:** a bag, such as a paper shopping bag. Used especially in the mountains.

- **reckon:** believe, think. Often used in interrogative statements that end in a falling tone, as in, "Reckon what we're having for dinner." (That is, "What do you suppose is for lunch?")

- **right:** Quite, very. Variations include "right quick" (soon, hurriedly), "right much" (often), and "a right many" or "a right smart of" (a great quantity).

- **sorry:** worthless, lame, shoddy. "I wanted to play basketball in college, but I was too sorry of an athlete."

- **speck so:** "I expect so," or, "Yes, I guess that's correct."

- **supper:** the evening meal (as opposed to "dinner," the midday meal).

- **sy-goggling:** see *cattywampus*. Used especially in the mountains.

- **ugly:** mean or unfriendly, spiteful. Sometimes referred to as "acting ugly." "Hateful" is a common synonym. The favorite Southern injunction that "God don't like ugly" does not mean that God wants us to be pretty, but rather that we should be nice.

- **wait on:** to wait for.

- **y'all:** pronoun used to address any group of two or more people.

- **yonder:** over there.

- **y'uns:** mountain variation of *y'all*.

individual artists, studios, and galleries can be found across the region.

Cherokee craft is an important aesthetic school comprising a wide range of techniques and media such as wood and stone carving, fiber arts, traditional weaponry, and avant-garde sculpture and painting. **Qualla Arts and Crafts Mutual,** located in the town of Cherokee, has a wonderful sales gallery that will dazzle lovers of fine craft.

Asheville is an epicenter of the arts, the heart of a vast community of artists that stretches throughout western North Carolina and includes such major folk schools as **John C. Campbell** in Brasstown, near the Georgia state line, and **Penland,** close to Tennessee in the northeastern mountains.

In Asheville you can see and purchase an infinite variety of crafts that include hand-made baskets, quilts, furniture, clothing, jewelry, and iron architectural elements. The **Southern Highland Craft Guild** (www.southernhighlandguild.org), an old and accomplished organization, deserves a lot of the credit for the thriving craft movement. Its website has a great deal of information about contemporary master crafters and their work.

As people become more accustomed to a world where almost every object we see and use was mass-produced far away, we develop an ever-deeper appreciation for the depth of skill and aesthetic complexity that went into the production of everyday objects in past generations. The artists of this region have always been great crafters of utilitarian and occupational necessities. As you travel, keep an eye out for objects that you might not immediately recognize as art—barns, fishing nets, woven chair bottoms—but that were made with the skill and artistry of generations-old traditions.

MUSIC

Asheville's a music-loving town if ever there was one. And the music scene revolves around the lauded, almost legendary, **Orange Peel Social Aid and Pleasure Club.** Everyone who's anyone in rock and improvisational music has played or will play here. The cool downtown venue offers shows just about every night of the week, including local and regional acts in addition to major players and the "next big thing" bands. The **Grey Eagle Tavern and Music Hall** is another of Asheville's long-running spots to catch a show. One of the biggest annual shows in Asheville is the **Warren Haynes Christmas Jam,** an all-star concert fund-raiser featuring a lineup of some of the top rock musicians playing with their bands, with one another, and in any mix imaginable.

If there is an epicenter of traditional Appalachian music, it may just be Gatlinburg and Pigeon Forge. Traditional music has been played here since the first European settlers arrived. As tourism increased and the towns grew into that "aw-shucks, we're hillbillies" character, traditional music also played a role. Today, you can hear everything from very strict traditional music to bluegrass covers of modern pop songs being played and sung on the streets and in any number of small theaters and shows. There's no marquee venue; the closest thing is Dollywood, which draws a big crowd and will do a lot to get a musician or band's name out there.

Knoxville has a busy college music scene; major musical acts roll through town, but smaller, no-less-talented bands come through as well. Traditional music is heard throughout the city; musicians from novices to virtuosos saw on fiddles, pluck banjo strings, and slap out bass rhythms on the street, in bars, and in concert halls like the **Tennessee Theatre** and **Bijou Theatre.**

FOOD

Up in the Great Smoky Mountains, the early spring is the season for **ramps,** sometimes called skunk cabbage—very pungent wild onions that grow along creek beds in the deep mountains. They're another of those foods passionately defended by those who grew up eating them but are greeted with trepidation by outsiders. The reason they're feared by the uninitiated is their atomically powerful taste, which will emanate from every part of your body for days if the ramps are too strong or not prepared correctly. Ramps taste like a cross between regular onions, garlic, leeks, shallots, and kryptonite. When they're young, they're perfectly pungent—not too overwhelming, but still powerful enough to let you know they're in the dish. Folks skillet-cook them, fry them up in grease, boil them with fatback, or just chomp on them raw. For a special treat and a gentle introduction to ramps, stop in at the Stecoah Valley Center near Robbinsville and pick up a bag of the Smoky Mountain Native Plants Association's special cornmeal mix with dried ramps, and make yourself a skillet of deliciously tangy cornbread. You can also try them at the local ramps festivals held in Robbinsville and Cherokee in spring. A growing number of restaurants from Asheville to Wilmington are buying ramps and **morel mushrooms** from mountain foragers and preparing them every way from skillet fried to pickled, so ramp lovers can get a taste of this springtime mountain delicacy even on the coast.

Vegetarians and devotees of organic food, fear not; most places are unusually progressive when it comes to healthy and homegrown grub. Nevertheless, if you want to avoid meat, you have to be cautious when ordering at a restaurant: Make sure the beans are made with vegetable oil rather than lard, ask if the salad dressing contains anchovies, and beware of hidden fish and oyster sauce. Traditional

Southern cooking makes liberal use of fatback (cured pork fat) and other animal products; greens are often boiled with a strip of fatback or a hambone, as are most soups and stews. Even pie crusts are still made with lard in many old-time kitchens.

You'll find organic grocery stores in the major cities. Ingles, Earth Fare and Whole Foods are common chains, but there are also plenty of small independent markets. Farmers markets and roadside stands are so plentiful that they almost have to fight for space.

Essentials

Transportation

GETTING THERE
Car

The north-south interstates I-81 and I-75 meet in Knoxville, Tennessee, just 30 miles northwest of the western entrance to Great Smoky Mountains National Park. Coming from the south, I-75 is a natural route from Chattanooga, Tennessee, and Atlanta; I-81 cuts a south-southwest diagonal through Virginia along the Shenandoah Valley, passing by or through Winchester, Lexington, Roanoke, Blacksburg, and Radford, Virginia, before hitting Bristol and Johnson City, Tennessee, and finally Knoxville.

Running east-west, I-40 carries westbound visitors directly by Asheville, across the Tennessee border just north of the national park, and to Knoxville; eastbound drivers will find Little Rock, Arkansas, and Memphis and Nashville, Tennessee, on the route.

To enter Smoky from Gatlinburg, follow I-40 to exit 407 for Sevierville, which connects to Highway 66 south. Upon reaching the Sevierville junction, stay straight to continue on U.S. 441 south, which becomes Newfound Gap Road on its way into the park.

From Cherokee, North Carolina, I-74 connects with U.S. 441 north into the park, where it becomes Newfound Gap Road.

CAR RENTAL

Rental cars are available at every airport, and if you take a train to your departure point, you'll find rental agencies in or near the station. Since many bus and train stations share a facility or are near one another, the same is true if you arrive by bus. The major rental players—Hertz, National, and Enterprise, among others—will be readily available with their standard fleet of cars, but if you are looking for a specific vehicle, like a 4WD or a convertible, check availability with the agencies and reserve your vehicle. Most of these vehicles will be available for one-way rental, allowing you to rent a car at one end and drive it to another, returning it there before boarding a plane or hopping a bus or train back home. Before you embark on a long one-way trip with a rental vehicle, be sure you can return it at the other end. Check with your car rental agency about additional fees for one-way rentals, because some charge hefty fees for this type of rental.

Air

Most visitors to Great Smoky Mountains

National Park arrive by car, but for those flying in, several airports offer reasonably convenient access to the surrounding regions.

Asheville Regional Airport (AVL, 61 Terminal Dr., Fletcher, 828/684-2226, www.flyavl.com) is located south of the city in Fletcher. The next closest airport in North Carolina is **Charlotte Douglas International Airport** (CLT, 5501 Josh Birmingham Pkwy., Charlotte, 704/359-4013, http://charmeck.org), two hours away. Charlotte-Douglas is the eighth-largest hub in the United States, with nonstop flights to and from more than 125 destinations worldwide.

The **Greenville-Spartanburg International Airport** (GSP, 2000 GSP Dr., Greer, SC, 864/848-6254, www.gspairport.com) is 80 minutes south of Asheville. Airlines serving Greenville-Spartanburg include Allegiant, American Airlines, Delta, Southwest, and United. It's a drive of a little over an hour from Greenville-Spartanburg to Asheville.

McGhee Tyson Airport (TYS, 2055 Alcoa Hwy., Alcoa, 865/342-3000, www.tys.org) in Alcoa, Tennessee, is about two hours from Cherokee and about 20 minutes south of Knoxville. Airlines serving McGhee Tyson include Allegiant, American, Delta, Frontier, and United. Gatlinburg and the western entrance to Great Smoky Mountains National Park is just over one hour away; Knoxville is closer, a drive of 20 minutes without traffic.

Bus

You can take a **Greyhound bus** (800/231-2222, www.greyhound.com) to Knoxville and Asheville, but other than those two cities, service is limited. Once you arrive, you'll need a rental car because meaningful public transportation in this region is virtually nonexistent. The **Knoxville Greyhound station** (100 E. Magnolia Ave., 865/525-9483) is not far from downtown, and taxis and ride-share services make it easy to get from the bus station to your accommodations. To get to the national park or North Carolina's Smoky Mountains, you'll need a rental car. The **Asheville Greyhound station** (2 Tunnel Rd., 828/253-8451) is also far from the real heart of downtown, and again, you'll need transportation once you arrive.

GETTING AROUND
Driving
SEASONAL CONSIDERATIONS

From where the Blue Ridge Parkway crosses the North Carolina line through to Gatlinburg, Tennessee, the weather can slow and stop traffic or even shut down sections of the route. Generally, though, the weather is quite pleasant and **winter** is the only time when there are widespread closures of the Blue Ridge Parkway. This route is high and exposed, making it vulnerable to ice and snow. With the expense of the equipment necessary for proper snow and ice removal, wintertime closures are inevitable. Newfound Gap Road through Great Smoky Mountains National Park is a public highway and is maintained throughout the year. It may still close if heavy snowfall is expected or is more than road crews can cope with, but closure is rare. More often you'll be delayed as crews clear the road. Road conditions are available by contacting the **National Park Service** (865/436-1200).

Spring generally brings a good amount of rain. During the earliest months, and even toward the first part of April in the highest elevations, you can experience road closures if a spring snowstorm visits the high passes. The rest of the season, it may rain, but it doesn't impede traffic.

In the **summer,** there is a chance of thunderstorms, and on rare occasions hail. Most likely you'll encounter a rain shower or fog. The fog can be quite dense, so slowing down or even pulling off at a socked-in overlook is advisable.

In the **autumn,** there are occasional rainstorms, and in the latest part of the season rare high-altitude snowstorms dust the tops of the mountains white. Autumn sees the highest number of visitors to Great Smoky Mountains National Park, and leaf-lookers often slow down well below the speed limit, causing some congestion on the roadways. Autumn color seekers also fill overlooks and line the sides of the road to snap pictures and take in the views, slowing traffic in these busy areas.

SPEED LIMIT

On Newfound Gap Road in Great Smoky Mountains National Park, the speed limit is 45 miles per hour, though it does slow in areas. Please observe the posted speed limit. Maintaining the speed limit allows you time to stop or avoid wildlife, debris, or other hazards on the road surface as well as pedestrians or other vehicles. Since long sections of the road are unprotected—read: no guardrails to break up the view—obeying the speed limit has the added benefit of keeping you and your passengers safe from leaving the roadway on an unexpected downhill trip. And if you think you can speed on the parkway or in the national park because rangers can't pull you over, think again: They can, and they will, delivering hefty fines to reckless drivers.

One reason for the low speed limits along this scenic drive is to keep wildlife free from harm. You'll see a number of woodland creatures on your drive, and as your route cuts through the forests where they live, you'll see many animals on or near the roadway. Be extra vigilant at dawn and dusk, when wildlife is most active. If you must stop in the road to allow an animal to cross, use your hazard flashers to alert other drivers, and try not to stop in blind curves or just over the crest of a hill where you'll be difficult to see.

PARKING

In Great Smoky Mountains National Park, parking is usually limited to designated parking areas at overlooks and trailheads; parking is permitted along the road shoulder, provided

Getting There

Knoxville **0.70/30**

Newport

0.75/25

0.70/24

Sevierville

0.3/14

0.5/16

Cosby

TENNESSEE

1/49

0.5/6.5

Pigeon Forge

0.6/21

Maryville

1/34

0.5/7.5

Gatlinburg

NORTH CAROLINA

0.70/24

Great Smoky

To
Asheville
(0.75/35)

1.2/37

Mountains

National Park

Chilhowee

Maggie
Valley

1/28

Cherokee **0.5/17**

Fontana
Dam

0.75/33

Bryson
City

Robbinsville

0.7/32

1/49

Franklin

↓ **Time/** = APPROX. TIME IN HOURS/
  Distance   DISTANCE IN MILES

0   10 mi

0   10 km

Murphy

© MOON.COM

all four wheels are off the road surface and your vehicle doesn't impede traffic. On interstates and other highways, stop only when necessary, and when you do, be sure to pull fully off the road so you're not a danger to passing motorists and so you don't put yourself in harm's way.

FUEL

You won't find any fuel inside Great Smoky Mountains National Park, but you will find it in Cherokee and the other towns on the North Carolina side. Gas stations are plentiful on the Tennessee side once you leave the national park.

Recreation

BACKPACKING

To go backcountry camping anywhere in the park, you'll need a permit and a reservation from the **Backcountry Information Office** (Sugarlands Visitor Center, 1420 Old Hwy. 73 Scenic, Gatlinburg, TN, 865/436-1297, https://smokiepermits.nps.gov, 8am-5pm daily, backcountry permits $4 per night, maximum $20 pp). The office can answer any questions about backcountry campsites, trail access, and trail shelters.

The **Appalachian Trail** (AT) runs nearly 2,200 miles from Georgia to Maine. The AT has 71.6 miles of trail in Great Smoky Mountains National Park, and stepping foot on it is a highlight for thru-hikers, segment hikers, and day hikers.

There are no fees or permits required to hike the Appalachian Trail; however, there are requirements when you hike the AT in Great Smoky Mountains National Park. Thru-hikers are defined as those who begin and end their hike at least 50 miles from the border of the park and only travel on the AT while in the park. Thru-hikers are eligible for a **thru-hiker permit** (www.smokiespermits.nps.gov, $20). Segment hikers must get a permit from the Backcountry Information Office. Day hikers do not require a permit.

For information about the Appalachian Trail, contact the **Appalachian Trail Conservancy** (www.appalachiantrail.org) or visit the **National Park Service's Appalachian Trail website** (www.nps.gov/appa) for trip planning information, maps, trail reports, and more.

For AT thru-hikers there's only one place to stay in Great Smoky Mountains National Park: Appalachian Trail shelters. Four spots are reserved for thru-hikers at all trail shelters, but they're first-come, first-served. If you're thru-hiking and a shelter is full, you can to pitch your tent next to the shelters. Segment hikers and backpackers can reserve spots in AT shelters or at any of the numerous backcountry campsites along and near the Appalachian Trail.

FISHING

There are 2,900 miles of streams within Great Smoky Mountains National Park, and some 600 miles of waterways are ready for anglers to come wet a line and see what they catch. While many think of these mountain streams as perfect for trout fishing with fly rods (these anglers are not mistaken; the Smokies are perfect for fly-fishing), just as many forget that smallmouth bass and rock bass are fairly abundant in these waters.

Smallmouth bass like a rocky-bottomed stream with lots of nooks and crannies where they can hide, so roots, boulders and rock formations, and debris fields are ideal; they also like deep pools where slow-moving currents make it easier to feed. In this region of the Smokies, look for smallmouth along the West Prong of the Little Pigeon River near Gatlinburg and the park's western entrance. You'll also find them in the Little Pigeon River near Greenbrier. Other places you'll find smallmouth and rock bass in the park include the Little River on the way to Cades Cove, Abrams Creek, and Fontana Lake, specifically the feeder creeks like Noland, Hazel, and Eagle Creek.

Fishing in the park is year-round, 30 minutes before sunrise to 30 minutes after sunset, and you can fish any stream in the park provided you have a license. Since Great Smoky Mountains National Park is in both North Carolina and Tennessee, a valid license from either state is accepted within the park and there's no trout stamp requirement. A special permit is required to fish in Cherokee and Gatlinburg. **License requirements** for North Carolina can be found at hwww.ncwildlife.org; requirements for Tennessee can be found at www.

tn.gov/twra. Though both states offer online license sales, a license can be obtained in person at most sporting goods stores near the park.

As for daily possession limits, you're able to possess five fish—brook, rainbow, or brown trout; smallmouth bass; or a combination—in total. Rock bass are the only exception; you're allowed to possess 20 of these in addition to the five-fish limit. There's no minimum size on rock bass, but smallmouth and trout are required to be at least 7 inches.

With regard to tackle, you're allowed one handheld rod and can only use single-hook artificial flies or lures. That means no fish bait, no liquid scents, and a healthy list of prohibited baits (including minnows, worms, corn, cheese, bread, and even natural baits you find alongside the stream). A full list of fishing provisions for Great Smoky Mountains National Park can be found online (www.nps.gov/grsm).

WATER SPORTS

Swimming and inner tubing are not recommended in the park due to a number of serious injuries and hazards—drowning is a leading cause of death in Smoky. Deep Creek (in the southern section of the park, near Bryson City, North Carolina) permits tubing on its waters.

White-water rafting outfitters are located in Gatlinburg, Tennessee, and in Bryson City, North Carolina. In North Carolina, Smoky Mountain Tubing in Cherokee rents tubes on the Oconaluftee River, while Dillsboro River Company will float you on the Tuckasegee River.

Your best option for white-water rafting, however, is the beautiful Nantahala River Gorge just outside Bryson City in the Nantahala National Forest. Nantahala Outdoor Company is one of several outfitters and guide services that will get you out onto the river in this stunning gorge.

Travel Tips

INTERNATIONAL TRAVELERS

Visitors from other countries must present a valid **passport** and **visa** issued by a U.S. consular official to enter the United States. Visas are not necessary for citizens of countries eligible for the Visa Waiver Program. For more information on traveling to the United States from a foreign country, visit www.usa.gov.

Foreign visitors who wish to drive should obtain an **International Driving Permit,** which is available from the nation that issued your driver's license. Driver's licensing rules vary from state to state. It's a good idea to familiarize yourself with the driving rules in the states that you'll be visiting (you can do this at www.usa.gov). Throughout the United States, drivers drive on the right side of the road, and distance and speed are measured in miles. Speedometers display both miles and kilometers; road signs display only miles.

If you're traveling to the United States from a foreign country, you'll need to exchange your currency at the airport, bank or currency exchange in your destination city, or, even easier, exchange your cash for dollars before you leave home; attractions, restaurants, and lodging on the route accept U.S. dollars only. Credit cards are widely accepted, but for moments when you need cash, there are plenty of ATMs in cities and towns along the route (though they will likely charge a fee for each transaction). Though ATMs are sorely limited in Great Smoky Mountains National Park, you will find them at some visitors centers.

TOURIST INFORMATION
What to Bring

Depending on the season, you'll need slightly different clothing, and your supplies will depend on the activities you plan to include as part of your trip. No matter what, you'll want

Leave No Trace

PLAN AHEAD AND PREPARE

- Know the regulations and special concerns for the area you'll visit.
- Prepare for extreme weather, hazards, and emergencies.
- Schedule your trip to avoid times of high use.
- Visit in small groups. Split larger parties into groups of 4-6.
- Repackage food to minimize waste.
- Use a map and compass to eliminate the use of marking paint, rock cairns, or flagging.

TRAVEL AND CAMP ON DURABLE SURFACES

- Durable surfaces include established trails and campsites, rock, gravel, dry grasses, or snow.
- Protect riparian areas by camping at least 200 feet from lakes and streams.
- Good campsites are found, not made. Altering a site is not necessary.

In popular areas:

- Concentrate use on existing trails and campsites.
- Walk single file in the middle of the trail, even when wet or muddy.
- Keep campsites small. Focus activity in areas where vegetation is absent.

DISPOSE OF WASTE PROPERLY

- Pack it in, pack it out. Inspect your campsite and rest areas for trash or spilled foods. Pack out all trash, leftover food, and litter.
- Deposit solid human waste in cat holes dug 6-8 inches deep and at least 200 feet from water, camp, and trails. Cover and disguise the cat hole when finished.
- Pack out toilet paper and hygiene products.
- To wash yourself or your dishes, carry water 200 feet away from streams or lakes and use small amounts of biodegradable soap. Scatter strained dishwater.

LEAVE WHAT YOU FIND

- Preserve the past: examine, but do not touch, cultural or historic structures and artifacts.

sunscreen and bug spray if you're traveling in the spring, summer, or fall, and sunscreen if you're visiting in winter (especially for skiers). Bring your binoculars and a camera with a zoom lens so you can enjoy the wildlife up close without disturbing it, keeping all parties involved safe.

If you plan to hike, dress in layers so you can easily regulate your temperature, and have a sturdy pair of hiking boots on hand;

trekking poles or a hiking staff aren't a bad idea either. Throw in some rain gear and a day pack with your first-aid kit, extra water, and some snacks, and you're good to go.

Many visitors enjoy water activities here, whether it's white-water rafting, wading in the streams, or going for a float on the river, and so you'll want a swimsuit. Since the white-water rivers can be cold even in summer, you'll want something warm, preferably

- Leave rocks, plants, and other natural objects as you find them.

- Avoid introducing or transporting nonnative species.

- Do not build structures, furniture, or dig trenches.

MINIMIZE CAMPFIRE IMPACTS

- Campfires can cause lasting impacts to the backcountry. Use a lightweight stove for cooking and enjoy a candle lantern for light.

- Where fires are permitted, use established fire rings, fire pans, or mound fires.

- Keep fires small. Only use sticks from the ground that can be broken by hand.

- Burn all wood and coals to ash, put out campfires completely, then scatter cool ashes.

RESPECT WILDLIFE

- Observe wildlife from a distance. Do not follow or approach them.

- Never feed animals. Feeding wildlife damages their health, alters natural behaviors, and exposes them to predators and other dangers.

- Protect wildlife and your food by storing rations and trash securely

- Control pets at all times, or leave them at home.

- Avoid wildlife during sensitive times: mating, nesting, raising young, or winter.

BE CONSIDERATE OF OTHER VISITORS

- Respect other visitors and protect the quality of their experience.

- Be courteous. Yield to other users on the trail.

- Step to the downhill side of the trail when encountering pack stock.

- Take breaks and camp away from trails and other visitors.

- Let nature's sounds prevail. Avoid loud voices and noises.

This copyrighted information has been reprinted with permission from the Leave No Trace Center for Outdoor Ethics. For more information or materials, visit http://lnt.org or call 800/332-4100.

a lightweight wool shirt; wool dries quickly and keeps you quite warm.

Other than these basics, you should pack any specialty gear that caters to your wants, needs, and plans—golf clubs, disc golf gear, skis, maps, rock-climbing gear, whatever it may be.

Maps

One of the best resources for exploring a new region is a good map. DeLorme's atlas and gazetteers are indispensable. The detail provided is enough to plan short day hikes or longer expeditions, and they point out everything from trailheads and boat launches to campgrounds, hunting and fishing spots, and back roads of all types. Look for the *North Carolina Atlas & Gazetteer* (Yarmouth, ME: DeLorme, 2016) and the *Tennessee Atlas & Gazetteer* (Yarmouth,

ME: DeLorme, 2017). If you're doing any backcountry camping, these guides will give you a good overview, but you may want to get quadrant maps for greater detail. Excellent guides are available from any good outdoor retailer, and since Great Smoky Mountains National Park is the most visited national park, quality guidebooks are always on hand.

Accommodations and Camping

In Great Smoky Mountains National Park, no unauthorized backcountry camping is allowed. Reserve a spot at a backcountry shelter or campground, or get a spot at a front-country campground. Adhere to Leave No Trace principles, and absolutely follow regulations and restrictions for campfires. Due to the hazard of fire, campfires are generally only permitted in front-country campsites. If you are front-country camping, be aware that you can't bring in your own firewood; you'll need to purchase or gather it on-site. This rule is to prevent the spread of insect infestations, parasites, and disease that may harm local plants.

For much of the year, you should be able to travel without reservations, though even in the off-season you may not be able to get into your first choice of campgrounds, lodges, hotels, or B&Bs. During peak seasons, namely October and late summer, you'll need reservations because visitors flood the area to see the autumn color show or squeeze in one more summer getaway. For some of the most popular campgrounds and lodging along the route, you should book months in advance.

ACCESS FOR TRAVELERS WITH DISABILITIES

The overwhelming majority of trails in Great Smoky Mountains National Park are not accessible for travelers with disabilities, particularly those that impede mobility. The one exception is the Sugarlands Valley nature trail (on Newfound Gap Rd.). Luckily, a huge number of attractions, accommodations, and restaurants are accessible. All visitors center restrooms are wheelchair-accessible.

TRAVELING WITH CHILDREN

There's no shortage of kid-friendly activities in Great Smoky Mountains National Park. Along the route, there are kid-friendly hikes, Junior Ranger programs, animals galore, and visitors centers and gift shops where you can pick up a little something to keep the youngest traveler occupied while in transit. In the cities, you'll find children's museums, parks, zoos, and playgrounds.

SENIOR TRAVELERS

Aside from stubble-faced and bearded bikers, one of the most common sights is the gray-haired couple tooling about in their Subaru, RV, or truck towing an RV. Many attractions, accommodations, and dining options offer senior discounts, so flash that AARP card and save a few bucks. Overall, the driving routes described in this guide are safe and leisurely ones for seniors and solo travelers.

GAY AND LESBIAN TRAVELERS

LGBTQ travelers may be pleasantly surprised at how tolerant the region is, despite being rural and, in some areas, part of the Bible Belt. In Asheville and Knoxville, you'll find open and active gay culture, and in most spots along the way the culture is open and accepting. This isn't to say everyone you meet is open to every lifestyle choice made, but it is to say that those closed-off individuals are fewer and farther between with each passing year.

HEALTH AND SAFETY

For the most part, your trip should be unremarkable as far as health and safety are concerned, provided you're attentive to your situation and surroundings, but there are a few things you should know. Those going on long hikes would also be wise to familiarize themselves with the **10 essentials** (www.

rei.com/learn/expert-advice/ten-essentials.html).

Emergencies

For emergencies anywhere in the United States, dial **911** on your phone for immediate assistance. In North Carolina, dialing *****77** connects you to the state police and *****67** puts you in contact with the highway patrol. In Tennessee, dial *****847** for police assistance. If you have to call, try to note your mile marker or a nearby exit or landmark as a reference point for any assistance that's headed your way.

Wilderness Safety

Hikers should beware of **ticks,** some of which can transmit Lyme disease. An insect repellant and some thorough body checks (use a partner for more fun) should keep you tick-free after a jaunt through the woods. If you do get a bite or if you notice a red circular rash that's similar to a bull's-eye, consult a physician; Lyme disease can be life-threatening in the worst cases.

You'll encounter woodland animals, including bees, wasps, yellow jackets, and hornets, so if you're allergic, be sure to have an **EpiPen** on hand. A number of **snakes,** including rattlesnakes and copperheads, live in these woods. Be alert and keep an ear open for that warning rattle, and if you unexpectedly smell cucumbers in the woods, you may be near a copperhead; in either case, back away slowly and detour around. **Spiders** can be a concern in places, namely woodpiles and some backcountry shelters. Most are harmless, though the brown recluse is seen from time to time, and the more commonly seen black widow spider is easily identifiable by the red hourglass on the female's abdomen.

Two of the most popular animals to look for in the park are **elk** and **black bears.** I've seen both many times, and frequent visitors can attest that they're quite the sight, but only when you're doing your wildlife viewing from a safe distance, and that means staying 50 yards (150 feet) from these animals. Why 50 yards? Because that's close enough for a good look but far enough away to keep the animals calm and keep you safe. If you see a bear or elk, keep an eye on it and monitor its movement; don't approach it; and try to maintain a safe distance between you and any wildlife. Most of the time bears and elk will take a look at you and get back to whatever they were doing, but if your presence causes the animal to alter its behavior (it stops feeding for more than a moment, moves toward or away from you, locks eyes and stares you down), you're too close. If you see any aggressive behavior (bears will run toward you, make loud sounds, or swat the ground), don't run. Instead, slowly back away and keep your eyes on the wildlife. Never, ever for any reason disturb or come between a bear or elk and their young; separating the mother and cub or calf, or coming between them, is often taken as an aggressive move on your part and may cause mom to get angry and do what angry moms do: protect her babies.

Because some visitors don't follow the rules and decide to feed bears and elk or elect to move closer for a better shot, some of these animals act differently around humans. If bears or elk follow you without making aggressive overtures, you need to take action. For bears, first try changing your direction of travel (head back down the trail or back to the car); stand your ground and talk loudly or shout; make yourself large by standing on something, raising your hands over your head, or even by raising your backpack overhead; as last resorts you can throw nonfood objects (rocks, sticks) at the bear or even defend yourself with a stick or hiking pole. If an elk approaches, retreat to your car or a safe spot, or put something like a tree between you and it. Bears that become accustomed to humans and associate us with food, and bears or elk that have an aggressive encounter with humans are often euthanized, and we don't want that.

Along the trails and roadsides you'll

likely encounter **poison ivy, poison oak, and poison sumac,** all of which deliver an itchy blister when you come in contact with the oils they secrete. These oils are active for several months, so if you walk through a field of poison ivy, be sure to wash your pants, socks, and boots well lest you inadvertently get poison ivy a month later. You may also come upon **stinging nettles,** which leave itchy welts akin to mosquito bites; these are harmless and generally go away quickly.

Resources

Suggested Reading

HIKING AND FISHING

Adams, Kevin. *Hiking Great Smoky Mountains National Park*. Guilford, CT: Globe Pequot Press, 2013. An excellent hiking-only guide to trails and on-foot sights in Great Smoky Mountains National Park, from Falcon Guides.

Brewer, Carson. *Day Hikes of the Smokies*. Gatlinburg, TN: Great Smoky Mountains Natural History Association, 2002. This pocket-sized guide covers 34 day hikes in the park, with maps, elevation profiles, and photos.

Johnson, Randy. *Hiking the Blue Ridge Parkway: The Ultimate Travel Guide to America's Most Popular Scenic Roadway*. Guilford, CT: Globe Pequot Press, 2010. A thorough trail guide to the Blue Ridge Parkway from Falcon Guides.

Rutter, Ian. *Great Smoky Mountains National Park Angler's Companion*. Portland, OR: Frank Amato Publications, 2002. Everything you need to know about fishing Smokie's creeks and streams, as well as fishing methods and seasons, written by a volunteer for the fisheries division.

Wise, Ken. *Hiking Trails of the Great Smoky Mountains*. Gatlinburg, TN: Great Smoky Mountains Natural History Association, 2001. This hike guide includes an overview of more than 125 trails in the park, with trailhead directions, maps, and points of interest along the way.

HISTORY AND CULTURE

Brill, David. *Into the Mist: Tales of Death, Disaster, Mishap and Misdeeds, Misfortune and Mayhem in Great Smoky Mountains National Park*. Gatlinburg, TN: Great Smoky Mountains Association, 2018. A look at some of the park's more macabre moments and how the rangers and local authorities responded.

Fisher, Noel C. *The Civil War in the Smokies*. Gatlinburg, TN: Great Smoky Mountains Natural History Association, 2005. How the Civil War impacted the region that is now the park, written by the winner of the Peter Seaborg Award for the best nonfiction Civil War book.

Hall, Karen J. *Building the Blue Ridge Parkway*. Charleston, SC: Arcadia Publishing, 2007. Narrative and archival photos combine to tell the story of the early days of the Blue Ridge Parkway, including construction, folkways, and cultural tidbits.

Holland, Lance. *Fontana: A Pocket History of Appalachia*. Robbinsville, NC: Appalachian History Series, 2001. This book explores the history, people, and stories of the Fontana region of North Carolina's Smoky Mountains, including the changes brought by the building of Fontana Dam and Lake.

TRAVEL

Duncan, Barbara, and Brett Riggs. *Cherokee Heritage Trails*. Chapel Hill, NC: UNC

Press, 2003; online companion at www. cherokeeheritage.org. A fascinating guide to both the historical and present-day home of the Eastern Band of the Cherokee in North Carolina, Tennessee, and Georgia, from ancient mounds and petroglyphs to modern-day arts co-ops and sporting events.

Fussell, Fred, and Steve Kruger. *Blue Ridge Music Trails of North Carolina: A Guide to Music Sites, Artists, and Traditions of the Mountains and Foothills.* Chapel Hill, NC: UNC Press, 2013. A guide to destinations—festivals, restaurants, oprys, church singings—in North Carolina, where authentic bluegrass, old-time, and sacred music rings through the hills and hollers. An accompanying CD gives you a chance to hear some tunes rather than just read about them.

Maynard, Charles. *Going to Great Smoky Mountains National Park.* Helena, MT: Far-country Explorer Books, 2008. A kid-friendly guide to the plants and animals in the park.

North Carolina Atlas and Gazetteer. Yarmouth, ME: DeLorme, 2012. Since I was in Boy Scouts, I have always been partial to De-Lorme's state atlases. This series represents in great detail the topography and other natural features of an area, providing users with far more useful and comprehensive information than the standard highway map.

Simmons, Nye. *Best of the Blue Ridge Parkway: The Ultimate Guide to the Parkway's Best Attractions.* Johnson City, TN: Mountain Trail Press, 2008. Beautiful photography of some of the most iconic and picturesque spots along the Parkway is accompanied by write-ups of some of the highlights.

Internet Resources

GENERAL TOURIST INFORMATION

North Carolina

North Carolina Division of Tourism
www.visitnc.com
This comprehensive guide contains trip itineraries in each region, including a dedicated section on the Blue Ridge Parkway. The site is rich with photos and videos, and it contains a wide-ranging index of accommodations, attractions, and more.

Explore Asheville Convention & Visitors Bureau
www.exploreasheville.com
The official website for Asheville, with lists of restaurants, breweries, hotels and accommodations, and an online visitors guide.

Bryson City—Swain County Chamber of Commerce
www.greatsmokies.com
The online visitors portal for Bryson City, including an index of restaurants and attractions, accommodations, trip ideas, and an online visitors guide.

Tennessee

Knoxville Tourism & Sports Corporation
www.visitknoxville.com
The official website for Knoxville, with lists of restaurants, hotels, and an online visitors guide.

Gatlinburg Convention and Visitors Bureau
www.gatlinburg.com
The official website for Gatlinburg, with a list of restaurants and attractions, a hotel

booking portal, and an online visitors guide.

**Tennessee Department
of Tourist Development**
www.tnvacation.com
The official site of Tennessee's state tourism office is user-friendly, allowing you to narrow your focus on one region with just a couple of clicks. Resources for the Smokies and East Tennessee include interactive maps that provide a great overview of the region's offerings from natural sights to built attractions.

NATIONAL PARK INFORMATION
Great Smoky Mountains National Park
Great Smoky Mountains National Park
www.nps.gov/grsm
An extensive history of the park, with details on flora, fauna, and natural features and downloadable maps and contact information for rangers and park offices.

Friends of the Smokies
www.friendsofthesmokies.org
Friends of the Smokies works to raise funds for park initiatives, trail maintenance and improvement, and a variety of other needs. They accept donations of time and money, so if you had a good time in the Smokies, consider lending them a hand or a few bucks.

Great Smoky Mountains Association
www.smokiesinformation.org
A nonprofit partner of Great Smoky Mountains National Park, the group operates retail stores in and benefiting the park; provides guidebooks, maps, logo-emblazoned clothing and gear, and other gifts; and helps with expenses associated in promoting the park.

OUTDOORS
Appalachian Trail
Appalachian Trail Conservancy
www.appalachiantrail.org

The Appalachian Trail Conservancy provides support to the Appalachian Trail, which parallels and even crosses the Blue Ridge Parkway in many places.

Hiking
www.gatlinburg.com
This website includes a brief list of hikes and waterfalls in the region of the park near Gatlinburg.

www.nchikes.com
All things hiking-related in North Carolina, including trails, books, and trip recommendations.

Sierra Club
http://nc.sierraclub.org
www.sierraclub.org/tennessee
Find information about upcoming hikes and excursions as well as an overview of each state's natural areas and environmental issues.

State Parks
www.ncparks.gov
http://tnstateparks.com
A number of state parks provide alternative camping options near Great Smoky Mountains National Park. Many travelers use the parks' campgrounds and facilities as resources and waypoints along their journey.

Wildlife
North Carolina Wildlife Resources Commission
www.ncwildlife.org
Information on fishing and boating in North Carolina, including easy-to-understand hunting and fishing regulations and online license procurement.

Tennessee Wildlife Resources Agency
www.tn.gov/twra
Need-to-know information regarding hunting and fishing regulations and licenses.

Index

List of Maps

Photo Credits

All photos © Jason Frye except page 6 © (top left) daveallenphoto/123rf.com; (top right) Alex Grichenko | Dreamstime.com; page 7 © (bottom right) Jon Bilous | Dreamstime.com; page 9 © (bottom left) James Vallee | Dreamstime.com; (bottom right) Dfikar | Dreamstime.com; page 10 © Jon Bilous | Dreamstime.com; page 12 © (top) Robert Philip | Dreamstime.com; (bottom) Narint Asawaphisith | Dreamstime.com; page 13 © Dfikar | Dreamstime.com; page 14 © Tang Man | Dreamstime.com; page 15 © (middle) Steven Bridges; page 16 © (bottom) alexandr grichenko /123rf.com; page 31 © (top left) Sayran | Dreamstime.com; page 45 © (left middle)Jon Bilous | Dreamstime.com; (bottom) alexandr grichenko /123rf.com; page 73 © (right middle)Anthony Heflin | Dreamstime.com; page 105 © (top left) Brenda Kean /123rf.com; (top right) Steven Bridges; page 109 © (top) Ritu Jethani | Dreamstime.com; (left middle)Sgoodwin4813 | Dreamstime.com; (right middle)Sgoodwin4813 | Dreamstime.com; (bottom) Sean Pavone | Dreamstime.com; page 120 © (top) Cynthia Mccrary | Dreamstime.com; (bottom) Anthony Totah /123rf.com; page 129 © (top) Jakub Zajic | Dreamstime.com; (bottom) Gilles Malo | Dreamstime.com; page 138 © Jill Lang /123rf.com; page 139 © (top left) Shester171 | Dreamstime.com; (top right) Jilllang | Dreamstime.com; page 156 © (bottom) Dpiano | Dreamstime.com; page 170 © (top) Florentino David | Dreamstime.com; (bottom) Jill Lang | Dreamstime.com; page 204 © Korzeniewski | Dreamstime.com

Trips to Remember

BALI & LOMBOK
CHANTAE REDEN

ECUADOR
& THE GALÁPAGOS ISLANDS
BETHANY PITTS

ICELAND
JENNA GOTTLIEB

TRIP OF A LIFETIME
MACHU PICCHU
WITH LIMA, CUZCO & CUSCO
ISTA POURJÉ

MOROCCO

NEW ZEALAND
JAMIE CHRISTIAN DESPLACES

NORWAY
DAVID NIKEL

TRIP OF A LIFETIME
PATAGONIA
INCLUDING THE FITZROY RANGE
WAYNE BERNHARDSON

PRAGUE, VIENNA & BUDAPEST

ROME, FLORENCE & VENICE
ALEXEI J. COHEN

ZION & BRYCE
INCLUDING ARCHES, CANYONLANDS, CAPITOL REEF, GRAND STAIRCASE-ESCALANTE & MORE
W. C. McRAE & JUDY JEWELL

Epic Adventure

CAMINO DE SANTIAGO
SACRED SITES, HISTORIC VILLAGES, LOCAL FOOD & WINE
BEEBE BAHRAMI

ROUTE 66
Road Trip
JESSICA DUNHAM

YELLOWSTONE TO GLACIER NATIONAL PARK
Road Trip
JACKSON HOLE, CODY, THE GRAND TETONS & THE ROCKY MOUNTAIN FRONT
CARTER G. WALKER

MOON

AMALFI COAST

MOON

ARUBA

MOON

BAHAMAS

MOON

BAJA

MOON

BELIZE

MOON

BERMUDA

MOON

COSTA RICA

MOON

DOMINICAN REPUBLIC

MOON

FIJI

MOON

FLORIDA KEYS

MOON

FRENCH RIVIERA: NICE, CANNES, MONACO & ST-TROPEZ

MOON

JAMAICA

MOON

MAUI

MOON

PUERTO VALLARTA

MOON

YUCATÁN PENINSULA

States & Regions

CHARLESTON & SAVANNAH
JIM MOREKIS

FLORIDA GULF COAST
JOSHUA LAWRENCE AINSER

MAINE
HILARY NANGLE

MICHIGAN'S UPPER PENINSULA
PAUL VACHON

NEW ENGLAND
JEN ROSE SMITH

NEW YORK STATE

NORTH CAROLINA
With Great Smoky Mountains National Park
JASON FRYE

RHODE ISLAND

TENNESSEE
MARGARET LITTMAN

VERMONT
JEN ROSE SMITH

VIRGINIA & MARYLAND
MICHAELA RIVA GAASERUD

WISCONSIN
THOMAS HUHTI

MOON.COM
@MOONGUIDES

MOON GREAT SMOKY MOUNTAINS NATIONAL PARK

Avalon Travel
Hachette Book Group
1700 Fourth Street
Berkeley, CA 94710, USA
www.moon.com

Editor: Rachael Sablik
Acquiring Editor: Nikki Ioakimedes
Series Manager: Kathryn Ettinger
Copy Editor: Christopher Church
Graphics Coordinator: Darren Alessi
Production Coordinator: Darren Alessi
Cover Design: Faceout Studios, Charles Brock
Interior Design: Domini Dragoone
Moon Logo: Tim McGrath
Map Editor: Kat Bennett
Cartographer: Brian Shotwell
Proofreader: Samia Abbasi
Indexer: Greg Jewett

ISBN-13: 9781640498457

Printing History
1st Edition — 2017
2nd Edition — April 2020
5 4 3 2 1

Front cover photo: Great Smoky Mountains National Park © Ethan Quin/Shutterstock
Back cover photo: John P. Cable Grist Mill was built in the early 1870s © Dndavis/123rf.com

Printed in China by RR Donnelley

Avalon Travel is a division of Hachette Book Group, Inc. Moon and the Moon logo are trademarks of Hachette Book Group, Inc. All other marks and logos depicted are the property of the original owners.

MAP SYMBOLS

Expressway	○ City/Town	✈ Airport	⚲ Golf Course
Primary Road	◉ State Capital	✗ Airfield	☐P Parking Area
Secondary Road	⊛ National Capital	▲ Mountain	Archaeological Site
Unpaved Road	★ Point of Interest	✦ Unique Natural Feature	⚑ Church
Feature Trail	• Accommodation		⛽ Gas Station
Other Trail	▼ Restaurant/Bar	Waterfall	Glacier
Ferry	■ Other Location	⚑ Park	Mangrove
Pedestrian Walkway	Λ Campground	❶ Trailhead	Reef
Stairs		Skiing Area	Swamp

CONVERSION TABLES

°C = (°F − 32) / 1.8
°F = (°C x 1.8) + 32
1 inch = 2.54 centimeters (cm)
1 foot = 0.304 meters (m)
1 yard = 0.914 meters
1 mile = 1.6093 kilometers (km)
1 km = 0.6214 miles
1 fathom = 1.8288 m
1 chain = 20.1168 m
1 furlong = 201.168 m
1 acre = 0.4047 hectares
1 sq km = 100 hectares
1 sq mile = 2.59 square km
1 ounce = 28.35 grams
1 pound = 0.4536 kilograms
1 short ton = 0.90718 metric ton
1 short ton = 2,000 pounds
1 long ton = 1.016 metric tons
1 long ton = 2,240 pounds
1 metric ton = 1,000 kilograms
1 quart = 0.94635 liters
1 US gallon = 3.7854 liters
1 Imperial gallon = 4.5459 liters
1 nautical mile = 1.852 km

More adventure east of the Mississippi with Moon Travel Guides

Road Trips

Cities